THE
GREATEST
MUSIC
NEVER
SOLD

THE
GREATEST
MUSIC
NEVER
S⬤LD

SECRETS OF LEGENDARY LOST ALBUMS BY
DAVID BOWIE • SEAL • BEASTIE BOYS
BECK • CHICAGO • MICK JAGGER & MORE!

BY DAN LEROY

Backbeat
Books

An Imprint of Hal Leonard Corporation
New York

Published in 2007 by Backbeat Books
An Imprint of Hal Leonard Corporation
19 West 21st Street, New York, NY 10010

Printed in the United States of America

Book design by Stephen Ramirez

Library of Congress Cataloging-in-Publication Data

LeRoy, Dan.
The greatest music never sold : secrets of legendary lost albums by David Bowie, Seal, Beastie Boys, Beck, Chicago, Mick Jagger & more! / by Dan LeRoy.
    p. cm.
Includes bibliographical references (p.   ) and index.
ISBN 978-0-87930-905-3
1. Popular music–Discography. I. Title.
ML156.4.P6L47 2007
781.64–dc22

                                                                        2007021641

www.backbeatbooks.com

With love and gratitude,
to my parents, who helped me start this book,
and to Kiena Page Nutter, who helped me finish it

Contents

Foreword

There is a business book called *The Long Tail*, written by Chris Anderson. The cover has a slug line that reads, "Why the Future of Business Is Selling Less of More."

Until recently, recording artists had always been stuck with the fact that their music had to fit on a small, round piece of plastic. Artists were allowed to release these discs every two or three years if the record label—often a committee of businessmen, accountants, lawyers, and the odd creative person—allowed them to do so. Yet during those two or three years of waiting to release their albums (and in-between touring, etc.), most musicians recorded miles and miles of tape, experimenting like a visual artist would make sketches on a notepad.

Often these "sketches" became massive hits that you and I would instantly recognize; sometimes they would turn into hybrids of songs—a verse from one section meets a chorus of a different sketch made a year earlier, for example. Some of these tape recordings, meanwhile, remained "sketches," and to this day have never been listened to again.

All of this "stuff" constitutes the "Long Tail" of an artist, and I personally find it fascinating when I discover the odd "sketch" that slips through the net (no pun intended). In this book, Dan LeRoy has tapped into this "Long Tail" and found not only sketches, but whole finished albums of material! And all of it remains unreleased, for one reason or another.

I personally now want to hear all these albums, just as I would love any of you readers to hear lots of my unreleased material, as some of it contains my personal favorite work out of everything I've recorded. So many times I've recorded stuff or produced albums and the label has either not released them or threatened not to release them—*Sweet Dreams*, by Eurythmics, being one of them!

I remember being told by the label at the time I was working on Imogen Heap's first album, *I Megaphone*, that we had gone crazy and ruined the record. They threatened to shelve it—yet when recently re-released, it got rave reviews, and it still sounds totally fresh and contemporary today, even though it was made more than ten years ago. There are hundreds of cases like this, just in my own career—so can you imagine the amount of amazing unreleased music out there?

In the end, just like water always finds its way through what seems to be an impossible, solid, obstructive mass, all of these unreleased gems will eventually find their way to us. And I somehow have the feeling that Dan may have a helping hand in this becoming a reality.

Read on . . .

Dave Stewart
Los Angeles, May 2007

P.S. My own "great lost album," *Platinum Weird*, will be released!

Acknowledgments

During the writing of this book, more than a few people I spoke with found it amusing to speculate about what seemed to be a deliciously ironic concept: What if a book about great unreleased albums were itself never released?

I quickly lost the ability to find the humor in this idea, but it is because of the following individuals that it did not become a reality. I owe them all the sincerest gratitude; the only parts of this project that are mine alone are the mistakes, for which I take full responsibility.

My love and most sincere thanks to Heather and Eric Lewis; Brenda Schanie Nutter, John D. Nutter, Devin Nutter and family; Paul, Gina, Abigail, Amanda, and Drew Martin-Ryan; Dan, Kelly, Rachyl, Jacob, and Joshua Berardo; Mr. and Mrs. C. Thomas Tallman; Jamie Tallman; and Nancy LeRoy and family.

I also thank the more than sixty people who agreed to be interviewed for this book, both on and off the record, and salute in particular Eric Matthews, Julie Christensen, Gus Isidore, Nick Launay, and Chris Fogel, who agreed to speak to me while I was still developing this concept.

Dave Lee Bartel, Bill Laswell, and Ginny Tura also took time from their busy schedules to send me crucial documents and music, as did Mark Laudenschlager of the amazing and invaluable Beastie Boys website Beastiemania.com. Justin and Nancy from adam-ant.net and Jen Hall at Silva Artist Management helped me make valuable contacts, while S. H. "Skiz" Fernando Jr. was generous enough to allow me to use his largely unpublished article about the Jungle Brothers' *Crazy Wisdom Masters*, which added immeasurably to that chapter of the book. (If you don't own Skiz's book *The New Beats*, your library is incomplete.)

Bob Nirkind at Billboard Books was very helpful in getting this book to its eventual publisher. I wish also to thank the first editor of this project, Richard Johnston, who offered a great deal of good advice in its formative stages, and my current editors—Carol Flannery, Jessica Burr, and copy editor Sarah Gallogly—for their patience, guidance, and eagle eyes as the book neared completion.

Brian Coleman is a fantastic writer, a savvy businessman, and a hip-hop scholar with few peers. He pointed me in the direction of two albums included in this book, the Jungle Brothers' *Crazy Wisdom Masters* and the Bubbleheads project. But I would implore you to buy all his writing—especially his new book *Check the Technique: Liner Notes for Hip-Hop Junkies*—even if he hadn't.

The *Charleston Daily Mail* is my former newspaper, and I am proud to have made so many friends there. Two of the best over the years have been Brad McElhinny and Chris Stirewalt, otherwise known as West Virginia's King of All Media. And a third is the saintly Monica Orosz, who has been as patient, as good, and as kind an editor as any writer could wish. I am lucky enough to work regularly with others who fit that description, including Eric Danton of the *Hartford Courant*, D. X. Ferris and Justin Farrar of *Cleveland Scene*, and Jason Pettigrew and Scott Heisel at *Alternative Press*.

Without Michael Lipton, I would probably never have become a writer (and would have been far less happy as a result). He gave me the chance to write professionally, and provided me the contacts and the opportunities to pursue a career in music journalism. Just as importantly, this phenomenal writer and musician taught me the humility of a true artist, and became not only a mentor but also one of my very best friends. Cub reporter Jimmy Olsen will always be grateful, Mr. White.

I am fortunate enough to work at the best high school in the world, and the support of the administration, faculty, and students at Lincoln Park Performing Arts Charter School has been a major reason this book was completed. In particular, I thank my fellow creative arts instructor Adam Atkinson, who helped keep our department running as this project went down to the wire. I thank also Dr. Nick Trombetta, who gave me the chance to be part of his vision.

Stephen Catanzarite is a great author, a great boss, and a genuinely great person. He has been my closest friend for more than twenty years, and I have never been as lucky to have his friendship and support as I was while writing this book. He read chapters and offered many valuable suggestions; more than that, he did what he has done since I have known him: he offered an example of the right way to live. His wife, Rachel, and sons, Thomas and Henry, also took me into their home for periods during the writing of this book, and I will always be grateful for their hospitality and friendship.

My brother, Drew LeRoy; his wife, Angie; and his sons, Alex and Mattie, were also gracious enough to share their home with me for an extended period. (This is what happens when you move twice during the writing of a book, something I emphatically do not recommend.) My sincerest thanks to all of them—especially to my brother, who has always been the most generous person I know, and whom I am always proud to claim as family.

Countless people claim to have the greatest set of parents, which is understandable. However, only my brother and I are correct when we say it. Louie and Polly LeRoy not only raised me and fed me, they raised and fed my dreams as well, supporting me unconditionally all the way. I love and owe them both more than I could ever say.

I can say the same of my three wonderful children, Carys, Greer, and Grant. They have all had to go without a father for long stretches while this book was being written, and the best thing about finishing it is the time I will be able to spend with them again.

Finally, often last but never least, is my beautiful wife, Kiena Nutter. No one has sacrificed more while I wrote this book, and no one could have suffered it all with more aplomb. She is the greatest person I know. Without her, there would be no book—or anything else.

And thank you to Father, Son, and Holy Ghost.

THE
GREATEST
MUSIC
NEVER
SOLD

Introduction

When I was a kid, I experienced a comic book obsession common to those with more imagination than friends. Every dark morning on the way to school I passed the Dairy Mart, its comic book rack fluorescent-lit in the window, and if I had lunch money to spend on a couple of new Marvels, I did, gladly going hungry later. After a few too many missed meals, my parents intervened and enforced a strict comic book rationing: one a month.

Of course, like the moonshiners and rumrunners of the past, and the digital pirates still in the future, I quickly found a way around the blockade. But if I'd had to choose a single comic book, it would have been an easy decision. My favorite title by far was debuted by Marvel in February 1977, and was called simply *What If?* It was a vehicle for exploring all the questions that resided in the back of every fan's mind. What if the Hulk had kept Bruce Banner's brain? What if the Fantastic Four had gotten different super-powers? What if Phoenix of the X-Men had lived? What if Spider-Man's Aunt May had died?

Comic book creators would one day overdose on this sort of alternate-reality crack, but I never quite got over the high. And many years later, after my media allegiance had shifted, I became aware that the same sorts of parallel universes existed in music—in the form of albums recorded, and then abandoned.

The Holy Grail, of course, was Brian Wilson's *Smile,* which should have provided the American counterpoint to *Sgt. Pepper's*

Lonely Hearts Club Band, and instead marked the descent of the head Beach Boy into creative paralysis and personal madness. It was a classic story—the musical equivalent of imagining Spider-Man stopping the thief who killed his Uncle Ben—but it had been done to death. I was more curious about the albums that showed up on my doorstep to be reviewed and then disappeared from the release schedules, leaving behind no trace or explanation. Most of them probably represented no great loss to Western civilization, yet even a dull or flawed creation gained mystique when it was dispatched to the shadow realm of the unreleased. Put more simply, someone had decided that people shouldn't hear this music. To the contrarian in me—in all of us, probably—that automatically made it interesting.

"I think there's something to the idea of a record that you'll never hear, something more stimulating or evocative," agrees Beck, who has recorded a few albums fitting that description himself. "They'll always be better in your mind."[1]

Undoubtedly, Beck is right. However, I couldn't shake the idea of trying to drag a few of those records out of the mists and into what I hope is some amount of illumination. The danger inherent in this demythologizing is always that it will reveal disappointingly mundane truths: that the Loch Ness Monster was created by camera trickery and unwitting schools of fish; that Bigfoot is really some guy in a gorilla suit. In researching this book, however, I found the opposite to be true. Stories as fascinating, and as little known, as the albums with which they are associated, were also dragged into the light. And in most instances, the mystery at the heart of every unreleased album—the reason it was consigned to limbo—remains.

I must admit that this is, at least in part, because of a circumstance I should have foreseen before I began writing. Artists do not, as a general rule, enjoy talking about their unreleased albums. Some have moved on unsentimentally, while for others, these rejected recordings are still too painful to revisit. "Devastated" was the most common adjective I heard while doing interviews, and with good reason. More than a few musicians can undoubtedly relate to Juliana Hatfield when she says of her unreleased album *God's Foot*, "It's like a child that was aborted against my will, a child they cut out of my stomach and threw in the trash can."[2] Rightly or wrongly, an unreleased album carries with it the stigma of failure. And not many of us relish discussions of our failures, real or perceived.

Even harder to solicit were the views of those who, in many cases, are the reason you are reading this book: the record company executives who made the final decision to leave these albums in the vaults. Sometimes that is because access was refused; label representatives are just as human as the rest of us, and also do not like being reminded of failure. At other times, the identity of the person responsible for rejecting the album in question was simply unknown. In either instance, the lack of such commentary represents a hole in this book, one that I fully acknowledge but do not believe is a fatal wound. The intent of *The Greatest Music Never Sold* is to tell the stories of these lost albums as completely as possible, yet also to introduce readers to the most important casualty of their disappearance—the music itself.

In fact, a more complete title for the book might be *The Greatest Stories Never Told About the Greatest Music Never Sold.* Rock journalism produces all too many volumes that are little more than rehashed news reports stitched together with commentary—often of dubious value—from the author. I did not want to contribute to this library, so early on I adopted this approach: if I could not get new information about an album from a primary source, I left it out of the book.

The albums I picked offered, in my opinion, the best combination of genuinely excellent music and intriguing backstories. The list is, of course, subject to your own additions, deletions, revisions, and outright disagreement—which is part of the fun.

Because of my desire to get firsthand information, however, several deserving albums were eliminated from the discussion. One of them, in particular, I regret excluding. Neil Young is the creator of any number of unreleased albums, but *Homegrown*—abandoned in 1975 in favor of *Tonight's the Night*—belongs on any list of the greatest music never sold. As Young's biographer Jimmy McDonough put it in his epic *Shakey*, "To hear *Homegrown* in its entirety is to hear Young at his best."[3]

However, the two primary sources for a behind-the-scenes look at those largely acoustic sessions are producer Eliot Mazer and Young himself. The latter has a well-known antipathy to the press in general and authors in particular (witness the lawsuits that greeted the publication of *Shakey*, which was supposed to have been an authorized biography), and Mazer, a longtime friend of Young's, understandably asked to get his permission before speaking to me on the record. That permission had not been granted at the time this book went to press; therefore I felt I could add nothing to the fair amount of ink already spent on this album. Here's hoping it will be featured in the "Volume Two" I not only hope to write, but believe is required.

I do feel the need to explain two additional exclusions. The unreleased music of Prince, perhaps the most consistently prolific artist of this era, deserves its own book, and has been discussed at length in at least a couple of excellent ones, including Per Nilsen's very thorough and engaging *Dance, Music, Sex, Romance*. However, the most frequent question I entertained while working on *The Greatest Music Never Sold* was undoubtedly "Are you going to write about *The Black Album*?" The answer was and is "No"; although this collection of risqué hard funk became legendary when Prince allegedly pulled it at the last minute in late 1987, Warner Brothers eventually did release *The Black Album*—albeit for what seemed like ten minutes—in November 1994, when declining sales of Prince's new material made a dip into the archives even more attractive. And any album that has seen official release, however brief or limited, was eliminated from consideration for this book.

Meanwhile, the most fabled unreleased album of our time is probably Guns N' Roses' *Chinese Democracy*, which has been evolving (or perhaps devolving) for more than a decade under the increasingly monomaniacal auspices of Axl Rose. It is yet another record that deserves its own book, and one day such a book will undoubtedly be written. At press time, however, word was that some version of this infamous artifact would indeed see daylight sometime in early 2007. What makes this promise about *Chinese Democracy* different than any of the dozens broken before it is impossible to say, but several people told me they'd heard the latest, "finished" version of the album. One of them was former Skid Row singer Sebastian Bach, who said, "Axl's always been a man of his word. If he says he's going to put it out, I believe him."[4] Your move, Mr. Rose.

For whatever it's worth, more than one person I interviewed about the record thought the reason for its failure to appear was a relatively simple one. In the words of one label executive who worked on *Chinese Democracy* for several months, "Axl is simply afraid to sing. He's psyched himself out, trying to create the perfect record, and now he can't even step up to the mic because he's so afraid to make a mistake. That's the biggest part of the problem."[5] But being afraid to make mistakes is the biggest reason so many other albums stay unreleased, as well.

We have reached a point in history where two irresistible and opposing forces will affect the future of unreleased albums and their what-if universe. The first is the insatiable desire for new product by a music industry that now pumps out more new releases than could have been imagined even a decade ago. An increasingly significant part of that glut results from labels trawling the vaults of recognizable artists, dead or alive, a trend unlikely to reverse itself. And the distribution possibilities offered by digital media (for example, download-only reissues of albums with appeal to only a limited market) seem to guarantee that the cynical declaration often made by fans and artists alike—that every note ever played is destined to be shrink-wrapped and sold—will eventually become reality.

The release in 2004 of that greatest of great lost albums, Brian Wilson's masterpiece, *Smile*, underscored this view; so did the decision, a year later, by Fiona Apple and Sony, to release *Extraordinary Machine*, an album originally rejected as too uncommercial. Fan pressure helped prompt the reversal, as did Internet leaks of the unreleased recordings. If such leaks have not performed the same service for the albums mentioned in this book—and bootlegs of several of these discs are regularly traded among fans—it may be only a matter of time. "If something exists in some sort of electronic form, we're in an age now where everything's coming out," insists the producer, remixer, and musician Bill Laswell, who oversaw the boundary-stretching hip-hop on the Jungle Brothers' *Crazy Wisdom Masters* and has made attempts to liberate the unreleased recordings. "I think nothing is gonna be overlooked. It just might not come out in a traditional format."[6]

Yet the second, even more irresistible force is a collective creativity that will always outstrip the capacity of even the freest global marketplace. Musicians will always record; the results will not always make sense as product. Even as labels dredge through tapes filled with insignificant outtakes for inclusion on re-remastered box sets, they will discard without a second thought a dozen albums that lack a certain hit or simply make more sense as a tax write-off. In an increasingly competitive and narrowly defined pop music world, the number of albums deemed unsuitable for release is likely to grow—and some will become mythical events as well.

Shortly after I began writing this book, I came across a remarkable novel about this sort of pop mythology. Written by Lewis Shiner and titled *Glimpses*, it is the story of a man who finds he has the ability to travel backward in time and help musicians like Brian Wilson finish their finest works. In the world of *Glimpses*, pop's "what ifs" are answered, with wildly unpredictable results. My hope is that *The Greatest Music Never Sold* will function as a nonfiction counterpoint to Shiner's novel, offering authentic glimpses into musical realities that came tantalizingly close to existing.

Some, however, would rather not peer behind that curtain. Not long ago, on a blistering July afternoon in New York City, the British singer Green Gartside reclined in the air-conditioned lobby of his hotel and recalled some recordings begun and abandoned by his group, Scritti Politti, almost twenty years earlier. "I imagine on a hot day like today, out in a tin cupboard somewhere in White Plains, those tapes are probably turning to powder," Gartside reflected. "But that's good. Pop music is disposable, purely ephemeral."[7]

At the risk of contradicting an artist I happen to esteem more than almost any other, I must respectfully disagree, and not just because my livelihood demands it. In tin cupboards all over the world sits music too vital to simply surrender to the ether from which it emerged. This book is a humble attempt to make a small portion of that music real once again. And if this project can, in some tiny way, help spur someone to consider granting any of these albums an official release, I would be happier than I can express.

Please forgive me if it sounds too melodramatic to say I feel a certain responsibility to the music in this book. Forgive me the same sin for adding that I have come to think of *The Greatest Music Never Sold* as a small and solitary candle, lit in the hope that these songs will all someday find their way home.

① Seal

Togetherland Falls Apart

*M*ention Seal, and the name Trevor Horn *is sure to follow. The towering, scar-faced singer, son of Nigerian and Brazilian immigrants, and the bespectacled British producer, responsible for signature hits by the likes of Frankie Goes to Hollywood, ABC, and his old band, Yes, appear to be music's true Odd Couple. Listen to their work together, however, and the partnership makes perfect sense: Seal's unmistakable silk-and-sandpaper croon breathes life into Horn's intricate studiocraft, creating pop-soul singles with dazzling surface and emotional depth.*

Yet while his pairing with Horn has made the formerly homeless singer a millionaire and global star via songs like the Grammy-winning "Kiss from a Rose," Seal has spent nearly his entire career trying to escape his mentor's guidance.

Almost every attempt thus far has been unsuccessful, and at least two unreleased albums still molder in the vaults as proof of Horn's hold on Seal.

"It's almost as if he's a prisoner, in a way,"[1] observes Nick Launay, an Australian producer who witnessed firsthand the strange, though undeniably successful, relationship between Seal and Horn. Launay's own brief alliance with the singer was interrupted, he alleges, by Horn spying on his work, and ended when Horn's notoriously hard-nosed wife and business partner, Jill Sinclair, reportedly dismissed the idea that a black artist could be successful making rock music.

The failure of Seal's latest break for freedom, however, is one that puzzles even his closest collaborators. Three years in the making, the ironically titled Togetherland *was shelved amid ruined friendships, label turmoil, and the large shadow Horn cast from afar. Seal himself has publicly disavowed the album on several occasions, most recently on his official website. "I will never release it as an album to buy," he wrote in early 2007, "because my feeling is that it really isn't that good."*

Yet it's a collection that more than one person involved considers far superior to its replacement, the Horn-produced Seal IV. *"Togetherland is a damn good album. It's just*

*a shame," says Gus Isidore, Seal's longtime gui-
tarist and co-writer, who played on both discs.
"To me, the new one just isn't Seal."*[2]

*But who, exactly, is Seal? That's a question
the self-produced* Togetherland *seems intended
to have answered—but with the album in limbo,
the answer is, too.*

When he began work on his fourth album in 1999, Seal was a star
on suddenly uncertain footing, an artist whose faith had been profoundly shaken.

He'd just returned from the road, after a disastrous tour behind
his latest effort, *Human Being.* Seal's label, Warner Brothers, had
abruptly pulled the plug on the tour in July due to poor ticket
sales, directly attributable to the problems that surrounded *Human
Being*—which Seal would later disparage as "the album that ten
people bought."[3]

In fact, it reached No. 22 on the *Billboard* album charts, and
went gold two months after its release. But that was a major disappointment after the improbable success of "Kiss from a Rose,"
a ballad with the stately feel of an Elizabethan madrigal that
became a No. 1 single in 1995 and made the exotic voice and face
of Sealhenry Samuel familiar across America. *Human Being* contained no follow-up hit; worse, its commercial failure exposed the
troubled relationship between Seal and his longstanding producer,
Trevor Horn.

Since signing Seal to his label, ZTT, in 1991, Horn had been the singer's closest musical ally. Horn, who had earned his Svengali reputation by turning five rockers from Liverpool who could barely play their own instruments into the global phenomenon known as Frankie Goes to Hollywood, saw in Seal—at the time a humble bike messenger—a raw talent he'd never had the opportunity to mold. And in Horn, some felt, Seal had found a replacement for the father who reportedly had abused him as a child, causing him to leave home at age fifteen for life on the London streets.

The pair produced two platinum albums and won sterling reviews for their futuristic fusion of dance, rock, and soul; yet things went sour between Horn and Seal during the making of *Human Being*. The two came to blows during the sessions, when Seal objected to Horn's meticulous rearranging of his vocal tracks, and for a time Seal was determined to produce the album himself. Horn later returned to oversee the project—"We fell out, and we kissed and made up and we finished the record," Seal summed it up for MTV[4]—but the bad blood seemed to have seeped into the songs, which contained little of the sparkle and majesty of the duo's previous work together.

With its dark, murky mix and its title track lamenting the deaths of rappers Tupac Shakur and Biggie Smalls, *Human Being* was a downer whose sales figures were entirely unsurprising. "I didn't like the sound of it," Seal admitted years later. "I thought that it suffered from having too many cooks to spoil the broth, and from me not retaining my focus. I think it had some good ideas, and quite possibly some of the best lyrics I have written, but it takes more than that to make a great album. And it is not a great album. It's an okay album."[5]

For the first time, Seal's surrogate father had let him down. And that failure gave him his best excuse yet to attempt something he'd been trying to do since 1992: take control of his own career.

Nothing else epitomized Seal's declaration of independence as did his selection of his first new collaborator. The man who had his choice of the world's finest session musicians picked up the phone one day in the summer of 1999 to ring Scott "piLL" McCall, a twenty-nine-year-old bedroom techno artist from Santa Monica, California, whose only public exposure to that point had come from posting his songs online. Yet Seal had discovered McCall's audio streams while surfing the Internet and proposed a partnership.

"He was telling me how he always wanted to get into the techno scene," McCall told *Rolling Stone* magazine. "After that I just started inundating him with MIDI files, like, 'Hey, check this out.'"

The duo would work together on at least three songs, one of which ("Breathe") would wind up reworked with live instrumentation for *Togetherland*. McCall explained their long-distance songwriting setup, conducted even while Seal was still on the road. "He recorded his voice in a microphone on his laptop, sent me the WAV file, and then I patched it in with the MIDI file. And that's the first time I heard his stuff to my music."[6]

That method of cowriting prompted one of Seal's most intriguing and obscure titles, "God Sits (at the End of Your Tongue)," an expression of his new freedom ("I go wherever I want / do whatever I feel") set atop billowing clouds of synth and a hard, trance-inspired rhythm that came from a $150 soundcard—the centerpiece of piLL's low-budget home studio. The pattering electronics of "Is It a Dream" and "Breathe," meanwhile, were subtler and more trip-hop-inspired, a clear precursor of the direction Seal would take on *Togetherland* the next year.

Seal's interest in electronica might have been a desire to explore cutting-edge sounds, but it could also have been viewed as a return to roots—and a chance to escape Horn's disapproval. After all, Seal had emerged from the acid house scene that engulfed Britain in the late '80s and produced electronic pioneers like Massive Attack and Tricky. And while most people remember his first album for its lush, Horn-produced hit "Crazy," other songs—including the breakthrough single "Killer," a collaboration with the London house DJ Adamski—had simple techno beats as their backbone. It was a sound Horn frowned upon; he told *Rolling Stone* in 1991 that Seal's infatuation with techno "was absurd, when you have that much talent. It's limited—you don't sit and listen to it. You can't go to concerts and things like that."[7]

But Seal's longest-standing collaborator, Gus Isidore, who was summoned from England in early 2001 to add guitar to the *Togetherland* sessions, immediately sensed the possibility that Seal was trying to recapture the spirit of his early career. "It was very much like I remember working on the first album—when there were no pressures, and it was very relaxed. He was very positive about it, and adamant about producing himself," says Isidore, a Londoner who first befriended the unknown Seal at a West End studio in 1987. "And the total feel of the album, I can relate more to the first and the second albums, particularly the first."

Work on *Togetherland* had officially begun a few months earlier, in the spring of 2000, at Seal's home in the Hollywood hills, near the summit of Mulholland Drive. Engineer Chris Fogel, best known for his work with Alanis Morissette, had helped convert Seal's gym into a studio, and a young English producer and programmer named Henry Jackman had been drafted to help with the album. The choice of Jackman, who had recently worked with Trevor Horn on an album that reunited the producer's high-tech, high-concept '80s pop consortium Art of Noise, was a hint that Seal wasn't ready to completely abandon his past. And it wasn't surprising that he felt immediately at home with his new collaborator.

"He was initially brought in to do a week's worth of programming on the record . . . and apparently Henry just blew him away with a rearrangement he did of a track," recalls Fogel. That led to an offer to coproduce the album, and "Seal liked him so much, he gave him a room at his house and let him live there for a year and a half."[8]

Jackman and Seal worked on songs through the winter of 2000, and by the time Isidore and Seal regulars like keyboardist Jamie Muhoberac, drummer and multi-instrumentalist Earl Harvin, and guitarist Chris Bruce—as well as percussionist Luis Jardim and Dr. Dre bassist Mike Elizando—were summoned to Los Angeles, much of the album was written.

It was evident to Fogel, who joined the sessions in May 2001, that Seal had immersed himself in the trip-hop and techno sounds of the late '90s. "It was sophisticated English electronica—it had a very Massive Attack feel to it," he says, "but with a lot more guitars. Granted, it might have been a little late to the party—that ship had already sailed—but Seal had added his own thing to it. The problem I always had with that kind of music was that it lacked emotion, but Seal definitely added that."

The approach was epitomized on "English Lover," a duet between Seal and one of the few guests on *Togetherland*, Emiliana Torrini, an Icelandic protégée of the singer Bjork. "I know we won't find the answers / if we don't live the questions," a restrained but romantic Seal crooned, over ping-ponging electronic beats. "Seal would sing the verses and she would sing the choruses," says Fogel. "It was really embracing the Bjork side, the Massive Attack and Goldie stuff."

Seal was also embracing a creative freedom rare among major label artists. His relationship with Warner Brothers had been strained over the failure of *Human Being,* and the label—which was also undergoing the turmoil common to the music industry at the time, as massive mergers and the threat of mergers meant constant layoffs and reshuffling—had evidently decided that it was wise to take a hands-off approach with one of its sensitive crown jewels. "There was a lot of question in the air about what was happening at the label, and he was kind of left to his own devices to make this record," Fogel says.

Like Gus Isidore, Fogel remembers the sessions as extremely relaxed, if occasionally intimidating.

> You'd walk into the kitchen and sit down for lunch and turn to your left and say, "Oh, there's Shaquille O'Neal." It was a star-studded affair.
>
> But we'd go up there for a week, and we'd work maybe two of the five days. The rest of the time would just be screwing off—riding in Seal's Ferrari, playing ping-pong, watching tennis. [Seal]'s a gigantic tennis fan. And to be honest, records don't get made in record time that way.

Yet as carefree as things seemed at the top of Mulholland, Fogel remembers one name that always aroused tensions:

> Whenever Trevor's name came up, there was this sense you got that it was the son who was trying to outdo the father. You got the feeling that there was a kind of father-son thing between Seal and Trevor, and that Seal really, really respected Trevor, but they'd had some kind of falling out and he was still bitter. It was understood all through the making of the album that, "We've gotta do better than Trevor."

"That was a pall that hung over the whole proceedings," recalls Fogel. "You didn't speak Trevor's name lightly in that house."

What Fogel, and most of the other participants, didn't realize were the striking parallels between the *Togetherland* sessions and the last time Seal had attempted to make an album in Los Angeles without his mentor. During that period, close to a decade earlier, Horn's presence had loomed uncomfortably over the studio, recalls producer Nick Launay.

"It seems to me now weird that it actually even happened," says Launay, an Australian who got his start by getting on the good side of the famously temperamental John Lydon during a Public Image Limited session, and made his name producing some of the biggest post-punk acts of the '80s, including Killing Joke, Gang of Four, Midnight Oil, and INXS. "It was as if it was all being done on the sly, although I knew that everything I did would be played to Trevor, and that Trevor would decide whether it actually came out."

Launay first met Seal in early 1992, shortly after the singer's debut had become a hit on both sides of the Atlantic. "Seal's manager at the time knew my manager, and there was some connection there. And then I remember meeting him at some club in London and we got talking," Launay says. "And he explained that he wanted to make a record very different from his last one, that he wanted to be an artist like Bowie was—where you never knew what kind of album he was going to make next. That impressed me."

The duo left England for California, where they set up shop in the home of famed producer and Eurythmics guitarist Dave Stewart, and began assembling musicians. "Absolutely everybody we called was interested, which was quite amazing. He was a new, exciting artist and everybody wanted to work him," Launay recalls.

The core of the band was to include a rhythm section drawn from two of America's premier funk-rock bands: the Red Hot Chili Peppers' bassist Flea, and drummer Fish from the Los Angeles septet Fishbone. (Launay remembers the Warner Brothers executive responsible for arranging the sessions asking incredulously, "You want me to book a Flea and a Fish to play with Seal?")

Pleading exhaustion, Flea was eventually replaced by top session bassist Doug Wimbish. The genre-spanning parade of superstars who joined the sessions, however, continued unabated, with Stephen Stills, Alice in Chains guitarist Jerry Cantrell, the duo Wendy and Lisa, Funkadelic guitarist DeWayne "Blackbird" McKnight, and jazz-fusion drummer Harvey Mason Sr. among the guests. Also on board was Gus Isidore, who'd earned his metal credentials with Thin Lizzy in the early '80s and was finally getting a chance to rock out alongside Seal.

Yet from the beginning, Launay says, "always hanging over my head was the knowledge that Seal was completely owned by Trevor Horn. Signed to his label, signed to his publishing company, almost managed by Jill Sinclair." At one point, he claims, Horn even "sneaked into the studio when we weren't there to listen to stuff, which was really uncool. They were definitely spying on us."

Although Launay says his relations with Horn remained cordial and that the two even discussed coproducing the album, there were also other clear signals that Seal remained Horn's artistic property. One of the many acoustic demos Seal played for his new producer was a fully realized version of "Kiss from a Rose," a song Launay fell in love with. "But I was told I wasn't allowed to record that one," he says. "Trevor wanted to do that one himself."

What did get recorded was "Love Is Powerful," a nine-minute Hendrixian jam. Seal had Jimi on his mind, having just completed a cover of "Manic Depression," with guitarist Jeff Beck, for the tribute album *Stone Free*. While Isidore believes now that "the rock stuff just wasn't Seal's thing," Horn apparently liked the tune enough to later whittle it down for single release in Japan.

However, another still-unreleased song, "Under the Wheel," was the killer cut, according to Launay. Two separate compositions stitched together into a thirteen-minute-long opus, it referenced classic California rock, with Stills on guitar and stacks of Beach Boys–style harmonies from Wendy, Lisa, and Wendy's sister, Susannah Melvoin. "It's *Pet Sounds*-ish," Launay says. "I've played it for lots of people and their jaws drop. It's pretty breathtaking." Isidore, who cowrote the track with Seal, also laments its suppression. "It had a very Beatles-like vibe," he says. Doug Wimbish, meanwhile, puts it even more succinctly: "It was *off the fucking chain*, man!"[9]

But after three months and $100,000, those two songs were all Launay had to show for the album he'd hoped would be a quickly recorded, back-to-basics rock record. In part, he claims, the sessions dragged because "Seal was, let's just say, really enjoying L.A." Seal himself would allude in interviews to his drug habits of the time: "I just thank my lucky stars that I'm not dead or maimed in some way," he reflected in 2003, "considering all I put my body through."[10] Wimbish, meanwhile, relates the story of Seal spending days on end with the girlfriend of a well-known pop star—who confessed to Wimbish years later that he'd been distraught enough to speak with a professional hit man about having Seal rubbed out.

There were more benign reasons for the delay, as well. As the hottest new star in Los Angeles, Seal was frequently sought out by industry legends, in particular a pair of musical magpies always eager to pick the brain of a bright young thing. "In one week, David Bowie and Mick Jagger had rung inviting him to dinner. I can understand why he wouldn't want to spend the evening in the studio with me!" Launay says with a laugh.

Yet he also echoes Chris Fogel's assessment of the *Togetherland* sessions: without Horn cracking the whip, Seal became easily distracted. "Seal is one of these people that is five hundred percent focused—for about half an hour a day. You could literally record a whole song in that half an hour," Launay says. "But you could spend the rest of the day waiting for him to turn up, or for him to be into it."

A break was called in recording, and when Launay returned home to London, he was quickly summoned to meet with Jill Sinclair. The interview went badly from its opening line, which, Launay remembers, was, "How do you justify what you have done to my artist?"

From there, things got worse, Launay alleges. "She said, 'I don't know if you've noticed, Nick, but Seal is a black person. And black people don't sell rock 'n' roll.' And I said, 'Does the name Jimi Hendrix mean anything to you?' And she said, 'The only reason Jimi Hendrix sold any records at all is that he died.' At which point I said, 'I can't even respond to that.'"

Launay called Seal to say he was quitting the project, but the singer resisted. "He said, 'Bollocks to that, this is what I want to do.'" So the pair, along with Isidore and Jamie Muhoberac, went back into the studio to cut the more R&B-flavored "Bird of Freedom," whose title and lyrics take on new interest given the circumstances.

"It's basically my attempt to sound like what Trevor Horn would do," Launay says of the ballad—which, in fact, Horn ended up producing himself for the soundtrack of the Spike Lee film *Clockers* in 1995. "But it took ages, and it was a compromise on what I wanted to do, and it just took the fun out of it."

The perfect excuse to end the project soon presented itself when Launay's countrymen Midnight Oil asked him to produce their next album, *Earth and Sun and Moon.* "I had to choose between working on this unknown thing that already sounded like it was never going to be heard," he says, "or working with a bunch of old friends."

A disappointed Seal wasn't ready to give up his dream of making a rock album so easily. He recruited Launay's close friend, the renowned producer Steve Lillywhite, to take over the sessions, and recorded several more songs during the winter of 1992–93. Isidore, who met with Seal and Lillywhite but was unavailable for the sessions, believes that some of Launay's work was redone at this time, and that early versions of songs from Seal's official second album were also tried.

But the end result was the same. "Steve had a similar meeting with Jill Sinclair, in which Jill basically trashed everything he'd done and told him he could learn a few points from Trevor," says Launay. "Now, this is Steve Lillywhite, who produced all of U2's early records, and who has made more important records than just about anyone in rock. He takes a job because he wants to do it, not because he's hired. So he said, 'Fuck you,' and walked."

Seal would suggest in 1994 that he immediately reunited with Horn after breaking with Lillywhite, claiming, "Steve was wrong for all the reasons Trevor was the right producer. Trevor's a musician first and foremost . . . he is, in my opinion, the only producer for me."[11] Yet at the time, Seal was evidently still not prepared to retake his place under Horn's wing. There are rumors of an unsuccessful collaboration with Chic guitarist and '80s superproducer Nile Rodgers (the pair would work together on a 1995 cover of "Fly Like an Eagle") as well as several more songs recorded under the supervision of Wendy and Lisa, who ultimately played on, and cowrote material for, Seal's official second album (and who years later would fall out nastily with Horn over an unreleased album of their own).

Besides his producer problems, in these difficult years Seal also had to overcome a case of double pneumonia, anxiety attacks, and the rush-hour totaling of his Ferrari on a California freeway. Launay recalls the enigmatic singer's passion for fast cars, and remarks on the insight Seal offered into his own personality late one night as he pushed his Mercedes to speeds well into the triple digits on Ventura Boulevard.

"If we'd crashed, we'd have been dead immediately. But that was the point. He was enjoying life while he had it," says Launay. "He explained to me that he'd been sleeping on the streets, and now here he was, working with all these great people. He got this big smile and told me, 'Nick, you're taking life way too fucking seriously.'"

The artist who reemerged before the public in May 1994 certainly seemed to have transcended his troubles; indeed, he appeared to have been reborn. His spiky crown of dreadlocks had been shaven, making his appearance even more striking, and the sophomore album Horn had patiently buffed over hundreds of studio hours gleamed, like Seal's newly bald visage, with an almost otherworldly aura.

The success of soaring, orchestral soul singles like "Prayer for the Dying" and "Kiss from a Rose," which hit No. 1 after its inclusion on the *Batman Forever* soundtrack, suggested Seal had finally resolved his creative and personal dilemmas, particularly those involving Horn. Subsequent events would prove that this was not the case.

"Trevor is an incredibly gifted guy, but he has to do everything his way. He'll work on something for as long as it takes to get it right. And the thing is, he *does* get it right. His records are unbelievable," Launay says. "But it is a particular style, and it's almost like Trevor is the artist, in a way.

"Then you've got Seal, and he wants to do his own thing. And there just isn't room for that in the formula."

But by the summer of 2001, Seal appeared at last to have found the artistic space he craved. *Togetherland* was turning into an album that acknowledged his approaching fortieth birthday with adult sophistication—the sort of album, Fogel believes, that would have given him the stature and critical respect of a Peter Gabriel or a Sting.

One of the completed songs that reminded Fogel of the former Police singer was "(Just a) Step Away," a stately, sweeping dance track that suddenly exploded with "a huge drum sound, and then just a breakdown for days in the middle," reminiscent of Sting's "Englishman in New York." Fogel adds, "That was Seal dry, no reverb on his voice, just belting it out. Seal's voice was just wonderful with that kind of thing."

Also in the can were the folk-rocking "Keep On" (originally titled "Champagne"), "Let It Ride," "Under the Sun," and "Love Is Better," all clear throwbacks to the first album, with brisk acoustic strumming underpinning the high-tech soul arrangements; and "This Could Be Heaven," a big, bold ballad that Fogel and Isidore both agree was the most pop-oriented song of the sessions. Retitled "Heaven," it would be the one composition that would survive *Togetherland* and see official release on *Seal IV*.

Seal hadn't finished writing, however. One afternoon, he overheard Isidore picking out a delicate progression on his acoustic guitar, "and Seal instantly, like he does, just jumped on it and turned it into a song in no time," Isidore recalls. The tune, "All I Wanted to Say," approached the beauty of another Isidore/Seal collaboration, "Fast Changes," from Seal's second album, with haunting arpeggios and a melody that owed something to Joni Mitchell. "It was just done acoustically," says Isidore, "with just a bit of effects and keyboards" beneath Seal's multitracked harmonies.

Another song, "Eliz," with links to Seal's first album—specifically, the "Crazy"-style synth line that pulsed through its verses—was also completed as the sessions drew to a close. Its surprisingly intimate chorus was dedicated to one of Seal's actress girlfriends, Fogel believes.

Isidore remembers the album's title track, which would close *Togetherland*, as perhaps the most tragic loss. "Originally he just did it with the Philharmonic Orchestra over here [in London], and it was just that and his voice, and it was amazing." Later, back in Los Angeles, "he put a totally different vibe on it, adding twelve-string guitar, although I preferred the original. But the message on it was just fantastic."

That message—a plea for understanding despite differences of race, religion, or nationality—was delivered via a song that suggested two lovers fighting to overcome such barriers (a theme touched on elsewhere on the album, and in the more pointed title of an abandoned track: "Interracial Immaculate").

"Seal manages to capture this emotional thing and spit it out— that's his genius, and it's all in that song," says Isidore. "It's on a scale where it's, if not better than, then on a scale with 'Kiss from a Rose.' It's just a massive song, massive."

Although there were almost no extra tunes recorded, one that didn't make the final track listing still has Fogel shaking his head. It was a cover of the 1971 Bill Withers hit "Ain't No Sunshine," recorded mostly by Jackman, with a slippery funk bass line "that just killed," courtesy of Mike Elizando.

"If anybody's got a copy of that, I would just defecate," Fogel says, laughing. "Seal nailed the cover of that. He absolutely nailed it. But that is going to be the hardest-to-find Seal track ever. I don't think it was ever even mixed."

In September 2001, just days after the terrorist attacks on America, Seal spoke about his first live performance since the *Human Being* tour (at a Los Angeles breast cancer benefit, where he closed out the evening with the new song "Love Is Better" and "Crazy") and the imminent release of *Togetherland,* scheduled for February. "I'm very excited. I produced this one myself. I thought [the concept and title of the album] was pretty poignant when I was recording it . . . but I think it is even more so now, given recent events," he told the website liveDaily. "It's an album that tries to promote the concept of togetherness and love and acceptance, the elimination of pointless barriers, the elimination of prejudice. . . . I'm mixing the last two tracks, but it's pretty much finished."[12]

In the same interview, Seal said he was happy about a recent shakeup at Warner Brothers. Former Interscope executive Tom Whalley had taken over the music division,

> and someone who I absolutely adore is his second in command, a gentleman by the name of Jeff Ayeroff. Jeff is an amazing person, a true music lover, and is someone who is extremely intelligent, one of the most intelligent people in the business. I consider both of those people to be allies . . . I think we have a good crew at Warner's. Everyone is excited about this record.[13]

Or maybe not. After allowing Seal carte blanche during the making of *Togetherland,* the label was finally giving a close listen to its investment.

The first hint of unrest came when Warner's ordered a remix of *Togetherland* by Steve Fitzmorris, who'd done the same job on Seal's first two albums. Fogel, who'd originally mixed *Togetherland,* and whose credits included mixing hits for acts like Alanis Morissette,

Aerosmith, and Sheryl Crow, remembers this as "a little freak-out stage. The work I'd done wasn't really in this genre, and they wanted someone they were more familiar with." The label was also searching, he believes, for some connection with the successful sound of Horn's recordings.

The second sign that the album was in trouble—and proof that the remix hadn't satisfied Warner's—came just before Christmas 2001, when Isidore got a call from Seal inviting him on a working holiday at Whistler, the Canadian ski resort.

"He wanted me to come with him and do more writing. He hadn't totally abandoned the album at that point, he just wanted to write some more songs to see if he could come up with other things to fit with *Togetherland*," remembers Isidore.

The trip never transpired, however, and shortly afterward, Seal began writing—at the encouragement of Warner's—with American producer and multi-instrumentalist Mark Batson, who'd worked with hit-making R&B acts like Beyoncé Knowles and india.arie. "They went to L.A. and hung out, and they got on really well and wrote a lot of things," says Isidore. "Mark was sort of producing at that point."

The producer's chair had become vacant because Jackman had left the now-sputtering project, allegedly in a dispute over money. Fogel says he and Jackman had both agreed to work on the album at low original rates: Jackman as a programmer, Fogel as an engineer. When they were both promoted—to producer and mixer, respectively—their salaries didn't change, he claims.

"The reality of it is, it was about money," Fogel says. "And Seal doesn't tolerate any dissension within the ranks."

With Warner's now "heavily involved" with the album and dubious about its commercial prospects, Seal's friendships with Fogel and Jackman had unsurprisingly cooled. "The six months I spent with him was an amazing relationship," says Fogel. "He would call me every day, and on the weekends, and say, come on up, let's just hang out. When I went to New York, he was like a baby that was missing his mother. He would call me every morning at 7:30 and talk for an hour. And the same thing with Henry. Henry was his boy."

However things ended up between Seal and Jackman, the latter has decided that discretion is the better part of valor—or at least, the key to continued work in the music business. "Talking about what happened is something that's really not going to help Henry right now," says his manager, David Surnow. "And in fact, it could hurt him."[14]

Fogel would soon follow Jackman out the door, after Seal accused him of theft early in 2002. Summoned into what he calls the "interrogation kitchen" of the house on Mulholland, Fogel was confronted by Seal and his guitar tech Steve McDonald. "They were both sitting at the table drumming their fingers, and they said 'Sit down.' Then Seal said, 'You're stealing from me.'"

The dispute, Fogel claims, had to do with some recording equipment he had brokered for the singer. After performing several other unpaid services for Seal, he says—from getting him free stereo equipment to remodeling his office—Fogel "finally got to the point where I said, 'I'm taking a commission.'" Seal, he alleges, objected.

"I walked out of there 100 percent confident not only that had I done nothing wrong, but that I had a pretty good case if it got any worse," says Fogel. But as he departed Seal's house for the last time that January afternoon, the door was also closing on *Togetherland*.

The album was taken off the Warner Brothers release schedule, and a planned spring tour—with music-generated computer graphics to have been provided by Andy O'Meara, creator of the "G-Force" program—was scrapped. When Gus Isidore next saw Seal, the singer had left his Los Angeles home of a dozen years and returned to his native England, where sessions began in London with Mark Batson as producer.

These sessions yielded at least six songs—"Love Divine," "Waiting for You," "Touch," "Loneliest Star," "Where There's Gold," and "Get It Together," all of which would appear on Seal's new album. Seal, however, "didn't feel [the material] was achieving its true potential," says Isidore, "and he knew what Trevor could do." Despite his best efforts to escape, the prodigal son was about to be reunited once again with his musical father.

The official announcement of Horn's involvement came in the fall of 2002, and Isidore recalls the ensuing recording, at the producer's Sarm West studio in London, as being remarkably fast and free of rancor. "It was pretty quick, the production of that album. Trevor just took what was there and worked his magic on it."

The sessions began while Seal was, in another irony, enjoying his first success without Horn in years. His latest attempt at techno, a collaboration with British house DJ Dave Lee (a.k.a. Joey Negro) on the song "My Vision," was a throwback to his career-starting work with Adamski. And the single, released in September under another of Lee's aliases, Jakatta, was a sizeable club hit in the U.K., begging the question of how the material from *Togetherland* might have fared.

But Isidore, for one, welcomed Horn back to Seal's musical life. "I've got total respect for Trevor; he's such a pleasure to work with, and it's such a pleasure watching him work. He's five, ten steps ahead of you. And Trevor really understands Seal, and knows how to get the best out of him, more than any other producer I've seen."

There are also those insiders, like Earl Harvin, the Texas drummer and multi-instrumentalist who's played and toured with Seal since 1995, who believe talk about *Togetherland*'s failure is overblown. "I did work on a lot of Seal material that either didn't see the light of day or ended up on *Seal IV* . . . and there isn't really anything to it except for 'Those songs didn't make it,' " said Harvin, during a break from European tour rehearsals early in 2004, adding that "as far as talking about it . . . I'm not really up for it."[15]

Despite Isidore's friendship with Seal and admiration for Horn, however, he makes no secret of his disappointment with *Seal IV*, aimed squarely at the urban-dominated pop charts. "I can't listen to it," Isidore confesses. "I hardly put it on, y'know." And Fogel's reaction to the stripped-down R&B of "Get It Together," the album's first single, was a simple "What the hell?!"

Of course, it's understandable that Fogel, whose employment and friendship with Seal ended after the *Togetherland* sessions, and Isidore, replaced as Seal's primary co-writer on *Seal IV* by Mark Batson, might prefer the unreleased album to its official substitute. And given the fact that *Seal IV* was the commercial success Seal desperately needed—reaching No. 3 on the *Billboard* album charts and going double platinum within six months of its release in September 2003—their criticisms can be refuted with cold, hard sales figures.

Yet reviews of the album were decidedly mixed, with many critics applauding the focus that Horn's unusually spare arrangements placed on Seal's voice, but lamenting the weakness of the material itself. The BBC's assessment—"Seal has the looks, the image and more importantly the voice of a successful artist; unfortunately right now he's not got the songs"[16]—was typical.

Meanwhile, some of Seal's most ardent followers—those, at least, who take the time to post their views on the singer's label-sponsored website—were also unimpressed. Although Seal's tight grip on his own studio outtakes is near legendary, a Russian fan site began posting sound clips from *Togetherland* (apparently taken from a Warner Brothers internal advance of the album) in the fall of 2003. The clips, and the site, would come and go over the next few months, but the verdict among Seal fans able to judge the samples against *Seal IV* seemed to be that Seal had erred.

Seal, however, seemed firmly convinced it was *Togetherland* that had been a terrible mistake. In fact, its failure became part of the marketing for *Seal IV*, as in interview after interview he repeated artistic mea culpas. "It was a complete and utter disaster," he told MTV. "It was unfocused and meandered into obscurity."[17] To VH1, he admitted,

> I started out by producing it myself, got two years into it, and in a word it wasn't good enough, basically. So I scrapped it and started again.
>
> It's quite simple. I'm not like somebody who has millions of dance moves like Michael Jackson or Justin Timberlake. I am the guy that has this voice that people connect with. There is an emotional quality in my music that resonates with people. If there's no emotion or belief in the song or the delivery, then there is nothing. It was not the easiest reality to come to terms with, but it was one that I had to accept. I had a lot of help from the record company and my management. They were very cruel to be kind, but

> I'm lucky they had faith in me as an artist. They knew that I hadn't suddenly forgotten how to sing or write songs. They knew I had to go off and find whatever it was that resonated with people in Seal's music.[18]

Despite such statements, Isidore believes it's only a matter of time before Seal changes his mind. "These songs eventually will find their home, or be released in some form on an album in the future," he says. "There's just so many great tracks."

Seal himself has occasionally softened his stance, suggesting that while the old songs have gone "in the vault," the book isn't necessarily closed on *Togetherland*—at least, as a possible source of material for other artists. Yet Fogel thinks the idea of the naturally reticent Seal ever plugging an album he's publicly disavowed is unlikely. "Seal is one of these guys, he likes to stay out of the limelight when he doesn't have to be in it. He's not in your face 24/7. He's kind of like the Tom Cruise of artists."

Whatever his differences with Seal, Fogel praises the singer's integrity—which he says would also prevent the release of the ill-starred *Togetherland*. "I think it would be seen as a ploy to make more money, or as something that just wasn't good enough," says Fogel. "No—I think that record's done."

In early 2007, Seal confirmed that opinion. Blogging on his official website, the singer promised fans he would try to post a version of *Togetherland*—"or at least the sections of it that I feel are worthy enough. . . . Sure there are moments in it that are definitively 'Seal,' but it is however wrought with inconsistency and this is the main reason why it wasn't officially released in the first place."[19]

And that may be the final word on Seal's great lost album—at least until he decides to let fans visit *Togetherland* and decide for themselves.

Seal: *Togetherland*
Recorded for: *Warner Brothers Records*
Scheduled release date: *February 2003*
Recorded at: *Seal's home studio, Los Angeles, CA; Sarm West Studios, London ("Togetherland"); 1999–2001*

TRACK LISTING:

1. (Just a) Step Away
2. Keep On
3. Love Is Better
4. Eliz
5. Under the Sun
6. Heaven
7. English Lover
8. Breathe
9. All I Wanted to Say
10. Let It Ride
11. Togetherland

Also recorded: *"Ain't No Sunshine" (B. Withers)*

Produced by: *Henry Jackman*
Engineered by: *Chris Fogel*
Mixed by: *Chris Fogel*
Remixed by: *Steve Fitzmorris*

Credits:
Seal—*vocals, backing vocals, acoustic guitar, bass, keyboards*
Gus Isidore—*guitar*
Jamie Muhoberac—*keyboards*
Chris Bruce—*guitar*
Steve McDonald—*guitar*
Mike Landau—*guitar*
Earl Harvin—*drums*
Luis Jardim—*percussion*
Mike Elizando—*bass*
Henry Jackman—*keyboards, programming*

❷ David Bowie

Broken *Toy*

*R*ock's great reinventor, David Bowie, has created and inhabited some of music's most memorable personas, from Ziggy Stardust to Aladdin Sane to the Thin White Duke to, periodically, just "plain ol' Cowboy Dave." Yet, believe it or not, some of the musicians closest to Bowie were, until recently, almost completely unaware of his earliest guises.

Then again, apart from his initial hit, "Space Oddity," Bowie had kept his '60s activities well under wraps for most of his career. The original tunes he cut as a Stonesey rhythm-and-bluesman, a dandified mod, and—most notably—as an Anthony Newleyesque crooner have remained available to fans, but received almost no acknowledgment from their creator. If he did speak about his early work, it was with scorn; "Aarrghh, that Tony Newley stuff,

THE GREATEST MUSIC NEVER SOLD

how cringey," he would say in 1990. "No, I haven't much to say about that in its favour." Unsurprising, given the fact that each of these songs had failed to give Bowie the hit he'd once desperately sought.

Over the years, revisionist history would begin the Bowie story in 1969 with "Space Oddity," which made for a far more satisfying bio. It skipped Bowie's years in the London wilderness, many of them spent under the guidance of impresario Ken Pitt. Also eliminated were embarrassments like "The Laughing Gnome," a 1967 novelty whose high-pitched, Chipmunks-style backing vocals marked a low point in Bowie's quest for a smash.

But Bowie has always considered his past ripe for plunder. And in 1999, as the fifty-two-year-old artist began touring to support the nostalgic 'hours . . . ', he decided it was finally time to revisit the least-known, least-appreciated stage of his professional life, by rerecording some of his '60s oeuvre on an album called Toy. Most of his bandmates were just as surprised as everyone else.

"Actually, I had never delved into that era at all," confesses Mike Garson, the pianist who first joined Bowie alongside the Spiders from Mars in 1972, and is the longest-tenured Bowie sideman. "So I recorded a lot of these songs never *having even heard the original versions. But that actually made it even more fun for me."[2]*

It also meant *Bowie's band wasn't aware that critics had long looked down on this portion of his repertoire. "I didn't know what songs were old or new," recalls Lisa Germano, who added a variety of instruments to the* Toy *sessions. "'Cause every song we worked on was looked at with fresh eyes and open-minded thoughts as to where to go with them."[3] Approaching the project in this fashion, Bowie's collaborators heard a set of tunes with attributes that had often been obscured by production and arrangements too dated, baroque, or cute. "All of these songs could have been written yesterday," thought Garson. "And the fact that a guy could write these songs in the '60s, that young, just let you know you were dealing with one of the heaviest rock artists ever."*

However, even Bowie would end up lacking the heft to get Toy *released. And while the project found longtime friend Tony Visconti working on a Bowie album again for the first time in almost two decades,* Toy *ended up a bittersweet experience for all involved, especially producer Mark Plati; first the job he had worked so hard to earn was reportedly usurped, and then the album that was to have been his first official coproduction with Bowie was shelved.*

It's more than a little ironic that the unreleased Toy *has become more obscure than the songs it was intended to re-introduce, and that an album full of rejected singles would receive an even more complete rejection the second time around. It's more than a little unfortunate that an album described by Mike Garson as "every bit as good as the last five or six we've done,[4] and some of it is better" turned out to be a corporate plaything instead of a genuine blast from Bowie's past.*

Despite all the indescribable highs of his fabled career, David Bowie had rarely been happier. It was the late summer of 2000, and Bowie was married to the internationally famous model Iman, had just become the proud parent of a healthy baby girl, and was on an artistic roll.

He had celebrated his fiftieth birthday three years earlier by appropriating the raucous electronic beats of jungle and drum-and-bass on *Earthling*. But it was a more reflective Bowie who returned in 1999 with 'hours . . . ', an autumnal album that examined middle age and looked back fondly on the orchestrated balladry of 1971's *Hunky Dory*. The tour for 'hours . . . ', which stretched into the following year, was a less melancholy affair, however, and found an upbeat Bowie delving deeper into his old songbook than he'd ever dared.

The first tune to be retrieved took both fans and collaborators off guard: "Can't Help Thinking About Me," which was exhumed for the taping of a VH1 "Storytellers" episode. An obscurity from 1966, recorded with Bowie's short-lived backing band the Lower Third at the height of his fixation with the Who, it was one of his finest early singles. But more than thirty years later, this tale of a boy who had "blackened the family name" by committing some horrible but unspecified crime, became the mod anthem it always should have been. Rocked up with buzz-saw riffing and a brisker tempo, it was a highlight of the VH1 show, and allowed guitarist Mark Plati, playing his first major gig alongside Bowie, to "work out a lot of Who fantasies, thank you very much."[5]

During the subsequent tour, Bowie would resurrect two more songs from his early career. "I Dig Everything" was a 1966 R&B stomper more notable for being Bowie's official solo debut than for its organ-driven tune. "The London Boys," which had been unfairly relegated to B-side duty[6] later that year, was a more inspired choice for revival, however. Generally acknowledged as the best of Bowie's pre-"Space Oddity" work, it was the cautionary tale of a small-town mod who had ventured to the capital and gotten lost in pills and loneliness. Other songwriters were exploiting this theme with more commercial success than the then-unknown Bowie; the Kinks' Ray Davies chronicled innocents despoiled in songs like "Polly" and "Big Black Smoke," for example. Yet Bowie's version of the story was genuinely haunting, with a somber brass arrangement and swirling organ; the new recording that would surface from the *Toy* sessions stayed faithful to that ambience, with a ghostly clarinet section provided by bassist Gail Ann Dorsey and backing singer Emm Gryner.

Mike Garson recalls running through a couple of other Bowie numbers from the same era—possibly "Karma Man" and "Conversation Piece"—which ultimately weren't played on the 'hours . . . ' tour. However, the old songs already on the set list were going down a storm with audiences, and a theme for Bowie's next album was emerging. In announcing the project to Gibson.com, the guitar manufacturer's official website, Mark Plati would explain,

> What we're doing is taking songs that David wrote in the '60s and recording them again—or for the first time in a few cases. These songs were from the same time period—1966–68—but the original versions all had different producers, so stylistically they're all over the place. Plus, David's voice wasn't very developed, and he didn't have enough experience in the studio environment to make the songs sound the way he wanted them to. Both of those are non-issues now, of course.[7]

During tour rehearsals in the spring of 2000, Bowie and his band began working up more of his old tunes, with an eye toward recording when the group came off the road. Shortlisted for what was then being called "the '60s album" were the aforementioned "Karma Man," a mildly psychedelic song from 1967 that had been influenced by Bowie's fascination with Eastern religion, and 1969's "Conversation Piece," another B-side given short shrift, considering its lovely melody and pointed lyrics about Bowie's creative struggles. The rerecording would flesh out those attributes with strings and full-bodied acoustic guitar, testing the more mature singer's lower register in the process.

Also hashed out during these rehearsals were new versions of "Baby Loves That Way," "I Dig Everything," "You've Got a Habit of Leaving," "In the Heat of the Morning," "Let Me Sleep Beside You," "Silly Boy Blue," and "Liza Jane," Bowie's very first single, from 1964, back when he was still known as Davie Jones and fronting a beat combo known as the King Bees. The remake eradicated most of the song's R&B swagger (which had been swiped unapologetically from Mick Jagger anyway), in favor of a lightly swinging arrangement that suggested trad jazz. It seemed an odd choice, but, as Mark Plati noted, "We weren't out to duplicate the original tracks at all—in fact, we wanted everyone to bring their natural musical sensibility to the party. We all got more psyched about the gigs, and the record, after each rehearsal."[8]

The band, at that point, consisted of Bowie mainstays Sterling Campbell on drums, bassist Gail Ann Dorsey, and Garson on piano. Plati, who had engineered *Earthling* and then filled in on guitar after Reeves Gabrels departed abruptly just prior to the 'hours . . . ' tour, would also return and coproduce, and 'hours . . . ' backing vocalists Holly Palmer and Emm Gryner were re-enlisted as well. Even the lone addition was a familiar face: guitarist Earl Slick, who had served stints with Bowie in the '70s and '80s and offered a dose of old-fashioned six-string heroics to the group. Well-practiced and fresh off the road, the band was at the top of its game that summer.

New York's oldest studio, the window-filled Studio C of Sear Sound in midtown Manhattan, was chosen for the recording because of its roomy, 2,500-square-foot interior. The facility included space for the entire band and featured two isolation booths—a "boudoir" for Bowie, plus a room for Garson and his keyboards. Sear had been selected by Plati and a relative newcomer to the Bowie camp: Pete Keppler, a New Yorker who ran live sound for alt-rock band the Eels. Plati had decided he wanted to focus on production, and needed Keppler's help to run a new recording software program called Logic, which gave them both some anxious moments and led Earl Slick to nickname Plati "Gameboy." "Pete and I share a basic sonic sensibility, so I rarely had to tell him anything," Plati would say. Still, the tapeless recording "took some getting used to, as I had to put a lot of trust in someone else and give up a degree of control. In the end, it was effortless—so much so that we've gone on to repeat the experience on other projects."[9]

After Slick joined the sessions from his home in Oregon, he was overcome by a strange sense of déjà vu. "We came into the studio together one day, after he'd been there a couple of days," recalls Keppler, "and he said, 'Man, this place feels so familiar to me—I can't figure it out!' And I said, 'There's another studio upstairs that's part of Sear Sound—let's go up to the sixth floor and take a look.'

"And so we went up and looked around, and he went, 'Oh my God—this is the old Hit Factory! This is where I did *Double Fantasy* with John and Yoko.[10] Holy shit!' He got really taken back for a minute—it kinda freaked him out."[11]

There was little time for reminiscing during the initial sessions, however. Over the course of a week in early July, Bowie and his band cut basic tracks for thirteen songs. "It all happened so fast," says Keppler, who was amazed to witness firsthand Bowie's legendary first-take vocal prowess. "I remember at times I was working on the console and David was in an iso booth, and he was about four feet off the mic, belting his brains out, and he would sound so good. And the band just roaring away behind him, it was incredible. It gives me chills even now just thinking about it."

Bowie would play no instruments during these sessions, according to Keppler.

Occasionally he'd walk out to Slick or Garson and say, "Hey, could you try this?" And he'd pick up the guitar or sit down at the piano. But as far as I can recall, he didn't actually play on any tracks. I mean, he's the first one to admit it: he's not really a great player. He really was there to sing and to provide reference for the rest of the band, and hopefully, get a great take. But when he has to concentrate on singing and playing, one thing or the other tends to get compromised. So it was really about the vocal for him.

Plati thought the fast pace and immediacy of the sessions had energized his boss,

more than I'd seen him at any point in the studio since the initial *Earthling* sessions in August '96. The way we were tracking, he'd sing on the first take of the song and be able to overdub himself on the band's second take. If we needed a third take, he'd add a third harmony or double. So . . . on a number of songs, his final vocals would be finished by the time the band had gotten it right! He'd emerge from the vocal booth, big Cheshire grin on his face, and say something like "Well, I guess that does it for me!"[12]

Garson, meanwhile, would get the chance to "do things I don't usually do on a David record," adding synth strings, Fender Rhodes, and Hammond B3 to the mix on various songs, in addition to his usual piano. And while he hadn't minded working on the electronic-oriented *Earthling*, he approved of the more traditional, melodic bent Bowie's music had since taken, on *'hours . . .'* and again on *Toy.* "As a writer of songs myself, and as a fan of classical music . . . I'm partial to a melody that rips your heart out," admits Garson. "And I felt that in a song like 'Conversation Piece.'"

The chance to share the hidden past of his very private employer touched an even deeper chord. In 1974, a cocaine-addled Bowie had told Garson he wanted him to be his piano player for the next twenty years; as it turned out, it was nearly that long before the two would work together again. But after returning to the fold in 1992, Garson had once again become an integral part of Bowie's studio and touring units. His jazz and classical background, as well as his sense of adventure—which had all first come to prominence during his unforgettably fractured solo on "Aladdin Sane"—added the air of unpredictability Bowie loved. Old misunderstandings had been forgiven, and old ties, Garson thought, were being strengthened. Proof of this occurred one day in the studio, while Garson was noodling around with "some nice chords and a melody" of his own. Bowie casually sat down and began scribbling down lyric ideas, and the two began working on this proposed cowrite during breaks in the sessions. "I don't have the tape, he's the only one who has the tape. And I have no idea what he was planning to use it for—maybe something that'll come out ten years from now, or maybe never," says Garson, who nonetheless treasured the experience.

"I remember my piano playing, specifically, was exceptionally inspired on these dates. Because I felt I was connecting to a deeper part of David, and I wanted to try harder, in a way, to show what these songs really were," recalls Garson. "Because the earlier versions were nowhere near as good as the versions we recorded."

Listening to the rough mixes, Mark Plati was similarly impressed, but thought there was something missing. As he sat in the audience at the Bowery Ballroom one sweltering August night, he heard exactly what he was searching for.

Pete Keppler had recommended that his friend Plati take an evening off and go see the Eels. The band was really the vehicle for the private pain and joyful noises of singer-songwriter Mark Oliver Everett, otherwise known as "E," but during this tour he'd expanded the Eels' lineup, and one of the additions was Lisa Germano. Accomplished on several instruments, Germano had first attracted notice as the fiddler in the band of John Cougar Mellencamp, a fellow Indiana native. She had gone on to work with a series of A-list artists, from Bob Dylan on down, and including Sheryl Crow, Iggy Pop, and the Smashing Pumpkins,[13] while also carving out a solo career for her own singular brand of poetic folk.

"After listening to a few songs, and being familiar with some of Lisa's solo records and her work with other artists . . . I knew I needed to have her play on *Toy*—her vibe would be just perfect for us," Plati later recalled. "I pitched my idea to David, as well as got Lisa to send him some of her solo CDs. After a week or so, we decided to go for it."

Plati scheduled two days of sessions at his East Village apartment in late September, inviting Germano and Bowie—who had taken some time off while Iman gave birth to the couple's daughter, Alexandria, that August—to attend. "At first it seemed odd having such high-profile folks sitting on my goofy Ikea couch, playing with my daughters' toys and combing through my fridge for milk.

David poked fun at the seashells I use for ashtrays," remembered Plati. However,

> we settled in, I put on the kettle, and we zipped through a number of songs that first day. Lisa really took to the material, putting down all sorts of parts on an arsenal of eccentric instruments, including an electric violin tuned one octave lower than usual, a 1920s Gibson mandolin, and an old, tiny tortoiseshell blue-green Hohner accordion with straps so old and tired we had to beg them to stay together (assisted by duct tape) for the duration of a song.[14]

Not only did Germano not know the material, however, she was also

> pretty nervous—being a fan and wanting to contribute, [but] not feeling too sure why I was even asked to do so. I brought my violins, an accordion, mandolin, and a recorder flute to see what colors I could add.
>
> But as soon as I arrived it was all clear that this was going to be fun. Mark made sure there were no rules or expectations, and that made the atmosphere comfortable for the "anything goes, all ideas welcome" attitude, which is all too rare these days in the studio. So we just were in major creative mode, and the feeling and energy was high, and the recordings show it. They are full of mistakes and life and the fun of experimenting. David even picked up the violin and played

some cool drones like a John Cale vibe . . . sounded good, but then he wanted me to do it.

He would get genuinely excited when he came up with an idea and Mark and I were able to see it to fruition, just like a child—curious and creative and unafraid. I loved being around this energy; it was inspiring.

Plati agreed:

David was completely into these sessions, having just as much fun as he did in July if not more. He'd not done any work on the album since late July, nor listened to it much. He seemed just plain *ready* to work, and he was thrilled with how great and fresh the songs sounded. [He] kept pulling ideas out of the air for Lisa to play, and it was great to see how well they got on and how in sync they were from the first few minutes.

The trio made a quick tour of the revitalized East Village—"I think both of them still had the late-'80s vision of it as junkie/anarchist hell," suspected Plati of his guests—and had lunch at an Italian cafe, then got back to work.[15]

Germano would play a violin solo that sounded "like it came from Mars, thanks to Mark's expertise" on the song "Baby Loves That Way." Yet another B-side, this time from Bowie's 1965 debut single with the Lower Third, the tune in its original incarnation was a fingersnapping but forgettable pop number, inspired by Herman's

Hermits and a sweet but faithless girlfriend. With its tempo and key dialed down—a trick used on several *Toy* rerecordings—and with a spacier arrangement, "Baby" gained an innocence unheard on the original, becoming "a drunken crazy recording" that still makes Germano laugh when she hears it.

Bowie was doing more than merely reclaiming the flip sides of his old singles, however. Two songs cited by band members as among the highlights of the sessions had never gotten past the demo stage. One of these, "Hole in the Ground," was a rarity from around 1970 and had featured assistance from Bowie's childhood friend George Underwood, as well as Herbie Flowers, Terry Cox, and Tim Renwick. Presented with the demo, Mike Garson and his bandmates promptly turned it into "this crazy little groove thing" that, as the *Illustrated David Bowie Discography* points out, bears a resemblance to Lou Reed's "Walk on the Wild Side."[16] "It was this very, very simple—but fun—jam that we expanded on," says Garson. "There was a lot of talk about that one." Germano would later add a recorder melody to the song, which she says delighted Bowie. "He got so excited when we came up with this simple line," she says. "That song rocks."

"Shadow Man," another demo technically from outside the '60s scope of *Toy* (it dates from the Ziggy Stardust sessions in 1971), was a more subdued affair. However, the new recording would add shades of melancholy to Bowie's original folk sketch, and is considered by many to be the highlight of the sessions. With Garson's delicate piano replacing Bowie's twelve-string, and violins and echoed vocals adding to the ethereal effect, the lyric about a man who can "show you tomorrow" took on a deeper meaning, especially when sung by its author—who has always had a fascination with the future, and foretelling it—almost thirty years after its creation. " 'Shadow Man,' " says Germano simply, "is beautiful."

Plati would soon invite another newcomer, Irish guitarist Gerry Leonard, to contribute overdubs to *Toy*. Leonard, who had recorded with the high priestess of art-rock, Laurie Anderson, also performed his own material under the nom de pop Spooky Ghost. It was an appropriate name, considering Leonard's spectral guitar style, and his contributions to the album would please Bowie enough that Leonard later became a full-fledged band member. Yet it was the addition of Germano that Plati was proudest of:

> For me as a record producer, Lisa could be one of my more inspired choices as far as an outside musician I've brought in to work on a project: it worked out much better than I could have imagined (I figured it'd work, but not *this* well), as her playing—especially violin— was simply magical and made some of the songs truly complete. It was as if she was a part of the band from the conception of the record, and not overdubbed afterwards.[17]

An important producer from Bowie's past, however, was about to push down the faders on Plati's plans.

Among David Bowie's close friends, Tony Visconti was not only one of the oldest, but also one of the most candid. The American-born producer had first worked with Bowie in the late '60s, when the singer was beginning the transition from pop fop to authentic rocker. Yet Visconti would turn down the chance to produce "Space Oddity," which became Bowie's breakthrough in the summer of 1969. Although he thought the song would be a hit, Visconti also believed it "a spectacular cheap shot" cynically timed to coincide with the first lunar landing.[18]

This frankness did not earn Visconti exile from Bowie's universe, however. After overseeing the work of Ziggy Stardust's main competitor, Marc Bolan, during the glam era, Visconti returned in 1975 to give sheen to the plastic soul platter *Young Americans*. And while Bowie's late-'70s trilogy of *Low*, *"Heroes"*, and *Lodger* is best known for Brian Eno's oblique studio strategies, it was actually Visconti who produced all three records—a fact even music writers often miss, to his annoyance.

> Things changed in December of 1982, a month Bowie had asked Visconti to leave free. The two were to reunite in New York to record Bowie's new album, which all parties involved knew would be a momentous release. Bowie was planning to leave his longtime record company, RCA, and a strong potential debut for a new label would send bidding into the millions. The album would also be Bowie's first recording free of the clutches of MainMan, the management company that had manufactured stardom for Ziggy Stardust—but had owned a big chunk of Bowie and his royalties ever since.

A chance meeting with producer and guitarist Nile Rodgers in the bar of New York's Carlisle Hotel instantly altered all Bowie's plans. "Looking for Ziggy Stardust," Rodgers didn't even recognize the plainly dressed Bowie; by the end of the evening, the pair had adjourned to Bowie's apartment to talk shop, and Rodgers had taken on the task of resurrecting his new friend's career. It was a job for which he was well qualified. As the driving force, with bassist Bernard Edwards, behind the R&B group Chic, Rodgers had a string of crossover hits like "Good Times" and the savvy to give Bowie the warm, funky—and chart-worthy—record he craved.

But Visconti, who was waiting by the phone for his summons, didn't find out about Bowie's new direction until recording had already begun. It was a bitter pill, made all the more acrid by the massive success of Rodgers and Bowie's work. *Let's Dance* became a hit that surpassed anyone's wildest expectations, and Bowie's sold-out "Serious Moonlight" tour helped win him the cover of *Time* magazine. The accompanying story carried one sour note, sounded—unsurprisingly—by Visconti, who reminded readers of Bowie's unconventional first marriage to the mercurial Angie Barnett. "Thursday was gay night. David would go to a gay club, Angie to a lesbian club, and they would both bring people home they found," Visconti recalled. "We had to lock our bedroom doors, because in the middle of the night, these people they brought home with them would come climbing into new beds, looking for fresh blood."[19]

That image was 180 degrees from the blond, tanned, and straight Bowie then topping the charts, and further Visconti interviews, which touched on the sensitive subject of Bowie's relationship with his son, Joe, were reportedly even less to Bowie's liking.[20] So the singer, who had made a habit of cutting off old acquaintances without warning, excommunicated Visconti from his inner circle. The silence would last for fifteen years, and was finally broken in 1998 when the pair began a series of collaborations on some soundtrack singles and outside projects (like the British band Placebo's *Without You I'm Nothing*). "We had both grown and changed, so the time was right to open the channels again," Visconti said at the time. "However, I've discovered how sensitive he is about his privacy, and I've learned to respect that."[21]

If Bowie was going to be reconciled to his '60s songbook on *Toy*, it was only fitting that Visconti be present as well. His initial collaboration with Bowie—on the 1968 single "In the Heat of the Morning," Bowie's first tentative foray into lewd rock 'n' roll—was on the set list, as was "Karma Man," produced by Visconti the same day, and "Conversation Piece," which Visconti oversaw two years later.

When Visconti joined the tail end of the initial *Toy* sessions in July, his brief was to help orchestrate a couple of the songs.[22] One on of those tracks—possibly the delicate "Silly Boy Blue"—Mike Garson was flattered to learn that Visconti had "used some of my piano lines to orchestrate it. And he did it in a very beautiful way. He's a wonderful string writer."

Before long, his role on *Toy* had apparently expanded. A friend of Bowie's who has requested anonymity observed the reunion with Visconti: "They just clicked, big time. And all of a sudden, Tony was kind of in on the project, in more than just a string arrangement way. And one producer kind of got edged out, and another producer took the helm. It just got a little bit messy."[23]

Plati, who had worked his way into a dream job, was reportedly crushed. The final blow would come later, when many of Lisa Germano's parts were erased from the completed mix. "Mark had positioned himself to produce the next few Bowie albums," the singer's friend adds, "and now that wasn't going to be the case.[24]

"I love David to death. He's a wonderful, wonderful man . . . but he knows what he wants. He definitely does not tend to make real bonds of loyalty with any certain people. It's not like Bruce Springsteen, where, till the day they die, the E Street Band will be who they are. David really picks from a palette of people."[25]

However, as recording on *Toy* continued that autumn, Plati remained the pivotal figure. He would lead a stripped-down, Big-Apple-residents-only version of Bowie's band—himself on guitars and bass, Sterling Campbell playing drums, and Bowie on various keyboards, including the Stylophone, first featured on "Space Oddity"—that worked on new material at Philip Glass's Looking Glass Studios. One of the songs was a version of Pete Townshend's "Pictures of Lily" for an all-star Who tribute album; like many of the songs on *Toy*, it dated from the '60s and was slowed down dramatically in its new incarnation. But Bowie had decided that *Toy* needed a couple of new songs as well. It was perhaps the first hint that he was having doubts about the project's viability, but the Looking Glass sessions would produce two strong tracks that fit nicely alongside their vintage counterparts.

"Afraid," like so many Bowie tunes, had its roots in a book he was reading at the time. In this case, it was the just-published memoir of former Rolling Stones manager Andrew Loog Oldham, which described how he had forced Mick Jagger and Keith Richards to write their own material by locking them in a flat. "We decided to try this approach, and so I sent David off to the Looking Glass lounge and told him not to come back until he had the goods!" said Plati. "It was all quite funny really, except that David really *did* come up with the goods, in the form of a song called 'Afraid,' which came into being courtesy of my mini Stratocaster."[26] A briskly strummed, straight-ahead pop number not obviously indebted to any particular Bowie era, "Afraid" returned to a familiar theme for its author: that of being an outsider, in this case one desperate to fit in.

The real knockout of the sessions, however, was "Uncle Floyd," a strange and moody composition "which began its life with a semi-out-of-tune piano and some grainy synth strings, which sounded like they were pulled off of an old 78 rpm record. Both sounds gave the effect of someone playing in a basement of some small, sad, lonely house," remembers Plati.[27] The effect was perfect, considering the subject matter. Bowie sang from the perspective of two abandoned puppets from *The Uncle Floyd Show*, a children's TV series that was a local favorite in New Jersey for twenty-five years, but never quite made the jump to a national audience. The singer had discovered Uncle Floyd in 1980 while working on Broadway in *The Elephant Man* and became a huge fan, lamenting when the series was finally canceled in 1999.

"Uncle Floyd" was actually completed during mixing sessions, Plati recalled.

> David went off on his own to complete the lyric while I started mixing the track. By the time I had a decent rough mix, he was finished. In typical style, he sang around ninety-five percent of it in the first take—it gave Hector [Castillo, Plati's assistant] and me the chills. It was intense, a feeling not at all hindered by the haunting violin from Lisa and the many spooky-isms from Gerry. It's ended up being a favorite of anyone who's heard it so far. For the outro, we employed a chorus of people rounded up on the spot—Sterling and Holly Palmer, Coco,[28] Sean McCaul of the Looking Glass staff . . . and a band called Stretch Princess who happened to be recording in Studio B with Pete Keppler.

Whoever was in the building with vocal cords got hauled in.[29]

Both "Afraid" and "Uncle Floyd" would survive the *Toy* sessions and be reprised on Bowie's next album, *Heathen*. The former would receive a new arrangement that included strings scored by Tony Visconti; the latter would be retitled "Slip Away" and expand its sweep, both musically and thematically. Given bolder production that evoked such classic Bowie ballads as "Life on Mars," the song's new name indicated a more universal approach: "Its meditative beauty effortlessly transcends the specific and eccentric lyrical references," offered Nicholas Pegg, author of the essential *Bowie Encyclopedia*. "As a song of loss and yearning, its themes are universal."[30]

Yet there were those who preferred the eccentricities of the original—including Lisa Germano, who had returned to New York for more overdubs and did some of her most inspired work on "Uncle Floyd." "[It was] full of emotion," she says. "The beginning bits that were left out on *Heathen* were kind of like a Mark Ryden painting ... sweet and strangely disturbing."

Engineer Pete Keppler also thought the first version was definitive. "The version of 'Uncle Floyd' that we did was way cooler than the one that came out on *Heathen*. The mix that Mark did on that song was so much more haunting and cool."

Mixing took place at Looking Glass in late October of 2000, according to Plati, but Visconti would reportedly become very involved with the final mix of the album submitted to Virgin. Bowie himself delivered a message to his fans upon completion of *Toy*: "It really has surpassed my expectations already. The songs are so alive and full of colour, they jump out of the speakers. It's really hard to believe that they were written so long ago." The music, Bowie would add, was "dreamy, a little weird at times, it rocks, it's sad, it's got passion . . . it's really good." He was also, he revealed, designing the album's cover art, which he described as "very odd," and thought the album would be out in March 2001, with a few gigs in support of the release, "at least in New York."[31]

However, as the holidays came and went, it would become clear that Virgin was not entirely pleased with the *Toy* Bowie had given it that Christmas.

What, exactly, was Virgin's objection to *Toy* has never been revealed. It is possible that the label simply back-burnered the project a time or two too many for Bowie's liking. Throughout the first half of 2001, he would update anxious fans via his Web journal, making references to "scheduling conflicts" and "unbelievably complicated scheduling negotiations."[32] It was certainly a complicated time for Virgin and its parent company, EMI, and not a good one by any interpretation. Profits were down dramatically at EMI—which had lost some forty percent of its market value in one disastrous year—and the company, like the rest of the record industry, was frantically jettisoning employees and artists as it tried to cope with the boogey-man of illegal downloading. In the autumn of 2001, things reached an embarrassing head. As former Polygram CEO Alain Levy was brought in to try to patch holes in the sinking ship, Virgin's $80 million prize signing, Mariah Carey, was by all indications having a nervous breakdown in public, and her first movie, *Glitter*, became one of the most universally reviled pieces of cinema in modern history. The company would end up paying Carey $28 million just to go away.

Against this chaotic backdrop, it seems not unthinkable that a collection of oldies—even by an artist of Bowie's stature—might fall through the cracks. There was also the prospect of a brand-new, Visconti-produced Bowie album for Virgin to consider. The two old friends had agreed to work together on a disc of fresh originals, and some initial work on the album had already gotten underway. It is not difficult to imagine Virgin taking a greater interest in this project than in *Toy*, which is exactly what Bowie would reveal to fans in October of 2001. "As I have said before, Virgin/EMI have had scheduling problems and are now going for an album of 'new' material over the *Toy* album. Fine by me. I'm *extremely* happy with the new stuff (I love *Toy* as well and won't let that material fade away)," he wrote on BowieNet. "If you've been following the newspapers you will have seen that EMI/Virgin are having major problems themselves. This has not helped. But all things pass."[33]

The passage of *Toy* came as an unpleasant shock to most of the participants, who had been waiting patiently for its release. "I would speak to David from time to time," says Pete Keppler, "and I'd say, 'Hey, what's up with the *Toy* record?' and he would say, 'It's coming out. It's coming out.' And then months went by and I didn't hear anything, and I thought, 'Well, there goes my calling card!' "

Mike Garson was "devastated" to learn the album had been rejected. "When you step aside and listen to any great artist, whether it's Beethoven or Miles Davis or Chopin ... you start to really realize the magnitude of the guy. And then you get some stupid company who doesn't want to release their work. That's what really pisses me

THE GREATEST MUSIC NEVER SOLD

off. Who is this person, to say they know more than this talented artist, who's put so much life force into this record?"

Whoever the person or persons were, however, they would not continue working with Bowie for long. In December, Bowie announced he was leaving Virgin and starting his own, independent label, ISO. Virgin had not picked up Bowie's option a year earlier; this oversight meant that a disgruntled Bowie was now unwilling to renegotiate his contract. "I've had one too many years of bumping heads with corporate structure," Bowie would say upon leaving Virgin, his latest head-bumping fresh in everyone's mind. "Many times I've not been in agreement with how things are done and as a writer of some proliferation, frustrated at how slow and lumbering it all is. I've dreamed of embarking on my own set-up for such a long time and now is the perfect opportunity."[34] He would ultimately take ISO—and his new collaboration with Visconti—to Columbia.

Still, Bowie pledged multiple times that he would not "let *Toy* slide away. I am working on a way that you'll be able to get the songs next year as well as the newie."[35] And indeed, he would make an attempt to live up to this promise. Over the course of 2002, five outtakes from the *Toy* sessions—"Baby Loves That Way," "Conversation Piece," "Shadow Man," "You've Got a Habit of Leaving," and "The London Boys"—would be used as B-sides and bonus material in conjunction with Bowie's new studio album, *Heathen*. In addition, new versions of "Afraid" and "Uncle Floyd" would feature prominently on *Heathen*, while *Toy*'s title track turned up the following year as a bonus for buyers of Bowie's *Reality*. Retitled "Your Turn to Drive," the song was an atmospheric mid-tempo rocker that boasted enigmatic lyrics and a Miles Davis–style solo from avant-garde jazz trumpeter Cuong Vu.

However, that laudable stab at getting *Toy* to the fans assumes they have deep pockets—as some of the tracks are on hard-to-find import singles—and still leaves at least a half-dozen songs to be accounted for. Included among them are "Silly Boy Blue," a stand-out from 1966 that evinced Bowie's deepening fascination with Buddhism, and the 1968 come-on "Let Me Sleep Beside You." Both new versions tried to amplify the originals' intent; with its beatific acoustic fingerpicking and soaring strings, "Silly Boy Blue" carried an even deeper undercurrent of spiritual yearning.[36] The latter song, meanwhile, was a trifle less sleazy than the '60s version, but its punched-up guitars were a reminder that it contained a great riff nonetheless.

Also MIA to date are "I Dig Everything," "Hole in the Ground," "In the Heat of the Morning," and "Liza Jane."[37] It's quite possible, despite the fact that Bowie evidently regained control of this material (given the official appearance of the aforementioned outtakes), that they'll stay that way. Bowie himself would admit, not long after the rejection of *Toy*, "Trouble is, as is usual with me, I'm already thinking about new songs and projects."[38] Since 2001, Bowie has completed two acclaimed albums, embarked upon a major world-wide tour, and suffered an enforced absence from the business due to heart bypass surgery, while *Toy* recedes further and further into the distance.

"One thing about David," says Mike Garson with a chuckle, "he does know the meaning of the words *move on*. You bring *Toy* up a few years later, and he's like, '*Toy* what?' It's not even in his world. He's off to his next creation. That's how he is."[39]

Tony Visconti, however, would claim that Virgin's thumbs-down on *Toy* wounded Bowie terribly. When contacted for this book, he would say only, "David would be the best person to comment about this album, but he won't."[40]

So Bowie's hidden past has become just a memory once again. Does it still have a future? "My instinct says 'Probably not,'" admits Pete Keppler, "but my heart says 'I hope so.'"

David Bowie: *Toy*
Recorded for: *Virgin Records*
Scheduled release date: *2001*
Recorded at: *Sear Sound, Looking Glass Studios, and Mark Plati's apartment, all in New York, NY; 2000*

TRACK LISTING (no official track listing is known to exist):

1. I Dig Everything
2. The London Boys
3. Baby Loves That Way
4. Conversation Piece
5. Shadow Man
6. Hole in the Ground
7. You've Got a Habit of Leaving
8. In the Heat of the Morning
9. Liza Jane
10. Let Me Sleep Beside You
11. Silly Boy Blue
12. Afraid

13. Uncle Floyd
14. Toy (later retitled "Your Turn to Drive")

Also believed to have been recorded: *"Karma Man"*

Produced by: *Mark Plati*

Credits:
David Bowie—*vocals, guitar, keyboards*
Mark Plati—*guitar, programming*
Mike Garson—*piano, Hammond B3 organ, synth strings*
Lisa Germano—*violin, mandolin, accordion*
Sterling Campbell—*drums*
Gail Ann Dorsey—*bass, clarinet*
Holly Palmer—*backing vocals*
Emm Gryner—*backing vocals, clarinet*
Gerry Leonard—*guitar*
Earl Slick—*guitar*

③ Chicago

Like a Rolling Stone

*Y*ou can play the "what if?" game during every chapter in this book, but not every unreleased album can be claimed as a career crossroads. David Bowie's Toy, for example, would have been a beautifully rendered collection of rerecorded early singles, and, had it come out as planned, Bowie might not have switched labels in 2001. However, Toy's failure doesn't seem to have caused a major artistic rethink on the part of its creator, and it's probable the disc would have become only a fascinating footnote to Bowie's legend.

Chicago 22—better known as Stone of Sisyphus—is a somewhat different case. Parts of it were an authentic return to form for a band that first made its name by fusing horns with rock, while certain songs represented a major risk for a group that, in its later career, had become *almost synonymous with easy listening. The album's surprising rejection in 1993, however, sealed Chicago's fate as an oldies act, an ensemble whose new material would henceforth be greeted by audiences as an unnecessary luxury.*

"If that record had come out, with some support, the band would have been doing all those songs live, besides a couple of old hits," says guitarist Bruce Gaitsch, a longtime friend of the group and major contributor to Stone of Sisyphus. *"It would have been revitalizing —instead of being an oldies band, they would have been a band that was really happening."*[1]

The reason Chicago didn't get that chance has been the subject of sometimes-heated debate over the last decade and a half. It's undeniable that the band's strange relationship with guitarist Dawayne Bailey played a role in the Stone of Sisyphus *debacle—yet that explanation doesn't cover the odd reaction the record received from Warner Brothers, and superproducer Peter Wolf, who remains stunned by the reception given* Stone of Sisyphus, *has his own theories about why his work was turned down.*

What makes the situation even odder is that, unlike most of the other albums mentioned in this book, Stone of Sisyphus *is now being withheld from the public by its creators. It has been reported—and seconded by those who spoke on the record for this book—that Chicago owns the rights to* Stone of Sisyphus, *and has chosen to keep it in the vaults. Save for the songs that have seen official release on compilations, the disc remains merely grist for the rumor mill.*

Over the years, the band has occasionally deigned to address those rumors during interviews and online chats. More often, the subject has been met with enforced silence; as of late 2006, that appeared to be the official policy. That summer, Chicago was promoting 30, *its first album of new originals in years. But David Millman, the group's longtime publicist, declined requests for interviews about* Stone of Sisyphus. *"At this time, the band is fully focused on the new album, and also the current tour," Millman wrote via e-mail, "so there isn't an opportunity to talk about the unreleased album."*

Others, however, have been waiting for the chance to discuss what they believe was, in many respects, Chicago's last stand. "It was like they felt, 'This is an album that's gonna make or break us,'" recalls Gaitsch. Ultimately, it may have done neither, but those close to Chicago during the creation of Stone of Sisyphus *certainly believed that its failure broke the group's creative spirit.*

When the members of Chicago met with producer Peter Wolf in 1992 to discuss working together, the group had achieved a level of success only a handful of artists would ever experience. Chicago boasted worldwide fame, a back catalog of hits that stretched across four decades, and more money than its members could ever spend in one lifetime. They were also a thoroughly defeated outfit nearly ready to part ways, their collective confidence eroded by a series of behind-the-scenes maneuvers that had kept the band in the charts, but had destroyed the sound and camaraderie that had once made Chicago unique.

"They were all at a point where it was really just a job," remembers Wolf. "They had lost that sense of, 'Why are we a band? Why are we still playing?'"[2]

To a casual observer, Chicago still appeared to be riding the wave of a comeback that had begun ten years earlier. The once-proud band that had emerged from the Windy City in the late '60s playing an ambitious blend of jazz and rock had floundered during the disco era. But teaming with producer David Foster had given Chicago a slicker, more radio-friendly sound built around the plaintive vocals of bassist Peter Cetera, and the 1982 album *16* returned the group to prominence with the mellow "Love Me Tomorrow" and "Hard to Say I'm Sorry."

The Foster-produced follow-up, *17*, was the band's biggest seller ever, spawning hit after hit and getting Chicago (or at least the blond and videogenic Cetera) heavy MTV airplay. Even after Cetera left the group in 1985 for a seemingly inevitable solo career, Foster and Chicago replaced him with the unknown but similar-sounding Jason Scheff and managed to cobble together *18*, which went gold and boasted the No. 3 tearjerker "Will You Still Love Me."

What not everyone realized was the price of this success. Foster's track record was impossible to dispute; the British Columbia native was an in-demand session keyboardist who had played with John Lennon and Barbra Streisand, and had written the 1979 prom anthem "After the Love Is Gone" for Earth, Wind and Fire. However, he had little interest in Chicago as a band. Not only did Foster take an active role in shaping the group's sound himself as a musician and cowriter, he brought in a familiar team of Los Angeles studio pros, including Toto's Steve Lukather and Steve Porcaro. "They say that I function best when I have my ringers around me," Foster once acknowledged.[3]

Legend has it that on the first day he worked with Chicago Foster asked the group, "OK, which one of you is the tenor?" When Cetera raised his hand, Foster reportedly told him, "Okay, you and me, we're gonna make the record, and I'll call you guys as I need you." What's undeniable is that the band's once-vaunted horn section played a far less important role in the new-look Chicago, and even musicians who had been mainstays, like keyboardist Robert Lamm, became sidemen.

"I think overall the Foster experience, from what they talked about amongst themselves on the road, was a balance of 'It's great' and frustration on the part of the guys like Lamm, who had to take a backseat to Foster's playing on the records," says former Chicago guitarist Dawayne Bailey, via e-mail. "By 18, Lamm was used to this, but it still didn't go over well."[4]

"David Foster badly, still to this day, badly wants to be an artist and he'll never be an artist. So what he does is he makes records using artists so that, you know, what he does can shine through using the artists as a synthesizer, if you will," Lamm would tell an interviewer from Goldmine in 1999. Still, Bailey believes, the band was willing to subject itself to "Foster domination" if that was the price of continued commercial relevance. "The '80s were such a Fosterized time anyway," he says, "and the band was just happy to be back and having an actual place on MTV."

That was true even after Chicago replaced Foster with producer Ron Nevison for *19*, an album that reflected Nevison's work with big-haired MTV favorites Heart. Crammed with power ballads—including the chart-topping "Look Away," by professional song doctor Diane Warren—the disc was another success costly to the health of the band, built on heavy guitars, outside writers, and a sound that took Chicago even farther away from its roots.

When this formula failed, the fallout was bound to be a shock. It happened on Chicago's *Twenty 1*, which had all the proper elements in place, including Nevison and a pair of Warren ballads, yet stiffed in the marketplace. The band reached a nadir during a performance on *The Arsenio Hall Show*; a run-through of the Tom Kelly / Billy Steinberg schlockfest "You Come to My Senses" was so dismal that trombonist James Pankow was ready to quit the group in disgust afterwards.

"I can't blame him. It was a song for Air Supply or even a female artist. Ultra-sensitive. That song took 'Chicago ballad' to an all-time low," says Bailey. "I have the greatest respect for the writers of that song, Tom Kelly and Billy Steinberg, but that song was just not right for Chicago. Especially on national TV on such a 'party' atmosphere as *The Arsenio Hall Show*. It was a huge mistake to play that song on that particular show. I can't believe someone in power chose that song."

Bailey's comment about "someone in power" represents an important reality of the resurrected Chicago. Since the group's early-'80s rebirth, it had been overseen by Howard Kaufman, whose management company was perhaps the most dominant in the industry. Like David Foster, Kaufman had an impressive résumé but also took a hands-on approach to his clients that at times conflicted with their artistic aims.

What was clear after the embarrassment of *Twenty 1* was that Chicago needed a hit. A producer would be brought in to guarantee that outcome, yet this producer had his own ideas. He was planning a resurrection of his own—but it was the old Chicago he wanted to raise from the dead.

Peter Wolf[5] had first encountered Chicago in 1975, shortly after moving to Los Angeles. A classically trained jazz keyboardist from Austria who had just joined Frank Zappa's band, Wolf was most impressed with Chicago's guitarist, Terry Kath, a musician compared to—and admired by—the late Jimi Hendrix. Tragically, Kath, like Hendrix, met an early end, accidentally shooting himself at a party in 1978. Despite the hits that followed his death, many observers believed Chicago had never truly recovered from the loss of Kath.

"I was fascinated by him. He was the most down-to-earth, real guy," says Wolf. "At that point in time I was in Zappa's band, making $500 a week, which was a little better than playing at the Holiday Inn. And Terry told me, 'You know, I have more money than I know what to do with.' And my jaw dropped."

By the early '90s, Wolf had made plenty of money of his own, producing Top 10 hits for the likes of Starship ("We Built This City") and the British band Wang Chung ("Everybody Have Fun

Tonight") by combining glossy synth-pop and hard rock. During this period, Wolf was in demand enough to turn down offers to produce Madonna and Tina Turner; his busy schedule, he says, even forced him to decline an offer to work with his hero, jazz trumpeter Miles Davis.

One of the bands crowded out of his schedule was Chicago, which had apparently first approached him about replacing David Foster and producing 19. But, after a meeting at drummer Danny Seraphine's Los Angeles home, Wolf turned the band down. "I had committed to two or three projects already," he says, "and I couldn't throw it all down the drain to work with Chicago."

However, Wolf's datebook was a bit more open in 1992, when his manager informed him that Chicago was once again interested in collaborating. There had been a reshuffling of the band's lineup: Seraphine, who'd struggled adjusting to Chicago's increasingly synthesized stage setup, had been replaced by drummer Tris Imboden. And touring guitarist Dawayne Bailey had become an important part of the group.

The thing that hadn't changed, Wolf realized, was an air of complacency, bred by years of success—and years of neglect of the band as a whole. As he saw it,

> the hardest part of the job—when somebody is that successful, like Chicago—is to get that spirit back. The guys in the band are all driving Rolls Royces. Then here comes a young punk producer, and he tells them, "Hey, guys—you ain't shit! You're only as good as your last thing. You have a style, and it's wonderful. But you have to sit down and work! And really hone into the things that are important in the life of

an artist. "It's hard when you have $20 million in the bank, and you don't have to think, and you can do whatever the hell you want. To motivate yourself is kind of hard! And that was my job.

Wolf's motivational tool was a simple one: he wanted to make an album that once again put the focus on Chicago's horns and songwriting. He challenged the group to rediscover itself, and met no resistance. "Because I knew that I was right. I knew that I had truth on my side, so I was very passionate about it. And they all said, 'You know what, you *are* right. We wanna make a great record. We are not dead yet! So let's buckle up and get this thing happening!' And they certainly did."

Woodwinds player Walt Parazaider would recall, "Peter told me, 'I want you to bring over your bass clarinet, all your saxes, your flutes, everything. We're gonna use everything the way you used to in the old days.' That was very exciting to all of us."[6]

Parazaider added that the band saw *22* as a chance to break out of its "ballad prison":

> That was a record that had to be made. We were frustrated that we weren't doing what we wanted to do, cranking out things that Warner Brothers wanted us to do, that sold. We're not looking a gift horse in the mouth, a hit is a hit is a hit, but there was other stuff for us to say, and that's where *Sisyphus* came in.[7]

What Parazaider declined to say concerned the band's relationship with Dawayne Bailey, who had begun dating Parazaider's daughter, Felicia. That pairing gave the new album its title and a vital creative spark, but would lead to Bailey's departure from Chicago—and perhaps played a role in the album's demise as well.

When he joined Chicago in 1986, prior to the tour for *18*, Dawayne Bailey represented the group's latest attempt to recapture some of the rock energy that had died along with Terry Kath. With his lanky build and long, blond hair, Bailey vaguely resembled Donnie Dacus, who had been Kath's replacement in Chicago during the late '70s. But Bailey wasn't just some aspiring rock god with flashy chops. Well-read, with a Zappa-esque sense of humor and the frequent urge to buck the status quo, Bailey had never been the easiest choice for the increasingly conservative Chicago.

"I didn't make much of an effort to fit into their visual image of short hair and conventional, safe male clothing such as macho denim jeans, slacks, etc.," says Bailey. "I also had a low tolerance/patience for playing the same arrangements, same set lists, no changing things up, not taking chances creatively, not being allowed to sing lead and being treated like a sideman.

"Chalk it up to my age at the time, and my growing and developing as an artist in my own right. To paraphrase Edgard Varèse and Frank Zappa," Bailey jokes, " 'The modern-day artist refuses to be a sideman forever and play "Colour My World" for the billionth time without breaking the repressive creative and financial chains that bind. . . .' "

A "Hendrix freak" since his youth, the Kansas-born Bailey had spent time in Bob Seger's Silver Bullet Band. Since that time, he'd developed into a more aggressive guitarist who loved shredding, heavy metal–style. Even though he hadn't played on *Twenty 1*, Bailey had still been a participant, singing "tons of backing vocals."[8] But when the sessions began for *22*, following a few rehearsals in the San Fernando Valley, he did not receive an invite. Instead, the guitar chair was filled by Chicago native Bruce Gaitsch, an old friend of the band.

Gaitsch had been suggested by Peter Wolf, who remembers the members of Chicago debating whether to fire Bailey before the sessions even began. "Dawayne was more a rock 'n' roll guitar player, a flamboyant soloist, instead of a solid rhythm player," claims Wolf.[9] "So I said, 'Guys, if you're already having your doubts, and I really need a solid rhythm player, why don't you get somebody?' And they all said, 'Yeah, yeah, of course. That's cool!'"[10]

Gaitsch remembers being surprised at his invitation to the sessions:

> I always thought Dawayne Bailey was an amazing guitarist. But I guess what they needed was somebody that could make up stuff that would fit this music. And Dawayne wasn't fitting in.
>
> I also think there was a problem between Walter and Dawayne then, they weren't getting along. [Dawayne] was dating his daughter, and [Walter] didn't like that. But I'll never understand, other than the Walter thing, why he wasn't included.

Those tensions dissipated as the sessions started in early 1993 at Wolf's home studio, on his Simi Valley ranch. The atmosphere was relaxed, and the musicians were all involved. This time around, the band's horn players wouldn't be forced to play air guitar if they wanted to appear in a video. Gaitsch recalls,

> The studio was a really cool setup—it had a balcony. And the horn players were camped out up there, working on arrangements, and voicings, while we're downstairs working on guitar parts. And the drum kit was set up above the garage, where we used to have lunch. And everyone was there, *working*. The roadies were there, changing strings. It was really exciting.
>
> Sometimes we'd start with a loop that Peter would come up with on the synthesizer, and just build stuff over that. Or sometimes we'd just start with a click and two guitars, me and Bill [Champlin]. And sometimes we wouldn't all be there; it would be Peter and whoever was the lead singer/writer. Because Chicago has three guys who could be solo artists.

Those three musicians—Champlin, Robert Lamm, and bassist Jason Scheff—would each contribute in different but significant ways to the sound of *22*. Champlin, who joined the group in 1982 and often sang Terry Kath's parts, had become the focal point of Chicago during the power balladry of *19*. But his "The Show Must Go On" was a surprising indictment of what the group had become in its quest for more hits.

In fact, the song had originally been entitled "Falling in Love" when Champlin and Greg Mathieson cowrote it, and that early version wound up on *Ink*, a 1991 album by British new wavers the

Fixx. "It was just really simple, with different lyrics," says Gaitsch. "Peter Wolf thought it was a little too simple to go on the other way. He wanted it to become more personal, and it did—it became incredibly personal—which I loved."

Champlin's "Plaid," cowritten with Mathieson and Robert Lamm, was even more pointed in its refusal to be a part of fad and fashion. And even "Cry for the Lost," originally titled "Proud of Our Blindness" and written by Champlin for Michael Jackson, carried hints of the band's dilemma amidst its "let's make a better world" lyrics.

Lamm's contributions, meanwhile, attempted to return Chicago to its past by giving the band an up-to-the-minute rethink. The swinging "All the Years" used a sample from the band's 1969 *Chicago Transit Authority* debut, yet despite its familiar horn charts the song is no nostalgia trip, with its sentiments about wasted years and vanquished dreams.

Gaistch, who had cowritten the song with Lamm the year before, doesn't remember whose idea it was to sample "Someday: August 29, 1968," which featured dialogue from the disastrous Democratic National Convention. "It was either Robert's or Peter Wolf's, but it fit perfectly. And really ties in with the history of the band."

Lamm's "Sleeping in the Middle of the Bed Again" seemed to be an even more radical departure; set to a hip-hop-influenced rhythm track and featuring chanted breakdowns, it is often described as "Chicago's rap song" and cited as a reason *Stone of Sisyphus* might have been rejected. But heard in the context of the album it is far less jarring, and Peter Wolf notes that Lamm's inspiration was not current hip-hop stars, but a proto-rap band from Chicago's early years.

Robert wrote this thing, and we all thought, "He definitely has something." It's very fresh and different. And he brought in all these records from the '60s, of the Last Poets, which is kind of where rap started. And we listened to that stuff, and it was fantastic—to me, coming from Europe, I'd never heard most of it before. Because they were never huge.

And Robert said, "Couldn't we do it in this kind of approach?" and I said, "Of course!" And we worked it out in the Chicago style, and that's how it happened.

Bruce Gaitsch concedes that the song

provokes angst among some people: "What is this guy *rapping* about?" But I loved it. There was no debate about it, at least when I was around. Robert brought it in, and everybody went, "That's cool! Wow!" Peter Wolf was the one who really had to make all the political decisions, about what songs would get worked on and which songs wouldn't—so that nobody in the band would get mad at each other and say, "Well, I'm not gonna play on that," or whatever.

And then any song that he thought any band member didn't like, he'd make them play it first, to get into it. He really knows how to work with a band, and make a record come alive.

Both of Lamm's major contributions make sense as political statements that reflect the disillusionment of an ex-hippie. Yet, coming from the band member who had probably chafed the most under the new management and production regimes, they can be easily interpreted as more personal expressions of dissatisfaction—not only with his disintegrating marriage, but with Chicago as well.

That, says Gaitsch, "was what was cool. The songs started out as love songs—a lot of 'em did—but then, by the end of the record, they were songs about the band. It was really exciting, because the songs got better as we worked on them." Lamm himself would opine, years later, that the song featured "some serious lyric writing, I think. Seriously good lyric writing."[11]

Despite the band's desire to return to a simpler, less overtly commercial time, completely abandoning the adult contemporary audience would have been an impractical decision. Hence the ballad "Let's Take a Lifetime"—described by Gaitsch, without rancor, as "the Jason Scheff vehicle"—became part of the running order. It was most notable, perhaps, for the soprano-sax solo, played on synthesizer by Wolf as the track was running, and never replaced.

"That's what I do—I'm a keyboard player. We needed a solo," Wolf says. "Walt is not a player who just throws down a great solo right off the bat. He has to work things out. I just threw it down—because I'm a jazz guy. And everyone just fell in love with it. I would happily have had someone play it, but Walt also was not fighting me."

Regardless, "Let's Take a Lifetime" had the sound of a hit, and "Mah Jongg" was a funky, mid-tempo groove goosed along by punchy brass, in the classic Chicago style. But it was Scheff's third contribution—completed late in the sessions—that would be the most significant.

Although barely known when he joined Chicago, Scheff had a sterling pedigree: he was the son of bassist Jerry Scheff, best known for his '60s work with Elvis Presley. Wolf remembers,

> That just totally fascinated me, that Jason's father was the bass player in Elvis's band. So I said to him, "Jason, why don't we write a song about your dad?" And he said, "Oh, I'd love to do that." And then my wife, Ina, came up with the idea—'cause when he was a little kid, right, he watched Elvis on TV. But he only watched the bass player. And he said, "Dad, to me, you were bigger than Elvis."

That sweet reminiscence would get an extra kick when Scheff decided to get his famous father to play bass on the track—without revealing to him what the song was about. "So I called him," recounts Wolf, "and said, 'Jerry, we'd love for you to play bass on this thing,' and he said, 'Aw, c'mon, my son is a much better bass player than me.' And I said, 'Yeah, but he wants your style and your sound.' And it was so sweet. He came in, and he had no idea."

For the finishing touch, Wolf enlisted the help of Elvis's old backing vocalists, the Jordanaires. "I don't remember whose idea that was—it was probably mine, or Jason's. Or we talked about who was in the original Elvis band," Wolf says. "We got a phone number from Jerry or something. And then we called them, and I flew to Nashville [to record]. They were so nice."

Scheff would deliver a CD of the finished song, with lyrics in place, as a birthday gift to his father. "And [Jerry] listened to it, and tears were running down his face," recalls Wolf. "It was such a meaningful thing, this love song to his dad."

Both Peter and Ina Wolf received cowriting credits on "Bigger Than Elvis,"[12] and in fact, while there are no outside compositions on *Stone of Sisyphus*, nearly every track on the album features a cowriter. This, says Wolf, was intentional, and part of his belief in producing quality songwriting through quantity.

"The problem is, people in bands, they think, 'Okay, I'm a band member. They have to do a song of mine on the record.' Regardless how good it is. And then they write one song, and present that one song," Wolf argues. "And I believe that you don't write like that. I like to write fifty songs, and then have ten possible contenders. And that's why we brought in cowriters.

"And since I'm a writer too, I would hear something and say, 'Ah, I love that! But it needs a chorus.' And they would say, 'Yeah, but I don't know what to write.' And I would come up with a little part. So that was my involvement."

Also part of his involvement was demanding that band members dig deeper for more personal lyrics.

> I tried to force them into it, y'know. I said, "Don't try to write a hit. You cannot have the hit idea in mind. You have to have your love in mind, and a hit record might happen." But you can't sit down and write a hit. That's bullshit. I believe that if you are trying to get rich, you will never have a penny in your life. You will get very rich when you do something that you love.

Wolf's admonition led the group to attempt a song in tribute to the late Terry Kath. "Because this was Terry's band. They all said Terry was the guy—his spirit started this whole thing, and [they] lived trying to live up to Terry's spirit," Wolf says. Titled "Feel the Spirit," the song, by Wolf and Robert Lamm, was not completed during the sessions, but Lamm would later finish it for his 2000

Like a Brother album with Gerry Beckley and Beach Boy Carl Wilson.

In his own way, Wolf wound up nearly as involved with *Stone of Sisyphus*, as a songwriter and musician, as David Foster had been on Chicago records during the '80s. The difference, he thought, was that "I'm a hands-on guy, but I'm not a guy who tries to muscle in. It just happens. As an arranger, I bring ideas for parts in—'Wow, I love that part. I'll write another part around it.' And musically, we were all absolutely equal—they accepted me right in."

Because the album sessions were taking place while the band was still on tour, the recording stretched out over the first half of 1993. After he was invited to join the sessions, Dawayne Bailey remembers, "The vibe was incredibly upbeat, positive, and exciting. We couldn't stop talking about the album to the audiences during and after the shows, as well as playing the roughs on the bus."

When the group reconvened at Wolf's home, the enthusiasm returned almost immediately. "I cooked—I love to cook. And I made Italian sausage on the grill. The only time I remember everybody in the same room, other than rehearsals, was when I made pot roast," Gaitsch recalls. "And everybody went, 'You makin' it the Chicago way? Oh, man!' Everybody loved that. And Pankow would bring a case of Old Style, which is a beer from Chicago. It was just so much fun. Just a bunch of old guys from Chicago, reminiscing."

"There were lots of fires in and around L.A. . . . when the album was in full swing," Bailey adds, "and we would often stand outside of Peter's studio, where you could see an amazing view from far away. It was intense, magical, tragic yet exciting in a twisted way." Something like how the *Sisyphus* sessions would turn out.

In 1989, while on the road with Chicago, Dawayne Bailey had begun writing a song he titled "Twenty Years on the Sufferbus." The tune had no lyrics, and sat unfinished until Peter Wolf heard Bailey's demo during the *22* sessions. The song was exactly what Wolf was looking for to round out the new album: melodic, but edgy and rock-influenced. He encouraged Bailey to write words to the track; when he did, returning with a tale based on the Greek myth of Sisyphus, not everyone in Chicago was convinced.

Trumpeter Lee Loughnane, according to Bailey, greeted "Stone of Sisyphus" with the exclamation "CAN'T YOU WRITE SOMETHING WE CAN ALL UNDERSTAND?!" But the dissent was quelled by Wolf, who "called me personally to tell me that 'Sisyphus is brilliant!'" Bailey says. "So no one else was against the idea. Once everyone else expressed their okay, Lee changed his mind and embraced it."[13]

In fact, the story of Sisyphus—condemned to push a rock up the same hill for eternity—carried inescapable parallels to the band's own hamster-wheel experiences in the music business. Robert Lamm had already argued that Chicago should abandon its long tradition (last broken on 1978's *Hot Streets*) of naming albums by their number. He suggested *Resolve*, but Bailey's song would become the band's title of choice.

Suddenly, Bailey was not only welcome at recording sessions, he was sought out as a valuable collaborator. Trumpeter James Pankow invited Bailey to his home to write another rock song for the album;

the result, "Get On This," was another big-beat anthem that made Chicago's horns part of its metallic stomp.

It was the lyrics for the song, however, that threw the band for a loop. Bailey incorporated a few lines of Felicia Parazaider's poetry[14] into perhaps the most bizarre set of words ever to grace a Chicago recording. With writing help on the bridges from James Pankow, Bailey created a song that referred to a dream about Hitler and Elvis and contained the line "I saw Jesus kissing the devil." The track was designed to make old fans sit up and take note: this was not your father's Chicago.

Walt Parazaider, Bailey recalls, was proud of his daughter's songwriting contribution and "immediately helped her set up her own publishing company called Nadir Moon, ASCAP." However, when it came time to cut lead vocals for the title track, Bailey would learn that his own position in the band was still tenuous. "Peter Wolf always wanted me to sing lead vocals on the whole song," he recalls, "but the band told him they couldn't have a sideman sing an entire song, and they must have an original band member sing at least part of it." Ultimately, the vocals were shared by Lamm and Bailey, with the latter tackling the choruses, bridge, and outro.

Bailey believed he was being held back because the band feared him taking too large a role, in the album or the group. He had played on the Los Angeles scene with Scheff in the early '80s, prior to both men joining Chicago, and was not in awe of his old band-mate. "One theory of mine is that Jason was not happy about my evolving as a lead singer because he knew our history," contends Bailey. "In our club band, we were both equals and shared lead singing equally. He was not my boss and I was not his full-time backing singer.

"And I knew that he knew that I knew that we both knew I was just as good a lead singer as he was, if not better. I'd been singing lead in bands years before Jason even touched a mic, and I'm certain he always knew I wasn't the type to keep on a leash for too long. If they had limited Terry Kath as a lead singer and writer the same way they treated me, Kath might have split from the very start."

Peter Wolf, who loved the song, sees some truth in Bailey's assessment. "If you have a hired gun, you feel very vulnerable. You're giving them a lot of power," he says. "Because all of a sudden they can go, 'OK, I'm the face of the band,' almost."

It would never come to that. In fact, before long, there would be no album for any "face" to promote.

In an acknowledgement that they'd been pushed around too long, the members of Chicago had recorded *Stone of Sisyphus* in complete secrecy. No one from the band's label, Reprise, or its management company, HK, had been permitted to hear a single note during the sessions.

So when Peter Wolf delivered the album to Michael Ostin, Warner Brothers' head of Artists and Repertoire (A&R), in the fall of 1993, there was no way of predicting the reaction. But, according to Wolf, "when I left that meeting, all I can tell you is, it could not have gone better. Michael listened to the tracks, he jumped up and down, he told me again and again, 'Oh, my God, now that's a hit! I love that! That's a hit! God, what a killer record. It's gonna fly out the first week!'"

Within a month, not only had the album been rejected by Warner's, but there had been no discussion about reviving it. No demands that songs be rerecorded or remixed, no assigning the album to a different producer, none of the many courses a label usually takes when an album doesn't meet expectations.[15] Chicago's power play had been checkmated with stunning finality. And after hearing the tracks, HK Management would side with Reprise. "I was flabbergasted," Wolf says.

The news, according to everyone involved, was devastating. It also opened up a schism within the band, Wolf says, between those members determined to fight for Chicago's artistic freedom, and those who believed that simply walking away from *Stone of Sisyphus* was the wisest course.

Backed by management, the latter faction—which included the band's entire horn section—would prevail. "The sad part about it was, after the fact, I heard from my dear friends in the band that there were guys in the band who believed that the record was not commercial," says Wolf.

> Robert Lamm loved the record. Loved it. Said to me, "Peter, this is nothing to do with you. This is coming from some other angle. I have no idea what's going on, but I love this record and it's total bullshit if they don't release it. I'm gonna fight for this." And he did, big time. But he didn't have a lot of pull back then.
>
> Tris Imboden, obviously, loved it. Didn't have a lot of pull. Champlin. Loved it. Didn't have *any* pull. Even at that point. They respected the guy's artistic input, but they said, "The guy's out to lunch." He had

already alienated himself from the band, because he always spoke his mind.

Gaitsch concurs, recalling Champlin telling him at the time, " 'The label doesn't like it. They're blaming me.' And I said, 'That's your problem, Bill—you're a bad influence.' It was probably because he was one of the newer guys. Musically, he's so advanced . . . but he also maybe just liked to think that they blamed him. But I think they blamed everybody."

Wolf refuses to blame the band's management—"the management, in all fairness, they only heard from the record company." However, he adds, "Howard is a great manager because he doesn't understand anything about music. He's the first guy to tell you that. Herb Cohen—he was Zappa's manager—once said to me, 'The more I hate music from someone, the better I can manage them.' So with Howard, I guess, it was a similar situation."

"I don't have a grudge against anyone. I love Lee. I love Jimmy. I love Walter. I just think that they backed away from it too early," Wolf says. "They had done twenty-one records before that, and if their manager would say something, they would go, 'OK, you're right.' It was, 'My manager, who I believe is God, says we should not force the issue. So I'm gonna shut up.' "[16]

Bruce Gaitsch and Dawayne Bailey each took the news badly; Bailey recalls simply, "A part of me died." Gaitsch would end up appearing on the project the band selected as a replacement: the ultimate conservative move, a big band album. But while he enjoyed the experience, he found it puzzling as well.

It was like, "What?! You're gonna do a big band record after you made that great record with all those great songs?" I just felt bad for them. Because they had to go out and keep touring—the show must go on. And yet they had no support from their label, and their management—sometimes I think the management doesn't have the band at all in their plans. They keep 'em out there, and they only want 'em to play the hits.

Bailey, meanwhile, had done his last—and probably best—work with the group. He attended a few rehearsals for the big band record before leaving Chicago for good; his four-year relationship with Felicia Parazaider, he felt, had "sealed my fate in that band."

Wolf has his own ideas, meanwhile, about what sealed the fate of *Stone of Sisyphus*:

This was the last record on their contract. If [Reprise] decided to go after it, a million dollars in promotion is normal. And if they had a big hit on their hands, it would only make sense for the record company to re-sign the band. To re-sign a band with the status of Chicago, coming off of a big hit, we're talking millions and millions of dollars. And I'm sure the head of Warner Brothers was sitting there thinking, "Is this really worth it?"

"And I'm telling you that's exactly what happened," he concludes. "Purely a business decision."

Many Chicago fans would not learn of the existence of *Stone of Sisyphus* for some time, until word of the album began leaking out during promotion for *Night and Day*, the big band album released in 1995. Lee Loughnane would confirm to at least one surprised interviewer that the album existed, and that year the title song and "Bigger Than Elvis" saw official release on a Canadian compilation.

Over the years, several songs would trickle out officially, either on compilations (most of the from overseas) or in rerecorded form. Seven of the album's twelve tracks have seen official release, although three of those ("Sleeping in the Middle of the Bed Again," "The Pull,"[17] and Pankow and Lamm's soulful slow jam "Here with Me (Candle for the Dark)") were issued only on a pair of hard-to-find, late-'90s Japanese collections, both titled *The Heart of Chicago*.

"Let's Take a Lifetime," meanwhile, first saw daylight in Europe in 1996, on *The Very Best of Chicago*. And three tracks from *Sisyphus*—"All the Years," "Bigger Than Elvis," and the title song—would finally show up on American soil a decade after their parent album was rejected, on Chicago's 2003 Rhino Records box set.[18]

Perhaps unsurprisingly, the three writers who contributed most heavily to the album would each rework some tunes on solo projects. Robert Lamm would rerecord "All the Years" in 1995; four years later, a much tamer version of "Sleeping in the Middle of the Bed Again" appeared on his own set *In My Head*. Elsewhere, Jason Scheff chose "Mah Jongg" to revisit on the 1997 solo album *Chauncy*, and, on 1995's *Through It All*, Bill Champlin gave "Cry for the Lost" back its original title and lyrics.

Chicago would leave Reprise following the rejection of *Sisyphus*, and apparently had sufficient clout to take the album with it. But, although the band went on to start its own label, and while members would occasionally hint at an official release—"The master tapes haven't been burned—this thing will get released," Parazaider claimed at one point[19]—fans remained disappointed, particularly when the group refused to even answer questions about the album.[20]

Concerns over access to the album were somewhat alleviated when bootlegs began appearing in the late '90s. The identity of the person who first made the boots available is an open question, but Bailey—who has devoted a portion of his official website, www.dawaynebailey.com, to an in-depth examination of *Sisyphus*, complete with audio clips—insists it wasn't him. Rather, he says,

> I never shared a copy of *SOS* until I returned from living in France in 2000 and found out that current Chicago members had shared their copy. It kind of angered me and I figured, "Well, what the hell—I guess I'll share mine then." Since my copy is different from the copies they shared, it was easy to tell whose copy went out first—and it wasn't mine.

Both Gaitsch and Wolf, however, admit they've circulated copies of the album to the curious. Wolf, in fact, relates the story of giving a *Sisyphus* CD to a young artist and Chicago fanatic he met in Nashville. The artist was Jay DeMarcus, bassist in the country band Rascal Flatts. DeMarcus not only went on to fame in his own group, but eventually realized his dream of producing a Chicago record of his own, the 2006 comeback *30*.

The mystique of *Sisyphus*—fueled in part by the bootlegs—is one reason Bruce Gaitsch is doubtful the album will ever be released. "I think there's more talk about it now that it isn't out. So if they put it out, what would be proved, other than to put all the rumors to sleep, and stop the bootlegging?" But Gaitsch, who continues to write songs with several band members, remembers Robert Lamm, as late as 2005, musing, " 'We could put that record out someday.' And I said, 'I hope you do.' " Gaitsch chuckles—" 'With credits.' "

Peter Wolf, meanwhile, is adamant that "If this record would come out now, people would *still* love it and buy it, and it would *still* be successful." The major casualty of *Stone of Sisyphus*, Dawayne Bailey, also remains hopeful. Even though he and the rest of the album's supporters appear to have made little progress in moving *Stone* closer to release, Bailey is confident it will happen "sooner, rather than later."

"I love Chicago, I love Peter Wolf and Paul Erikson, and I love *Stone of Sisyphus*. I believe we all helped create a great record and it shows in every song," Bailey says. Years of waiting for the public to hear it haven't eroded his optimism; in fact, he now views the condemned Sisyphus as a heroic figure instead.

"Sisyphus believed he could tackle that rock one more time," offers Bailey, "and that's the kind of faith you have to have in yourself and your work."

Chicago: *Stone of Sisyphus*
Recorded for: *Reprise / Warner Brothers Records*
Scheduled release date: *1994*
Recorded at: *Embassy Studios, Simi Valley, CA; The Jordanaires recorded in Nashville, TN; 1993*

TRACK LISTING:

1. All the Years (Lamm, Bruce Gaitsch)
2. Stone of Sisyphus (Bailey, Loughnane)
3. Bigger Than Elvis (Scheff, Peter Wolf, Ina Wolf)
4. Sleeping in the Middle of the Bed Again (Lamm, John McCurry)
5. Mah Jongg (Scheff, Brock Walsh, Aaron Zigman)
6. Let's Take a Lifetime (Scheff, Walsh, Aaron Zigman)
7. The Pull (Lamm, Scheff, P. Wolf)
8. Here with Me (Candle for the Dark) (Pankow, Lamm, Greg O'Connor)
9. Plaid (Champlin, Lamm, Greg Mathieson)
10. Cry for the Lost (Champlin, Dennis Matkowsky)
11. Get On This (Bailey, Pankow, Felicia Parazaider)
12. The Show Must Go On (Champlin, Mathieson)

Produced by: *Peter Wolf*
Engineered by: *Paul Erikson*
Mixed by: *Tom Lord-Alge at Encore Studios, Burbank, CA, in 1993 and 1994*
Remixed by: *Peter Wolf and Paul Erikson*

Credits:

Robert Lamm—*keyboards, lead and backing vocals*

Walter Parazaider—*woodwinds, backing vocals*

Lee Loughnane—*trumpet, flugelhorn, backing vocals*

James Pankow—*trombone, backing vocals, horn arrangements, co-horn arrangements (track 2)*

Bill Champlin—*keyboards, rhythm guitars, lead and backing vocals*

Jason Scheff—*bass, lead and backing vocals*

Dawayne Bailey—*rhythm guitar, lead guitar (tracks 2, 3, and 11), lead and backing vocals, co-horn arrangements (track 2)*

Tris Imboden—*drums, percussion, harmonica*

Guest artists:

Bruce Gaitsch—*guitar*

The Jordanaires—*backing vocals on "Bigger Than Elvis"*

Sheldon Reynolds—*guitar*

Jerry Scheff—*bass on "Bigger Than Elvis"*

Joseph Williams—*backing vocals on "Let's Take a Lifetime"*

Peter Wolf—*arranger, keyboard bass, keyboards*

4 The Jungle Brothers

Too Crazy for Hip-Hop

*T*hey were no-going-back moments, seismic
eruptions that altered the landscape of
popular music forever. Elvis Presley's Sun sessions. The Beatles on Ed Sullivan. Woodstock.
Altamont. The birth of the Sex Pistols, and of
hip-hop. And in Brooklyn, New York, on a sweltering evening in June 1992, Bill Laswell was
certain he was witnessing another.

At Laswell's Greenpoint Studio, the propri-
etor was down on the floor, playing bass in the
middle of a furious jam session that included
avant-garde saxman John Zorn, Napalm Death
drummer Mick Harris, and members of the
British industrial band Godflesh. When Laswell
raised his sweaty head, however, he saw twenty
local youngsters writing rhymes to accompany
the punishing noise. Alongside them were the
Jungle Brothers, one of hip-hop's better-known

acts, trying to find ways to incorporate their own raps into the racket.

"Now that was something to see," recalls Laswell. "And at that moment, I thought, 'This shit could actually go somewhere! And if it does, it's gonna be a revolution in music.'"[1]

For Laswell, who had spent most of the '80s trying to advance this revolution via every conceivable musical hybrid, this was quite a statement. But it was a feeling reinforced by the rest of the evening. The Jungle Brothers attended Godflesh's gig "and bugged out," according to Laswell; members of both groups would cement their unlikely bond by scoring weed together in the Bronx during the wee hours.

"It was this little period where it looked like there was kind of a new world forming," says Laswell. "Which was an illusion, because ultimately it's controlled by business. But it was encouraging."

The fate that awaited the most tangible manifestation of this new world, however, was discouraging, to say the least. When high school friends Mike G and Afrika Baby Bam began recording Crazy Wisdom Masters with Laswell, they were determined to spend the commercial capital they'd accumulated through hits like "Jimbrowski" and "I'll House You" to advance hip-hop. What they received *for their pains was an official release shorn of nearly every innovation, the eventual loss of their major-label deal, and ultimately the disintegration of their partnership. In short, the Jungle Brothers gambled their career on* Crazy Wisdom Masters—*and lost it all.*

"That was our most creative record. That was our peak, right there. But it was such a disgusting time," says Mike G, with a sigh. "You can try to fight the battle, but two things are important as an artist: You gotta stay productive, and you gotta be timely. For better or worse, you gotta put somethin' in front of people."[2]

And yet, interest in the album the Jungle Brothers never got a chance to put in front of their fans remains constant. It has become hip-hop's great lost artifact, a casualty of the genre's seemingly insurmountable divide between commercial success and artistic ambition, and a touchstone for scores of indie rappers today—whether they realize it or not. As this book was going to press, there were even rumors that an unidentified independent label was trying to negotiate an official release of Crazy Wisdom Masters.

"There always comes a time," the Jungle Brothers would warn with some prescience, on the song "40 Below Trooper," "when you must sacrifice." The sacrifice they made on Crazy

> Wisdom Masters *was a heavy one, which will probably never be fully repaid. Hopefully, sharing some wisdom about their missing masterpiece will at least be a start.*

By any measure, 1991 was a momentous year in hip-hop history. It is seen now as the final, glorious twelve months of the music's "golden age," when hip-hop had reached Middle America, but had not yet fully succumbed to the demands of the marketplace. No less an authority than Tom Silverman, the founder of seminal hip-hop label Tommy Boy Records, believes 1991 represented the proverbial line in the sand. "After '91, there seem to be a lot of hit records, but not that many reinventors," says Silverman. "Hip-hop was revolutionary then; after '91 it was evolutionary."[3]

Yet 1991 was also a year in which the evolution of hip-hop's next, turbulent decade was being charted. A young rapper named Tupac Shakur made his official debut on "Same Song," from the Bay Area collective Digital Underground, while in Southern California an ambitious producer named Andre Young and a lazy-voiced MC called Calvin Broadus—a.k.a. Dr. Dre and Snoop Doggy Dogg—were beginning a partnership that would create G-Funk and help spark a bloody bicoastal rivalry. Across the continent, their New York counterparts—producer and would-be entrepreneur Sean "Puffy" Combs, and ex-con-turned-rhymer Christopher "Biggie" Wallace—had started their own collaboration.

And another unknown Big Apple rapper, Nasir Jones (or simply "Nas"), would introduce himself to the public via a cameo on "Live at the Barbeque" by Main Source. It was perhaps the most symbolic release of this auspicious year; the rapper who, for some, would come to personify the corrupting effects of hip-hop's new commercialism got his first taste of fame courtesy of one of the Golden Age's most thoughtful and uncompromising groups.

The positive-thinking "Daisy Age" that Native Tongue rappers De La Soul had heralded two years earlier already seemed quaintly outmoded in the new decade. De La, in fact, would write its epitaph on the 1991 release *De La Soul Is Dead,* which made the sense of disillusionment explicit by featuring a broken flowerpot on the cover. But their Brooklyn brethren, the Jungle Brothers, had not yet given up on the Afrocentrism, the positivity, or the spirit of musical adventurousness that characterized hip-hop's Native Tongue movement.

Formed by Mike Small and Nathaniel Hall, graduates of Lower Manhattan's Murry Bergtraum High School, with DJ Sammy B[urwell], the Jungle Brothers had displayed early on a desire to stretch hip-hop's musical vocabulary. Their 1988 debut, *Straight Out the Jungle,* featured a collaboration with house music producer Todd Terry; the follow-up, 1989's *Done by the Forces of Nature,* was a critical smash that found Small (Mike G) and Hall (Afrika Baby Bam) saluting black women, black history, and vegetarianism, without neglecting the dance floor.

The album was the trio's first release for Warner Brothers, but sales peaked below 300,000 copies—well short of gold status. Company executive Benny Medina, who had signed the band on the promise of *Straight Out the Jungle*, would later admit to journalist S. H. Fernando Jr. that the label's black music division hadn't been ready for *Done by the Forces of Nature*, and in fact had done the group "a disservice in our handling of the music."

However, the disc had sold well enough to keep the J. Beez on the road, and the group trekked around the world to support the release. It was an eye-opening experience for three teenagers who'd never left the streets of New York City. "We got to do a lot of travelin.' Passin' through different cultures, crossin' borders," remembers Mike G, "and we brought a lot of that right back into the studio while it was hot on our tail."

Exposure to the wide, wide world outside hardened the group's resolve: in 1991, they would begin recording a third album that would definitely break them "out of the cookie cutter mold" into which hip-hop was increasingly being shoved. They couldn't have found a more willing collaborator than Bill Laswell.

Laswell's hip-hop credentials were impeccable. He and collaborator Michael Beinhorn had helped put the genre on the map via "Rockit," an instrumental that appeared on Herbie Hancock's 1983 album *Future Shock* and introduced the art of turntablism—via the contributions of Grandmixer D.ST—to America's heartland. But Laswell was far too restless to capitalize on the commercial success of "Rockit," and instead used it to explore a series of groundbreaking musical mash-ups, producing everyone from Mick Jagger to legendary Beat poet William S. Burroughs to metal monsters Motorhead. His own group, Material, would also play host to such far-flung excursions; it was on one of them, 1991's *Third Power*, that he first hooked up with the Jungle Brothers.

Laswell and the Jungle Brothers already shared a manager, Tony Meilandt. And Laswell was pleased to discover that Mike G and Afrika, who began to hang out at his Greenpoint studio, were extremely open-minded. I just always assume that people could go further. That's just how I look at things. And I was at that moment, working with George Clinton and Bootsy [Collins] and a lot of P-Funk people on the one hand, and a lot of jazz artists on the other hand. So I didn't really take the time to analyze the Jungle Brothers' potential, as far as how far they could go. I always just naturally assume people can go as far as possible, and I think in some cases I overestimate that a lot with hip-hop people.

It didn't seem that way in 1991, as Laswell, Mike G, and Afrika began collaborating on the third J. Beez album. In fact, the newest Jungle Brother was one whose sense of adventure would be impossible to overestimate.

Colin Julius Bobb comes to the phone just moments before he's due to catch a flight to England. His upcoming European tour, under his hip-hop alias Sensational, will offer him a welcome respite from harsh realities at home: when Bobb returns to the U.S., it will probably be to take up residence once again at a homeless shelter.

Then again, Bobb has been manufacturing his own reality for some time now. A Guyanese native who moved to Brooklyn as a child and first met the Jungle Brothers at age sixteen, Bobb has a well-documented penchant for pharmaceutical excess. "He's just *way* out there. He gets a little money from whatever projects he's workin' on," says Mike G, "and he gets ridiculously drunk or high."

On this afternoon, however, Bobb is lucid—so much so that S. H. "Skiz" Fernando Jr., the journalist and producer who has long been a champion of Bobb's music and will be accompanying him to Europe—remarks afterward, "You really caught him on a good day today."[4] Or maybe it's just that discussing the twisted reality of *Crazy Wisdom Masters* is a natural fit for Bobb's one-of-a-kind mind.

"That's the Matrix, *main!*" Bobb exclaims, comparing the album to the popular film. "It just naturally happened, y'know. It was done by the forces of nature," he adds, punning on the Jungle Brothers' debut album title. "That's the zone I was in—the zone we was in, at the time."[5]

At that time, Bobb was known as Torture, an aspiring rapper who'd got his start dancing with the *Forces of Nature*–era J. Beez. His own four-track musical experiments, however, soon came to the attention of the group, and of Laswell, who was hosting informal get-togethers with the Jungle Brothers at his apartment. At one of them, he remembers hearing Torture scratch out a rhythm from an unlikely source: one of his Stockhausen LPs.

Hearing the experimental German composer drafted into the service of hip-hop convinced Laswell that his charges were on an exciting new track. "I had a huge record collection, and I would just let them stay there and listen to my vinyl. And I would come home at four in the morning, and Torture would be listening to, like, Anthony Braxton and Derek Bailey and shit. Never rhythm music. So I knew that they had the potential then, to really bug out. But I never realized how dangerous it was."

Torture, he says, "was kind of the detonator" for the sessions. "Because he was so young, the Jungle Brothers looked at him and thought, 'Maybe this is what the young people like.' They just didn't realize," Laswell adds with a laugh, "that he was one weird young person."

Not everyone agrees with Laswell's assessment of Torture's role—including Torture himself. "Nah, I wouldn't say that," he demurs. "Remember, Af was a real interesting dude. He was just appreciatin' the whole scene."

Indeed, it is Afrika whom Mike G credits with spearheading *Crazy Wisdom Masters*. "Afrika was in there, totally headstrong, always tryin' to put his ideas first," says Mike. This, he hastens to add, was not something he resented. Despite growing up the nephew of legendary DJ Red Alert and frequently rubbing shoulders with Afrika Bambaataa and other members of the early hip-hop elite, Mike had always been ambivalent about his own musical career. "I think Af had more . . . dreams about the music business," he admits. "Even though I grew up in it . . . I never really had aspirations of becoming a hip-hop artist. That wasn't really where my head was at."

Afrika, however, was another story. He would claim a direct link to Bambaataa through his own nickname ("Baby Bam") and had manifested his ambition by overseeing the Jungle Brothers' material, as well as producing cuts for British hip-hop and R&B acts Monie Love, Stereo MCs, and Soul II Soul vocalist Caron Wheeler. Laswell recognized Afrika's hunger for knowledge and tried to indulge him, introducing him to some free jazz pioneers. "I remember taking Af to Ornette Coleman's house, and I think Ornette kinda blew him out. And then I remember taking him and Mike to see Ornette play, and Cecil Taylor play. So that was interesting."

But Afrika's dedication would create tension with the Jungle Brothers' other member, Sammy B. There had first been problems after the success of *Forces of Nature* and its subsequent tour. "Sam would be on the road, gettin' sick and sayin' he wanted to go home," recalls Mike G. "It was like, 'Gimme a break.'" When the group did return to Brooklyn, "Sam just kinda got caught up with the street stuff. I think he just had cats in his ear, y'know what I'm sayin'? And there was a little bit of a clash with Af. [Sammy] just wasn't motivated, he wasn't comin' in the studio and offerin' ideas."

Eventually, he stopped coming altogether, and Torture, who always seemed to be hanging around the studio, stepped into the breach. In 1991, the reconfigured Jungle Brothers would record an album's worth of new material at Greenpoint with Laswell, engineer Bob Musso, and programmer David Williams. Out of those sessions would emerge an EP that would debut the startling new direction the group had chosen.

The leadoff track, "Simple as That," was a dense but catchy collage that began with the pertinent couplet "You see, I choose to be a trendsetter / Which means I have to do much better." Fusing programmed beats with snippets of live funk—some of which probably included contributions from Laswell's friends in the P-Funk universe—the song took the rare groove plundering then at its peak in hip-hop to an ambitious new level. "Trials of an Era," which followed, packed even more innovation into a minute and a half. Clearly inspired by the flow of free jazz, the heavily echoed lyrics cascaded atop a clattering beat for the first half of the song; a more regular, yet still raw and lo-fi, rhythm took over for the final thirty seconds before cutting off abruptly.

Even that dose of lunacy would pale next to "Troopin' on the Down Lo," which took hip-hop to galaxies undreamed of in 1991, and seldom imagined since. Long stretches of its seven minutes featured break-neck lyrical flows keeping pace with what sounded like improvised jazz, but the rhythms shifted almost constantly, encompassing every-thing from uncut funk to techno to thrash metal, before concluding with the drunken, out-of-tune chant "40 B-L-O-T / I'm troopin' on the down lo." Lurking somewhere in the mix was a sample of "Five Percent for Nothing," from *Fragile*, the 1972 opus of prog-rock gods Yes.

"That shit is insane!" exclaims Laswell, who appeared on the track alongside avant-garde stars Amina Myers on piano and John Zorn on saxophone.

> It was the most progressive thing that ever happened in that genre, I'm sure. Amina comes from more of a gospel and blues background . . . but she played very free, almost like Cecil Taylor kind of stuff. Moments of that piece are really intense—like really up-tempo. I think there's live bass—no live drumming—but there's all these kinds of weird loops, and dissonance. And it's long. Over five minutes for that area of music is long.[6]

Of Zorn's involvement, Laswell adds, "He was just curious 'cause he couldn't believe that people involved in [hip-hop] would be interested in anything that he was doing. And they were."

Next to "Troopin'," the final EP track, "Headz at Company Z," seemed deceptively sedate. In fact, it hailed from a similarly far-flung universe; a mostly instrumental collage of found sound, fractured piano runs, and organ stabs, its sole nods to convention were its familiar-sounding drum break and its length of three min-utes, fifteen seconds.

In retrospect, it's not hard to imagine why Warner Brothers, in Laswell's recollection, "brutally rejected" this EP. And indeed, Warner Brothers A&R Benny Medina and his representative, Peter Edge, would both tell S. H. Fernando Jr. that they had "real problems with the tracks." Edge, in fact, thought the EP "real wild, and kind of very free-form. It almost sounded drug-induced, y'know ... definitely a very radical thing."[7] Edge's assessment was certainly accurate in several respects, but Laswell, who was busy with other projects, could see the handwriting on the wall. He would pull back from the album, leaving the Jungle Brothers in the hands of his young protégé, an engineer named Matt Stein.

Warner Brothers executives, Mike G recalls, had by this time made it clear they "wanted more like *Done by the Forces of Nature*. They didn't see the connection with this new stuff." But the Jungle Brothers and Stein weren't about to give in to the forces of Warner Brothers just yet.

As Matt Stein remembers it, the way he got his position with the Jungle Brothers was reminiscent of the famous scene in *Scarface* where Tony Montana executes his old boss, then calmly turns to the man's quaking bodyguard and asks, "Do you want a job?"

In this case, the bloodbath was only figurative, but it occurred at a time when Mike G and Afrika were beginning to butt heads in the studio with Bob Musso and David Williams over technical issues. The group had already recorded about twenty tracks at Greenpoint,

Stein says, but "they had ideas about things they wanted to do, and were getting frustrated."[8]

The bearded, long-haired Stein had already proven himself a problem solver. He had first met Laswell in 1990, when he managed to solve a computer glitch that was holding up recording of the Bootsy Collins album Laswell was working on.[9] A year later, when a similar problem interrupted a Jungle Brothers session, Bob Musso remembered the young whiz kid and summoned him back to the studio. Stein's reward was an invitation to join the sessions on a $50-a-day retainer, which he eagerly accepted. And when the Jungle Brothers, Musso, and Williams reached the end of their collective tether during one heated studio excursion, Stein would inherit *Crazy Wisdom Masters*.

He was a better choice than the group probably realized at the time. An early pioneer of computer recording and digital editing, Stein was able to translate some of the J. Beez' more difficult concepts. "He really put his touch on *Crazy Wisdom Masters*," an admiring Mike G says now, "'cause at the time, I don't think anyone in hip-hop was using digital editing. We was chopping *everything* up, chopping, like, one-bar samples. We was just like, 'You can do that?!'" Stein, meanwhile, found himself impressed by the J. Beez' adventurous spirit. "I don't think they always had a good grasp of how to get from Point A to Point B," he says, "but they wanted to get to Point B really badly."

They would continue that journey at Stein's second-floor, East Village apartment, which was soon christened "Bush Camp." A frequent guest was Gary "Mudbone" Cooper, the P-Funk vocalist who had joined the project under Laswell's watch and was renting a room nearby. Stein's home studio was cramped, but the ambience was relaxed, with a perpetual haze of marijuana in the air and frequent home cooking to satiate the ensuing munchies. "Af's mom would come and cook for us a lot," remembers Stein.

Over the next six months, the Jungle Brothers would record basic tracks at Stein's, then take the tapes to Greenpoint, where Laswell would do additional recording and mixing. There were already "tons of backing vocals" from Cooper, and various P-Funk luminaries—including keyboardist Bernie Worrell, and possibly Bootsy Collins and George Clinton himself[10]—would add parts to the already busy mix.

Some of the more conventional songs recorded during these sessions eventually saw the light of day. The hypnotic "Spark a New Flame" sugared its drone with female backing vocals, while "I'm in Love with Indica," which sampled Eugene McDaniels's "Supermarket Blues,"[11] was a love letter to the herb that was perhaps the greatest single influence on *Crazy Wisdom Masters*.

"To be honest, we were smokin' so much fuckin' weed, it was ridiculous. Even when we kinda downsized at Matt Stein's studio," says Mike G, laughing. "And we were stayin' up for days and days. And Af did his little experimentation with whatever kinda paraphernalia was around at that time"—including, some observers believed, much stronger psychedelic drugs.

The haze of dope smoke hanging over the project, Mike also admits, helped soothe any doubts he might have had about the more out-there material. "Yeah, some things I looked kinda cross-eyed at. Maybe thirty percent of the songs . . . I couldn't see the big picture on 'em," he says. "But what was most important was the productivity. We were doin' high energy songs."

That was a good description of "Spittin' Wicked Randomness," which lived up to its title with a series of off-kilter verses ("Filofax / concrete drumbeat / bare feet antics / givin' me tactics of survival") that reflected pleasure in the pure sound of words, and became even more disorienting when Echoplexed. Set against a single, repeated piano chord and vocal sample, the song was another effort leagues away from hip-hop's then-dominant sound, and was one of Mike G's personal favorites.

But, unsurprisingly, it was a vehicle for Torture that epitomized both the "high energy" and "out-there" labels attached to the album. "Ra Ra Kid" paid titular homage to ra-ra, a Haitian carnival music associated with both political rallies and voodoo ritual, and reflected Torture's Caribbean roots. The song began with twenty-first-century studio backchat—the sound of various records being cued up—and then plunged into three minutes of what could only be described as a hip-hop version of an old-fashioned jazz blowing session. Galloping along to a breakneck rhythm that uncannily anticipated the pulse of jungle (which would not surface in the clubs of Great Britain until the following year), "Ra Ra Kid" incorporated various bits of sonic flotsam and jetsam around Torture's machine-gun verses, and broke down periodically into a fingersnap-assisted chorus: "Ra ra caper / I got some more wicked rhymes on the paper." The whole thing finally collapsed rhythmically, as if the players simply couldn't maintain the manic pace, and the song closed with the distorted thump of a digital heartbeat.

However, it would not be that uncompromising track that would incur the wrath of Warner Brothers. In April 1992, the Jungle Brothers, along with Stein and Laswell, went to Masterdisk in midtown Manhattan to master the album. When they arrived, according to S. H. Fernando Jr., there was a FedEx delivery awaiting them. The letter, from Warner Brothers headquarters in Burbank, California, directed the group and its producers to remove the title track from *Crazy Wisdom Masters.*[12]

Mike G would tell Fernando that the label was unhappy with a line of his from the song—"Majors that treat us like minors / pack of bullshit sold to every signers." Someone at Warner Brothers "took that line seriously," Mike said. But Matt Stein thought the label was responding instead to a rhyme of Afrika's that described "GQ niggas"—an unflattering reference, Stein believed, to Benny Medina.

"I don't think Benny was the right man to A&R the project," Stein says now. "The Jungle Brothers were coming from the underground, and Benny was working with [rapper turned TV star] Will Smith. They were just worlds apart." However, other cracks that had so far been papered over in the relationship between the J. Beez and Warner Brothers were also beginning to show.

In Afrika's estimation, the Jungle Brothers had created an adventurous album worthy of the same sort of patient promotion Warner's had extended to pioneering rock acts on its roster, like the Red Hot Chili Peppers. But Peter Edge would tell Fernando that "there was not enough confidence at Warner Brothers in terms of the marketing and promotions side to really go with that." This rejection brought to the fore simmering resentments about the way the Jungle Brothers had come to Warner Brothers in the first place. The group's contract with the independent label Idlers/Warlock had been bought out for a sum believed close to $1.5 million, but according to Fernando, Afrika, Mike G, and Sammy B had each netted only $15,000 from the deal. "They sold us to Warner Brothers like slaves, you know what I'm sayin'?" an embittered Afrika would later remark.[13]

The failed Warner Brothers campaign behind *Done by the Forces of Nature* had also not been forgotten. Afrika would tell Fernando that he "started hating myself for what happened" to the album. "It shouldn't have mattered what the record company did. It should have just blew the fuck up anyway." However, by this point the Jungle Brothers' contact with Warner Brothers was reportedly almost nonexistent. All communications were being handled through their manager, a potentially streamlined setup that instead might have further alienated the group from its label. "I don't think Tony Meilandt had the best relations with Warner Brothers," says Stein, noting that there were rumors Meilandt had actually been banned from Warner's because of a dispute with another client. "Tony was always leading us to believe everything was peachy, but I'm not sure that it was."[14]

An additional factor beyond the group's control was a high-profile incident that summer involving another Warner's client. Ice-T's controversial "Cop Killer" wasn't even a hip-hop track—it was recorded with his thrash-metal group, Body Count—but the furor that surrounded its release was so great that it even spilled over into the presidential campaign between incumbent George Bush Sr. and Bill Clinton. As S. H. Fernando Jr. observed, Warner's-affiliated rappers would subsequently come under the microscope, with certain releases being altered and some acts—most notably, the Bay Area provocateur Paris—being dropped. The timing couldn't have been worse for a group hoping to test the boundaries of hip-hop—even if, as Fernando pointed out, the Jungle Brothers' recorded test "did not take potshots at the cops" or "rely on sex, violence or profanity."[15]

With a studio bill approaching half a million dollars and an album deemed unsuitable for release, the showdown between the J. Beez and Warner's had reached an unhappy stalemate. "I think if they had money, they probably would not have bothered with the corporate thing and would have gone independent, which is what we were all hoping," says Laswell. "But I don't think they had enough strength to do it." The situation would finally be resolved that fall when hip-hop producer and mixer Bob Power was drafted by Warner Brothers to remix *Crazy Wisdom Masters.*

Power came with gold-plated credentials—he had worked with Native Tongue acts like A Tribe Called Quest and De La Soul, and was already renowned for the warmth and live vibe he brought to his projects. The work he did on *Crazy Wisdom Masters,* however, would prove more controversial. The running order of the album would be reshuffled, with some songs salvaged from the original 1991 sessions with Laswell, and others abandoned completely. Meanwhile, although certain tracks would barely be changed— "Book of Rhyme Pages," which arrived almost completely intact from the original EP, and "Spark a New Flame" being two notable examples—others were stripped of their more outré elements. "40 Below Trooper," for example, which would become the first single from the revamped album, was a succinct and commercial edit of "Troopin' on the Down Lo,"[16] playing up the familiar sample from Billy Squier's "The Big Beat." However, for those who had heard the original, it was a pale substitute—as were other surgically altered tracks. "The long breaks, the eighteen-bar breaks, the P-Funk stuff," laments Mike G, "that shit was gone."

These sometimes-radical reworkings of the songs may be what Mike G is referring to when he claims that some of the master tapes from the *Crazy Wisdom Masters* sessions were lost by Warner Brothers. Matt Stein, who isn't aware of any missing tapes, was nonetheless stunned at what was absent from the resultant album, retitled *J. Beez wit the Remedy* and released in the summer of 1993. Mike G dropped off a copy of the disc at Stein's apartment, but "I couldn't even listen to the whole thing. I fast-forwarded and listened to about ten minutes total," says Stein, who later guessed that the album featured "maybe twenty-five percent" of *Crazy Wisdom*

Masters. "It was just like, *Fuck.* Whole pieces of music were gone. It was kind of sickening to me. I didn't touch it for two more years."

There is a long silence when Mike G is asked whether *J. Beez* was a difficult record to promote. "Yeah. Yeah," he says finally. "But you do what you gotta do, y'know?" Given his nature, however, it is perhaps not surprising that Torture takes a contrary view of the album. "I liked it. I loved it," he says, noting that *J. Beez wit the Remedy* was his own title. For Torture, being forced back into the studio by Warner Brothers was in fact a pleasure. "That's what I liked—especially the [studios] that looked like spaceships," he enthuses. "To me, that's like I'm in the candy shop, *main*. It was like, 'We goin' back in the studio! That's the shit!' "

To the hip-hop community, *J. Beez wit the Remedy* was assuredly not the shit. Most reviews would note the uneasy-sounding compromise between commercial considerations and the group's stranger side. *Village Voice* critic Robert Christgau, who gave the album a B+ and praised its experimentation, nonetheless noted that "the JBs sound as dissociated as some tortured hippie manqué or privileged gangsta."[17] Others would not be as kind. The album would spawn no future singles and sold a paltry 34,000 copies, according to Soundscan, making it a full-fledged disaster when its recording costs were considered.

Still, the album anticipated a number of musical trends. Only a year later, Stein noted, "everybody started using P-Funk stuff," underpinning what became the hugely successful West Coast mutation known as G-Funk. And by the mid-to-late '90s, underground rappers like Company Flow were beginning to try the same experiments with rhythm and rhyme that the Jungle Brothers had already conducted. "[*Crazy Wisdom Masters*] was part of that sensibility, which I really didn't see again until later, when Kool Keith and

THE GREATEST MUSIC NEVER SOLD

Rammellzee did some stuff I thought related," Laswell says. "Or, in recent days, Killah Priest—his mind can go there. He's probably the most advanced writer in the business."

S. H. Fernando Jr., who had gotten acquainted with Laswell and the Jungle Brothers around the time of *J. Beez*, would become an important fan of the group. He was an author of note, having written the influential hip-hop study *The New Beats*, published in 1994. Fascinated by the history of *Crazy Wisdom Masters*, Fernando successfully pitched a feature story on the album to *Vibe* magazine. In an unfortunately ironic parallel to its subject matter, the piece would eventually appear, in heavily edited form, as a mere sidebar.

However, Fernando would also play a more tangible role in bringing the sounds of *Crazy Wisdom Masters* to the public. Also a producer—who recorded his experimental electronic music in several guises, including the alias Spectre—and label owner, Fernando approached Laswell in the mid-'90s about releasing some of the Jungle Brothers' material through his Wordsound Recordings.

Laswell, Afrika, and Mike G would okay the distribution of four of the most adventurous tracks from the *Crazy Wisdom Masters* sessions. "Battle Show," "Ra Ra Kid," "Spittin' Wicked Randomness," and "Headz at Company Z" composed an EP sold for a limited time through Wordsound's Black Hoodz imprint.

The *Crazy Wisdom Masters* EP, which featured Laswell's master tapes and did not specify the name of the group involved, was essentially a bootleg. But Laswell, who had plenty of experience with labels sitting on his projects, certainly wasn't losing sleep about its release. "I just think music ought to be free. You could put [*Crazy Wisdom Masters*] out today," he scoffs, "and people from Warner Brothers would say, 'Who are the Jungle Brothers?'"

That was, unfortunately, the reaction that awaited the Jungle Brothers, post–*J. Beez.* When S. H. Fernando Jr. tracked the group down for his *Vibe* feature, Afrika had become a born-again Christian and moved to Florida. Mike G was still in New York, "but was living uptown at his mom's, sleeping on a bunk bed or something," remembers Fernando. "Their fortunes had pretty much reversed."[18]

It would be four more years before the group—with Sammy B back in the fold, and minus Torture—returned on the Gee Street label with *Raw Deluxe*, an album that harked back to the sound of the group's Daisy Age heyday. That made it welcome to reviewers and listeners disgusted with the materialistic hip-hop then ascendant, but it also ensured a continued commercial irrelevance. The sole single, the mellow "Brain," stalled outside the Top 20 of the rap charts and was invisible elsewhere.

Three years later, Afrika and Mike G would connect with British producer Alex Gifford on *V.I.P.,* an album that reflected Gifford's work with his electronic duo, Propellerheads, and also reminded longtime fans of "I'll House You," the Jungle Brothers' first foray into club music. Unfortunately, there were fewer and fewer of those fans still around. By the time of 2002's *All That We Do,* helmed by old friend Todd Terry, the J. Beez had decided to self-release their material.

The current status of the group could best be termed active but uncertain, and is illustrated by a wistful juxtaposition. As Mike G answers questions about *Crazy Wisdom Masters,* he is driving around Brooklyn, showing his younger brother points of family interest. Passing a familiar-looking building, Mike motions toward a window. "Right there," he tells his brother excitedly, "there's where me and Af came up with the name Jungle Brothers!"

Yet, a few moments later, Mike admits that he doesn't even have a current phone number for his old friend. "Af texted me a week or two ago," he says, "but I deleted it." With Mike now living with his family in North Carolina, and Afrika located in Florida, regular contact has become a thing of the past.

Both men are now pursuing separate musical paths as well: Mike has contributed to the Playmakers, Matt Stein's current musical venture with ex-X-Ecutioners DJ Total Eclipse, while Afrika is now the CEO of Baby Bam Records, a label whose MySpace page boasts of Afrika's affiliations with gangsta rappers like 50 Cent and Rick Ross, but makes no mention of his Jungle Brothers past. Afrika also declined a chance to speak about *Crazy Wisdom Masters* for this book; "He's told me," an apologetic Mike G says, "that he really doesn't wanna talk about it anymore."

Afrika's startling career rethink might be seen by some as an epitaph to the J. Beez' career. However, there is still the matter of *Crazy Wisdom Masters*, which refuses to go gentle into that good night. All the principals in this story have been made aware of an unspecified label's interest in the album, and Laswell and Stein both have master tapes ready to supply should a deal be reached.

"Now there's so many ways to do it right," says Stein. He describes the chance to talk about *Crazy Wisdom Masters* as "just like a therapy session," but the possibility of finally making the album available—whether it's via conventional means, electronically, or otherwise—has him even more excited. "It's just full of heart and soul," he enthuses, "and that never goes out of style."

Years earlier, a defiant Afrika had predicted that *Crazy Wisdom Masters* would eventually win release—and respect. "They'll put that record out forty years from now, when they want the world to look at hip-hop as something foreign that happened in some distant past," he told S. H. Fernando Jr. "That shit will come up, just like Jimi Hendrix's shit comes up, but back then, niggas in Harlem didn't give a shit who he was. That's what that album is gonna be like."[19]

On that point, at least, he and his old partners remain in complete agreement. "Put it back out! *Put it back out!*" demands Torture. "You got me wantin' to hear that shit again. Let's do it. Let's make it happen!"

"It's like a crackhead. They chase after that one hit," adds Mike G, slowly patrolling the drug-haunted streets of New York as he mulls over his sometimes-crazy past. "*Crazy Wisdom Masters . . .* that was that one hit, right there."

The Jungle Brothers: *Crazy Wisdom Masters*
Recorded for: *Warner Brothers Records*
Scheduled release date: *1992*
Recorded at: *Greenpoint Studio, Brooklyn, NY; "The Bush Camp,"
    New York, NY; 1990–92*

TRACK LISTING:

Unknown

Produced by: *the Jungle Brothers, Bill Laswell, Matt Stein*
Mixed by: *Bill Laswell, Greenpoint Studio, Brooklyn NY*
Mastered by: *Howie Weinberg at Masterdisk, New York, NY*

Credits:
Afrika Baby Bam—*vocals*
Mike G—*vocals*
Torture—*vocals*
Bill Laswell—*bass, programming*
Matt Stein—*bass, guitar, keyboards, programming*
John Zorn—*saxophone on "Troopin' on the Down Lo"*
Amina Myers—*piano on "Troopin' on the Down Lo"*
Gary "Mudbone" Cooper—*vocals*
Bernie Worrell—*keyboards*
Bob Musso—*programming*
David Williams—*programming*

⑤ Mick Jagger

Sympathy for the Devils

A musician has to be ready for anything. It's practically part of the job description. But how could you hope to be prepared for a late-night phone call telling you to be at one of the world's most famous studios the next morning—to back up Mick Jagger on a selection of his favorite blues songs?

According to Dave Lee Bartel, who once got such a call, you couldn't. "It's a pretty hair-raising endeavor. It's like going into a lab, and you're under the microscope," recalls Bartel, the former rhythm guitarist for the Red Devils, who were summoned to record with Jagger. "You think about Keith Richards and Ronnie Wood and Charlie Watts, and you just feel self-conscious. It's heavy pressure, man."[1]

In fact, Bartel and most of his fellow Red Devils didn't even know some of the vintage numbers Jagger wanted to record. Yet the Hollywood bar band came through the one-day session on June 18, 1992 with flying colors, learning and tracking a baker's dozen blues chestnuts with the Rolling Stones' frontman.

The gambit employed by Jagger and producer Rick Rubin of keeping the band in the dark until the last possible minute had evidently worked. "Mick didn't want us to do a lot of rehearsing. He wanted it to be dirty, and he told us, y'know, 'I want this to sound like the original guys playing it.' He wanted it to sound like black musicians playing," reflects Dave Lee's younger brother, Johnny Ray Bartel, the Red Devils' bassist.[2]

"A lot of the changes in the songs are unpredictable—the counts weren't mathematically correct. And he got that from us. That's why people liked us, 'cause we could get that weird blues thing."

For a while, it looked like "that weird blues thing" was going to become Jagger's next solo album. Yet when Wandering Spirit *was finally released in 1993, the material from the Red Devils session was nowhere to be found. Jagger and Rubin instead offered a contemporary-sounding mixture of rock and funk, the same approximate formula followed on the Stones singer's previous two solo outings.*

That was a disappointment to the Devils, who continued their association with Rubin long enough to back his major reclamation project—the Man in Black, Johnny Cash—in the studio, and to record their own sophomore album as well. In both cases, the results were a further letdown: the Cash material would go unheard for years, while almost all the Devils' studio work remains unreleased. Singer and harmonica player Lester Butler, the hard-living heart of the band, left not long after those sessions, and later met a bizarre and tragic end.

Yet those who have heard the results of Jagger's return to the blues may have Butler to thank. Who leaked what bootleg of the Red Devils sessions is still open to debate, and some of Butler's former bandmates believe he helped circulate one version. But even mastered from cassette, the copies in circulation are still a significant document. You can hear a singer stripping away the varnish and studio-bound safety that had surrounded him for years, in an attempt to get back to the sounds and attitudes that had first captivated him as a London schoolboy. And behind him, an exciting American blues band very much in its prime—a strange mixture of slicked-back rockabilly cool and primal rock fire, something like the Stray Cats fronted by Jim Morrison in full Lizard King glory.

"To use a poker analogy, we just had a full house. Standing there onstage without even playing, people'd be staring, like, 'What's this?'" recalls drummer Bill Bateman. "The music moved people."[3] Perhaps someday the music Bateman and his bandmates recorded with this wayward Rolling Stone will get its official chance to move listeners as well.

When Mick Jagger approached the tiny stage of the King King one evening in May 1992 and politely asked the house band if he could sit in on a couple of songs, the Red Devils were not surprised. They'd been warned earlier that afternoon through their producer, Rick Rubin, that Jagger might be in attendance. The only startling thing was how small the rock 'n' roll legend was in person. "I thought *we* were little and skinny," says drummer Bill Bateman. "Hell, no! We looked like well-fed Americans."

The Devils were also not intimidated. The quintet's Monday-night residency at the King King had been the buzz in Los Angeles for months. As bassist Johnny Ray Bartel now remembers with some self-deprecation, that might have been partly because "we were the only thing happening in Hollywood on a Monday night." But boredom alone wouldn't have been enough to attract the guest list the Devils had begun to pull.

One of the Devils' more frequent onstage collaborators was actor Bruce Willis, who had released a couple of albums in the late '80s and still enjoyed playing blues harp. He liked the Devils so much, in fact, that he once flew them to his Idaho retreat and had them spend the night. In the morning, breakfast was served by Willis's wife at the time, actress Demi Moore. "In her robe and slippers, and those eyes lookin' at you," recalls drummer Bill Bateman with a laugh. "'How would you like your eggs, Bill?' 'Just like your eyes. I mean, your boobs. I mean, your ass.'"

Meanwhile, the Devils were also drawing interest from the likes of ZZ Top's Billy Gibbons, Angus and Malcolm Young of AC/DC, and the then-red-hot Black Crowes. Queen guitarist Brian May showed up to jam one night,[4] and supermodels had begun to queue outside. "It was reminiscent of old Hollywood," says Bateman. "But it was still first come, first served at the King King."

When Jagger hopped onstage that May 18, alongside Bateman, the Bartel brothers, Lester Butler, and lead guitarist Paul Size, he led the band through the Bo Diddley classic "Who Do You Love" and "Blues with a Feeling," by Chicago harpist Little Walter. Even for a crowd grown accustomed to celebrity spotting, it was an electric moment. "There were girls standing on guys' shoulders. People were standing on the bar. It just got really crazy in there. The whole club just raised up about three feet as soon as he got onstage. Everybody was all of a sudden very tall," laughs Johnny Ray Bartel.

What the Devils didn't realize was that they had passed an audition of sorts. With the Rolling Stones on hiatus following the *Steel Wheels* world tour, Jagger had turned his attention to the blues of his youth, with an eye toward tackling some of his favorites. It was evidently a project he had been giving consideration for some time: drummer and author Doug Hinman, who spent some time in the band of blues guitarist Duke Robillard, recalls Robillard receiving a call from Jagger's management as early as 1990. Nothing would come of the contact, but "I got the sense that Mick was feeling out blues bands," says Hinman.[5]

On the recommendation of Rick Rubin, Jagger had already scouted the Devils at the King King, and after joining them onstage, he knew he had his band. Exactly one month later, he would summon them for another jam session—this time with the tape running.[6]

For Jagger, who had cut his teeth watching and playing blues shows at London's iconic Marquee Club, part of the appeal of the Red Devils might well have been the way they'd made their own night-spot part of their legend.

In fact, it was the King King that had been responsible for the band's formation. Bill Bateman and guitarist Greg "Smokey" Hormel both had day jobs in the Los Angeles roots-rock collective the Blasters. But in December 1988, they'd agreed to put together a house band for Monday-night jam sessions at their new neighborhood club: the King King, a converted Chinese restaurant on Sixth and LaBrea.

Behind the red lacquered door lay a room that officially seated less than 150 patrons. The walls were black, the bar was blue Formica, and the old restaurant's Oriental exotica—and poor sightlines—had been retained by owner Mario Melendez. Yet while concert conditions were less than ideal, that didn't stop crowds from gathering.

"There was a very high density of hipsters and artists and musicians in the neighborhood, and the King King was in walking distance," explains Dave Lee Bartel. "They could get sauced and then walk home. Which is unusual in L.A."

The King King would host a variety of shows: ska acts like Jump with Joey; hip-hop up-and-comers such as Digable Planets; even the occasional theatrical production. But it was the house band, christened the Blue Shadows, that began packing the club. The roster shifted week by week, with Blasters Dave Alvin and Gene Taylor sometimes sitting in on guitar and piano, respectively.

By the summer of 1989, the Shadows' lineup included both Bartel brothers, as well as a long-haired, tattooed vocalist and harmonica player who was the missing, manic link between Little Walter, the Rolling Stones, and punk rock. Not that Lester Butler had the words to explain the connection. "When people ask me why I play the blues, I'll have to look back far and think hard. It's so deep in my soul," Butler once said. "It's just like you ask a fish, why do you swim? A fish doesn't know he swims, he just swims."[7]

Born in Arlington, Virginia in 1959, Butler moved to Santa Monica with his mother and sisters when he was six, after his parents split up. "Lester was the typical California kid," says his sister Ginny Tura. "He surfed, body surfed, skateboarded, and skied." But another of his hobbies would make him anything but typical. "He started playing the harmonica at around eight years old. He played it night and day for the rest of his life," Tura adds. "I remember him riding around on his skateboard playing harmonica all over town when he was young."[8]

"He had everything: the voice, the harp chops, and just a crazy attitude," says Dave Lee Bartel. His brother, Johnny Ray, adds, "Lester always thought he was Jim Morrison, this kind of shaman, trying to achieve some kind of crazy state like that. And he used us to get there." One of the bandmates he began using was a raw young guitarist named Paul Size, who replaced Smokey Hormel in the autumn of 1990. Transported from small-town Texas to Hollywood at the tender age of nineteen, Size was so naïve and wide-eyed that he was immediately nicknamed "Kid." "But he was a natural, just like Lester," Dave Lee Bartel says.

Word began to spread about the Shadows' fiery Chicago blues, and lines began forming outside the little red, green, and black building. By early 1991, one of the people who had gotten the message was Rick Rubin. After leaving behind his native New York and Def Jam, the groundbreaking hip-hop label he had formed with Russell Simmons, Rubin had relocated in Los Angeles and set up his own, Def American imprint. This gave him a chance to work with bands he championed, like the controversial speed-metal group Slayer, but at this point he was ensconced in an old Laurel Canyon mansion, producing the album that would send his reputation into the stratosphere: the Red Hot Chili Peppers' *Blood Sugar Sex Magik*.

Rubin would sometimes leave the allegedly haunted mansion to check out the happenings at the King King, bringing along his friend George Drakoulias. Both men were interested in the Shadows, and Dave Lee Bartel now says he and his bandmates had hoped Drakoulias—a successful producer in his own right, after the release of the Black Crowes' Def American debut—would work with them. "He was more of a normal person," Bartel says. "But it was totally Rick's band, and there was no question he was gonna do it."

That much was made clear when Rubin ordered a name change for the Shadows. After finding out that the Bartel brothers had played in an '80s rockabilly band called the Red Devils, he demanded a switch. "He liked that name," says Dave Lee Bartel. "He was like, 'Ah, that's tougher. You gotta use that one!' " Rubin would also take over the recording of the rechristened group's debut for Def American, a debut he insisted had to be live. "He picked out the songs and brought in a mobile studio, and we recorded it over about four nights," Bartel says. "We didn't even know when we were gonna record. We just knew we had to play good whenever that truck was in the alley."

Rubin would even take charge of the cover art. "He had the vision of it all," says Bartel. That vision was of a one-take, no-over-dubs release, titled simply *King King* and released to much acclaim in 1992. A combination of unimpeachable source material by the likes of Little Walter and Howlin' Wolf, as well as a trio of Chicago blues–inspired originals—including the frenzied "Goin' to the Church"—the album would become the sweaty document by which the band and its scene would be remembered.

"Maybe Rick Rubin was really brilliant," acknowledges Bartel. As far as the Red Devils were concerned, he was about to come up with his most brilliant idea yet.

That Rubin was calling Bill Bateman's home at all was unusual. To the annoyance of the Devils, the producer now seldom deigned to make contact with anyone but Butler. "He would take one person out of a band and only communicate through him," says Dave Lee Bartel. "Usually the lead singer, who isn't always the best leader."

But on the evening of June 17, 1992, the news was important enough to warrant a personal call to the other group members as well. The Devils were to report to Studio B at Ocean Way Recording in Hollywood, at ten sharp the next morning. They would be recording with Jagger, but had no clue what songs he wanted to try. It made no difference to the Devils: "It was like Christmas Eve," says Johnny Ray Bartel. "We were like, 'We're gonna be in the studio with *Jagger?*'"

When Christmas came the next morning, the band assembled at Ocean Way still feeling disbelief. Jagger was in the midst of the regular sessions for *Wandering Spirit* there, and the Devils got a glimpse of the piles of equipment being used by the session pros in his backing band. It wasn't exactly a confidence builder: "I figured we'd get about halfway through it, and then he'd fire us, and call in some studio people," remembers Johnny Ray Bartel. "This isn't like playing with Bruce Willis—this is one of the most famous musicians in the world. So I figured after about an hour and a half, they'd bring in the bass equivalent of Jim Keltner, y'know."[9]

Bartel's brother, Dave Lee, agrees. "I don't even think I belonged there. I'm not that great a musician," he says frankly. "But I got by, and the people liked my personality."

The contract the band members signed for Arnold Dunn, the Stones' road manager, was a further reality check. Each Red Devil was to receive a flat $750 fee for the day's work, with no claim toward future royalties.[10] The group would be joined by pianist Rob Rio, a local player whose expertise in jump blues and boogie-woogie styles had earned him the nickname "Boss of the Boogie."

"Jagger wanted an Otis Spann–type character to play piano, and I was the Otis Spann guy in town," says Rio.[11] Dave Lee Bartel recalls, "In between takes, Rio would just read the newspaper, the business section. I was like, 'This cat is from Wall Street!' But he was very relaxed, and he had some serious chops." Rio would have ample opportunity to display them, as he played a prominent role in almost every song.

Jagger brought to the studio a scarf, which he wore draped around his throat; a young Swedish girlfriend who stood well over six feet tall and worked on her knitting during the session;[12] and a small case full of vintage blues music on CD, much of it drawn from the old Chess records he had loved growing up.

"And he said, 'OK, guys, these are my favorite records. I'm gonna play 'em once for you, and then we're all gonna jam along to the original versions. And then we're gonna record it,'" remembers Johnny Ray Bartel. "Basically what he wanted was ultimate spontaneity, and not a whole lot of rehearsing at all, and just nail it down really quick and let's see what we get."

The track list for the day included a trio of songs each from Little Walter and his mentor, Muddy Waters, the man who had given the Rolling Stones their name. Slide-guitar pioneer Elmore James and harpist Slim Harpo each contributed a pair of tunes, while the remainder was drawn from '50s and '60s sides by Sonny Boy Williamson II, Bukka White, and Howlin' Wolf.[13]

Some of it was obscure enough to concern the Devils—Muddy Waters' "Still a Fool," for example, was a song Dave Lee Bartel admits "I didn't know well enough to play in my fucking bedroom." However, Bill Bateman was enough of a blues veteran that he was not only familiar with all the material, but could assist Jagger in interpreting lyrics that had remained a puzzle for almost forty years. "I sat down with him at the board, and we wrote the lyrics out. 'Cause he couldn't understand a Muddy Waters song, he couldn't understand a Slim Harpo song. He'd say, 'What's he saying there, Bill?' And I'd say, 'I think he's saying this, Mick.' And he'd write it down."

The format for the following thirteen hours was simple. Jagger and the Devils would rehearse each track, then quickly lay down a take together, in the old-fashioned way. There were no overdubs, and most songs were left in their original key. On a few occasions, four or five tries were necessary to nail down a song, but most were completed in three or fewer takes. And Jagger alone would venture into the control room to check the playback with Rubin between takes.

The rush of working so fast erased most of the Devils' worries, and brought out a side of Jagger the band had scarcely imagined. "It turns out, he comes in, and he's acting like he's been our friend forever. Not only that, but he was acting like he was twenty years old the whole time. He was running around making faces at us while we were recording," says Johnny Ray Bartel. "He actually walked up to me during a take, and had his fingers around his eyes upside down, making that hawk face. You know, your elbows up in the air? And he kept trying to get me to look at him, and I had to keep looking away, like, 'Stop it, Mick! I'm trying to do you a favor here!'"

First up was "Mean Old World," a song credited to Little Walter, who had cribbed it—at least in part—from T-Bone Walker's 1942 hit "Mean Old World Blues." Led by Butler's distorted harmonica and Rio's rippling piano runs, the song was a brighter version of the more deliberate Little Walter original, which had been a Top 10 R&B hit in 1953 and featured Muddy Waters on guitar.

Another unhurried shuffle by Walter, "Blues with a Feeling," followed. Despite having played it together just a month earlier, Jagger and the Devils required five takes to record it to everyone's satisfaction. The song's breakdown threw the band on the first couple of passes, but by take four things had tightened up appreciably, providing Butler and Rio with another slow-paced showcase.

The third Little Walter number attempted was a much jauntier march, driven by a spiky guitar riff from Paul Size and completed in one energetic try. "You Better Watch Yourself" had reached No. 8 on the R&B charts in the fall of 1956, when a teenaged Jagger was first discovering the blues. Now he was rediscovering his voice at Ocean Way, handling the shouted verses and the deeper-voiced choruses with an ease that suggested he was rounding into form.

By the time Jagger decided to tackle Muddy Waters' ominous 1951 hit "Still a Fool"—which the Stones had recorded in 1968, yet never released[14]—another musician had joined the proceedings. Former Devil Smokey Hormel was known in particular for his slide-guitar skills, so "Lester called him and said, 'I think you need to get down here,'" Dave Lee Bartel says. "And Mick was real happy." Especially since "Still a Fool" was one of Waters' raw, early sides dependent on his signature bottleneck playing—which Hormel approximated with ease on the song's three takes. "He's one of those historian cats who can just duplicate a certain tone," says Dave Lee Bartel admiringly.

The confident stride of "Checkin' Up on My Baby" sounded tailor-made for Jagger and the Devils, and their loose-limbed (if somewhat more leisurely) version of the 1965 Sonny Boy Williamson II song was a fitting tribute to the legendary harpist. Three tries were evidently necessary, but the take that has circulated was spot-on. Butler took the solo, and it is a testament to Jagger's respect for his style that Butler would be the only harmonica player heard throughout the day. "At one point I heard Rick [Rubin] call out, 'Hey Mick, play some harp!' recalls Dave Lee Bartel. "But he said, 'No, I'm just here to sing.' Later on he pulled Lester aside and said, 'I really admire your playing.' Lester had that raw and gritty sound—he had a certain gift, man. He could sound black without sounding fake."

Evening was now approaching, and Jagger and the band were peaking. Elmore James had been a particular favorite of the embryonic Stones, and the pair of his tunes now attempted came exactly at the right time. "One Way Out" undoubtedly offered Jagger a familiar situation, if not a direct scenario: it was a cheatin' song about a lover trapped in the bedroom with no exit but the window. And the tune was mastered in a pair of takes that barely topped two minutes each. Once again, the fervor of the original,[15] which had been bolstered by honking baritone sax, was swapped for a more relaxed shuffle, with Rio's tinkling keys the instrumental highlight.

The rolling Chicago blues of James's "Talk to Me Baby," another of the slide guitarist's early '60s recordings, followed; Jagger was in full-throated Stonesey yelp, and the Devils were demonstrating the qualities that Bill Bateman had deemed intrinsic to their success: "No extraneous notes, no typical white-blues-band stuff, no going back to the five after the one."

The session nearly ground to a halt, however, when everyone's attention turned to Howlin' Wolf's "Evil." Under any circumstances, it would have been difficult to match the Wolf's 1956 hit. Written by Willie Dixon (who also penned Muddy Waters' "Hoochie Coochie Man"), it was an ideal showcase for the larger-than-life persona of Chester Burnett, the towering, 300-pound singer who was as imposing in person as he was on wax. Over the course of five takes, Jagger and the Devils tried to meet the Wolf's mammoth mojo head-on, but the sluggish pace didn't help, and Rio's busy boogie-woogie riffs lightened the mood a trifle too much. "That," says Bateman, "was the hardest one for Mick."

The Devils recovered quickly, knocking off Slim Harpo's "That Ain't Your Business," and then nailing the Bukka White classic

"Shake 'Em on Down" in a single go—a feat more impressive considering the song's irregular structure, which reflected its country blues origins. Originally recorded in 1937, the tune was redone by its author more than twenty-five years later, after White, one of the early delta bluesmen, was rediscovered by folk fans. Staying faithful to the raw Mississippi drone of the original, the Devils gave Butler the spotlight, and he rose to the occasion with some of his most primitive harmonica licks.

The energy of that take seemed to carry over onto a run through Muddy Waters' "Don't Go No Farther," another Willie Dixon composition.[16] Jagger managed the nifty trick ending in full growl, but by this time he had been at the mic, off and on, for upwards of ten hours. Even given a constitution atypical of most forty-nine-year-olds, this was a lot of punishment, and by the time he and the Devils attempted a version of Slim Harpo's heartbroken swamp blues "Dream Girl," the strain was beginning to show. "He was getting tired on 'Dream Girl,'" confirms Bateman; the languid tempo, faithful to the original, gave Jagger some breathing room, but it's hard to imagine he couldn't have bettered the vocals he turned in on both takes that have circulated.

Still, he reached back for whatever he had in reserve on "Forty Days and Forty Nights," an R&B hit for Muddy Waters in 1956. Written by a Gary, Indiana butcher named Bernie Roth (who also composed "Just to Be with You" for Waters), the song turns the search for a lost love into an ordeal of Biblical proportions. It's a suffering reinforced by the raggedness of Jagger's voice, which held out for at least two takes.

By this time, it was growing late, and the work at Ocean Way was done. "That should be it for tonight," Rubin told the band over the control-room intercom. Thirteen songs had been completed in as many hours. The Devils collected their cash; Jagger collected his girlfriend, his blues CDs, and the masters of the session.

"And then he took his tapes and ran away, and we never saw him again," jokes Johnny Ray Bartel. That wasn't precisely true, but subsequent events would give the Red Devils an authentic case of the blues.

Because the session at Ocean Way had been arranged so hurriedly, it had never been made clear to the participants exactly what was planned for the recordings. As Dave Lee Bartel understood it, the original expectation was that at least a couple of the songs would end up on *Wandering Spirit*, which Jagger and Rubin were in the midst of completing.[17] Rubin himself confirmed that the session generated much more material than expected. "We were going to record just one or two songs with [the Devils], but we did fourteen[18]—all in one day—and it sounded so great we thought it should be a whole other album," he told the *Los Angeles Times*. "I assume it will come out someday."[19]

So did some members of the press. At various points during the summer of 1992, it had been reported that the Red Devils session would constitute the next Jagger album. The source of this rumor was unknown, but it was cleared up by the fall. Reinforcing Rubin's views, *Billboard* noted, "The thirteen tracks Jagger recorded this summer with Def American act and Rubin pet project the Red Devils may see the light of day in the future, but will remain on the shelf for the time being."[20] Jagger would underscore this further in an interview with *Rolling Stone*'s David Wild: "People should know that I'm not making a blues album," he said, adding, "As far as I know, I'm not."[21]

That Jagger and Rubin would decide against releasing an album of vintage blues covers was hardly surprising. Substantial work had already been done on *Wandering Spirit*, and while substituting a bunch of old blues songs would have likely been a critical success, the fact remained that Jagger's solo career had still not produced a substantial commercial hit.[22] The Red Devils tracks were unlikely to change that.

However, the session offered a rare and revealing portrait of Jagger. Rob Rio, who had come to the studio "not really a Stones fan," and who wasn't crazy about hearing Jagger do straight blues covers, left impressed. "He's a lot better singer than I thought. A great singer, in fact." Yet even Dave Lee Bartel, who thought Jagger's vocals and Butler's harmonica work were the highlights of the session, admits, "We always figured Mick probably would want to rerecord his vocals, when he wasn't so rushed." He adds dryly, "At some point, he might be on vacation in the south of France or something, and might want to recut them."

As the year changed, however, the Devils had no word about the fate of the session. That frustration may have been the source of a report that appeared in journalist Rick Sky's "The Limit" column in London's *Daily Mirror* on February 9, 1993. Sky described the Devils as "livid" about the unreleased recordings, and quoted Bill Bateman:

> Mick said he wanted to do a solo album of old blues and R&B songs. When we finished, he said it was some of the best music he'd ever recorded. Then he

took the master tapes, jumped into his limo and split. He wouldn't let anyone have a copy of the music. We tried to call him but he never phoned back.[23]

In response, a Jagger spokesman told Sky, "Mick loved the stuff he did with the Red Devils, but in the end he decided to release something different." A response was swift: later that month, the U.K. magazine *rpm* carried a notice from Richard Wootton, one of Britain's leading publicists. According to Wootton, any suggestion that the Devils were unhappy with Jagger was incorrect. "The material recorded did not make it on to Jagger's *Wandering Spirit* album, but the band are keen to point out that both parties were extremely happy with the fruits of their labours, and there are plans to release the recordings 'in the future,'" the magazine reported.[24]

The source of this damage control is now lost to the passage of time, but it probably had something to do with the reunion of Jagger and the Devils in England that spring. Bateman offers,

We did a little tour. Because Mick got a hair up his ass and wanted to play some parties. Private parties, in central London, for his friends. So that's where we ended up a few times, driving around the block several times cause we needed to finish the fattie that Mick and brother Chris had lit. Y'know, like, "Here, bloke—smoke this!"

It was pretty funny. 'Cause we just looked like geeks from Santa Monica, or Downey, or something. Wearing plaid shirts and walking into these high-class parties with all these supermodels. But it was still Red Devils songs.

One of the gigs took place at the London Borderline in late March. At this show, Jagger was only an observer, but a reviewer from *Metal CD* claimed the Devils played "one of the tightest sets this club has ever witnessed . . . segueing rapidly into one musical highlight after another." Butler, who was described as looking "like an extra from *Wild at Heart*" in his long leather jacket and shades, "whipped up his cohorts into a scorching display of musical muscle tempered with some old-fashioned passion and fire. . . . What a bunch of cool bastards!"[25]

A few nights later, the band played the Chelsea nightspot Roberto's—a small and "smoky basement club in the King's Road," according to the *Evening Standard*, with a capacity of just 150.[26] Jagger joined the Devils to reprise "Who Do You Love" and "Checkin' Up on My Baby," the Sonny Boy Williamson number they'd recorded the previous summer. Photos of the event even seemed to show the singer, otherwise dressed down in sweater and jeans, with a tattoo of a red devil on his left wrist. This apparent token of devotion aside, the Devils chose not to question Jagger about his plans for their session work.

The band stayed in England to open some shows for Lynyrd Skynyrd, but when they returned home there was still no news about the album, save for a *Musician* magazine interview in which Jagger said of the songs, "We don't know if we're going to put them out. We did it just for fun."[27] In retrospect, it seems clear that Jagger had already moved on; by this point, he and Keith Richards had patched up their latest round of differences and were already beginning to plan a new Rolling Stones album—the group's first without bassist Bill Wyman.

Meanwhile, the Devils didn't even have copies of their work to play for friends. But that situation would soon be rectified in a couple of different ways.

According to his sister, Ginny Tura, Lester Butler lived most of his adult life fairly straight. He had begun experimenting with drugs in junior high school, and loved smoking pot. However, "He didn't drink or do drugs, from his late twenties on, on a regular basis," Tura claims. "He would have a binge, I would say, about once a year when he would drink and do drugs. Usually after he came into big money for his music." The Jagger recordings, some of his bandmates believe, might have fueled just such a binge.

One day, according to Dave Lee Bartel, Butler suddenly turned up with a ninety-minute cassette of the Jagger session. When asked where he'd gotten it, Butler was cagey: "Some guy gave me this," Bartel recalls him saying. Bartel believes the cassette might have come from the tape deck that was run alongside the multitrack machine during the session.

Bartel's brother, Johnny Ray, further believes that Butler sold the cassette, or a copy of it, to bootleggers. "Lester got some really bad cassette copies from Rick, 'cause he was palling around with Rick," Johnny Ray Bartel says. "And I'm pretty sure he sold it to some Italian guys for some drug money, so he could keep getting high. That's where those came from."[28]

"Those" were the bootlegs of the session that began to proliferate. Johnny Ray Bartel has had one of them for years, his only proof of a historic day. But he was stunned during the interviews for this book to learn that his bandmates had been listening for years to a

CD-quality copy of the songs. An amused Bill Bateman explained to Bartel how those copies found their way out of Rick Rubin's office.

According to Bateman, Jagger's touring guitarist Jimmy Rip and a source within the Devils

> hoodwinked, or paid off, or something, Rick's right-hand gal. And she called in one afternoon and said, "OK, Rick's gone now." And she got the keys, went into a locked drawer, got the DAT of the sessions, and gave it to him. They raced over to Jimmy's, burned a copy on CD, made a copy of the DAT, and raced back, gave her back the DAT. She put it back in the spot, locked the drawer, and nobody was the wiser.

Obviously not, since Rubin would summon the Devils to Ocean Way's Studio Two in the fall of 1993 to back yet another legend. Perhaps the only thing more intimidating than the thought of spending the day backing Mick Jagger was the prospect of spending one playing alongside the Man in Black.

It was Labor Day in Los Angeles, and evening traffic was reaching its 5 P.M. critical mass when the Red Devils arrived at Sunset Boulevard. Awaiting them at Ocean Way, clad in his traditional dark attire and holding a Martin acoustic, was a man who had been reshaping popular music while Mick Jagger was still wearing out Elmore James and Muddy Waters records in his London bedroom.

The years had not been kind to Johnny Cash, especially not the past few. His album sales had plummeted during the '80s, as a new label, Mercury Records, directed the once-proud singer to rerecord old hits in a desperate attempt to keep him relevant. Yet the glossy crossover pop that passed for relevance in Nashville had little to do with Cash. The outlaw stance that fueled "Folsom Prison Blues" and his prison concert from San Quentin, in fact, had more in common with the rebellious alternative rock and hip-hop of the '90s.

This was something Rubin, who had worked with acts from both genres, quickly understood. "I don't know if it was so much his music, per se, that drew me to him," Rubin would say years later. "It was more his overall persona. Obviously, I love his music, but his attraction was greater than music. . . . He really lived an extreme life in different directions."[29] In 1993, he began a partnership with Cash that would continue for the final decade of the singer's life. The intimate music that followed—especially the duo's first album together, 1994's *American Recordings*—is now considered some of Cash's finest.

One of Rubin's goals at the beginning of the collaboration was to pair Cash with younger artists and songwriters, without a clear goal in mind. "We tried a lot of different things before we settled on what that first album was," Rubin admitted.[30] Although the Devils only spent five hours with the singer that September evening, their session embodied the experimentation Rubin had in mind for Cash.

"He was sitting on this big chair, teaching us these songs," remembers Bill Bateman. "And he'd go, 'You got that, boys?' And we'd go, 'Yeah,' and then we'd just play the shit out of it."

The initial song they attempted was the 1927 Jimmie Rodgers standard "'T' For Texas," which had been the first in the pioneering country singer's series of "blue yodels." With Butler's harp supplying counterpoint, Cash and the Devils gave the tune a low-key but swinging reading, which would later show up on the 2003 box set *Unearthed*.[31] So would a rowdy version of a much more contemporary track—Steve Earle's "Devil's Right Hand"—but Rubin chose to wipe the Devils off the finished mix.[32]

In between those two efforts, Cash and the Devils also recorded "Bad News," a song from "Tobacco Road" author John D. Loudermilk that Cash had made a Top 10 country hit in 1964. The rerecording, however, has never been released. Perhaps more disappointingly, although they apparently got first crack at "Thirteen"—a song Misfit-turned-metalhead Glenn Danzig had written specifically for Cash—the Devils' version never made it onto tape.

However, after Cash vacated the studio at 10 P.M., Rubin had a surprise for the Red Devils. "He said, 'OK, we're gonna record your next album right now,' recalls Dave Lee Bartel. And for the next three and a half hours, the band tore through nine songs, a mixture of originals like "Blackwater Roll,"[33] covers like B. B. King's '50s hit "She's Dynamite," and even a tune—Muddy Waters' "Louisiana Blues"—shortlisted for the Jagger sessions.

The Devils left Ocean Way early the next morning on an adrenaline high. They had no way of knowing they'd spoken to Rick Rubin—and recorded with Lester Butler—for the last time.

In truth, by the time of the Johnny Cash session, the Devils had already begun to flame out. Earlier that summer, lead guitarist Paul Size, an exciting player still barely out of his twenties, had quit the band and returned to his native Texas. "He'd been around the world with us, and he'd had enough," says Dave Lee Bartel. "He was homesick."

For the Cash session, Size had been replaced by Smokey Hormel, while West Coast session man Zach Zunis filled in on the Devils' second album recording. But the group soon had a much bigger problem than finding someone to take over on guitar.

In short, Lester Butler and the Red Devils had reached an impasse. According to Butler's sister, Ginny Tura, he had decided to find himself another group; according to his bandmates, his excesses were helping fuel that decision. "It was getting harder and harder to get Lester to want to rehearse," says Dave Lee Bartel. "Other than live performances, it was just hard to get him out of the house in the daytime. He'd say, 'I just have to feel it. It'll come out onstage. It'll be all right.' And I'd say, 'That's okay for you, but the rest of us don't know what's gonna happen!' "[34] Soon Butler stopped showing up for gigs as well.

This behavior had not escaped the disapproving gaze of Rick Rubin. Despite his long hair, leathers, and shades, Rubin had a decidedly low tolerance for the stereotypical rock 'n' roll lifestyle. "He was a straight edge kid. He looked down on that stuff," says Bartel. "Rick was probably tired of dealing with Lester."[35]

That, the Devils would come to believe, was why Rubin finally broke off contact with the entire band, which was now regularly struggling to find replacements for Butler. "We heard from someone later that he thought Lester needed to clean up," Bartel recalls. Once Rubin's decision was made, there was no chance of getting more answers. "He didn't take calls from people, and he especially wouldn't dig any calls from musicians," Bartel notes, "unless you were Johnny Cash or Mick Jagger."

Despite the high-profile collaborations of the past couple of years—and a growing popularity in Europe, where the band had played a series of prestigious festivals during the summer of 1993—the band Bill Bateman thought had a full house decided to fold its hand. By the end of 1994, the Devils were essentially finished; to underscore the point, even the King King had shut its doors. Each member began pursuing other musical projects, with Butler's inevitably attracting the most attention. His collaboration with guitarist Alex Schultz, dubbed simply 13,[36] gave Butler top billing and a chance to prove himself as a songwriter. The group's lone, self-titled album was composed mostly of his originals, which modernized blues with hints of alternative rock and impressed most reviewers when released by Hightone in 1997.

European audiences, in particular, continued to adore Butler. Even minus his long mane, and clad in the alt-rock uniform of T-shirt and soul patch, his charisma was undiminished. So was his desire to make his bandmates take him higher. Video clips that survive of Butler rehearsing with 13 offer proof; so does a segment filmed at the 1998 Moulin Blues Festival in Holland. "At the end of the video it flashes to Lester sitting in a room, watching his performance on TV," says his sister, Ginny Tura. "I could just see his mind working on what he liked and didn't like about the show."

Just one week later, Butler was back in the underbelly of Los Angeles. The details of what happened on that weekend in early May have been sketchy for years. What is certain is that Butler spent some time in the company of April Ortega and her boyfriend, Glenn Demidow, who were later changed with second-degree manslaughter in his death.

At some point during the weekend, Butler had reportedly been shot up by Ortega with a dose of heroin so potent it caused him to pass out. Over the next few hours, Ortega and Demidow tried to revive Butler with injections of cocaine, but he failed to regain consciousness. The pair then put Butler into his van and made several stops around town, without seeking medical attention for their comatose passenger. Butler was dropped off at Bill Bateman's house on Saturday evening; the drummer believes his former bandmate was already dead by that time. A formal pronouncement would come Sunday morning at Los Angeles County Hospital, in the early hours of Mother's Day. The modern-day blues shaman left behind a devoted girlfriend, Lori Peralta, and an equally devoted and loving family. He was thirty-eight years old.

Ginny Tura and the rest of Butler's family pushed for a murder charge against Ortega and Demidow, but the two defendants—who would claim they had not sought medical help for Butler because they were afraid of getting him in trouble—accepted the plea bargain offered by prosecutors. It was a heavy blow for Butler's family, especially given some of the details that later emerged about Butler's last hours. Even as Lester lay unconscious and in need of a doctor, Tura was told by police, one of his companions had scrawled on his body, "I am fucking stupid."

"Lester was a truly gifted musician," Tura says now, making a dignified segue from questions about her brother's death. "He was passionate about his music and would have done it for free."

In the years that followed, bits and pieces of the Red Devils' past would re-emerge. After almost a decade, Mario Melendez found a new building on Hollywood Boulevard to house a new, larger King King. A reformed version of the Blue Shadows would even entertain at the club's grand opening.

Yet Butler's surviving bandmates admit that without him, a longer reunion would seem hollow. "Lester would take it to a crescendo inside his mind, and he wouldn't stop until he'd achieved it," remembers Bateman with a sigh. "And by the time we got up where he wanted us, we were almost in a trance. And playing *hard*. You could definitely say it was spiritual, in a sense."

But the spirit has flown, gone to join the ghosts he helped summon in the bright studio sunlight one summer day in 1992. And the blues Dave Lee Bartel sings now are of a more practical nature. "Let's face it: without Lester, it ain't really that great," he says matter-of-factly. "Without Lester . . . it's not really the Red Devils, is it?"[37]

Mick Jagger and the Red Devils: *(no title given)*
Scheduled release date: *Unknown*
Recorded at: *Ocean Way Studios, Los Angeles, CA;*
June 17, 1992

TRACK LISTING:

1. Mean Old World
2. Blues with a Feeling
3. You Better Watch Yourself
4. Still a Fool
5. Checkin' Up on My Baby
6. One Way Out
7. Talk to Me Baby
8. Evil
9. That Ain't Your Business

10. Shake 'Em on Down
11. Don't Go No Farther
12. Dream Girl
13. Forty Days and Forty Nights

Produced by: *Rick Rubin*

Credits:
Mick Jagger—*vocals*
Johnny Ray Bartel—*bass*
Dave Lee Bartel—*rhythm guitar*
Bill Bateman—*drums*
Lester Butler—*harmonica*
Paul "Kid" Size—*lead guitar*

Guest artists:
Greg "Smokey" Hormel—*slide guitar*
Rob Rio—*piano*

The Beastie Boys

Reading the News in the *White House*

*T*he Beastie Boys are almost certainly not the artists with the most unheard music stashed in their vaults. That honor would likely go to either Prince or Neil Young, the co-patron-saints of the unreleased album. But imaginary unreleased albums are a different story.

From Adam Horovitz's "five solo albums of a rather risqué bent,"[1] which Capitol Records reportedly turned down, to a nautically themed disc allegedly recorded in a submarine at the same time the trio was working on the 1998 release Hello Nasty, to the group's claims to have recorded with everyone from the Traveling Wilburys to Queen, the Beasties have built up one of the most amazing back catalogs in music—with the help of a bemused, or simply gullible, press.

However, two of the many purported projects that have involved the Beasties deserve special mention. The first, though it was, like so many others, merely a concept and never an album, stands out in that it easily might have come to pass—and if it had, there would probably be no Beastie Boys as we know them today. The other unofficial release, meanwhile, was shocking: not only because it revealed the down-home side of the downtown New York trio, but also because it actually existed.

The legends of White House *and* Country Mike *have both passed into Beastie lore, and to call Mike's lone album some of the greatest music never sold might be stretching the claim. Yet while fans of Waylon and Willie—or, even more pointedly, Carrie Underwood and Rascal Flatts—likely won't need it in their collections, the conceptual brilliance behind Country Mike and his collection of greatest hits is hard to argue. If all of it isn't great music, the entire album qualifies as something almost as rare: great fun.*

When Beastie Boys fans discovered Country Mike, they immediately noticed striking similarities between the troubled, kerchief-wearing singer and the group's own Michael Diamond. Over the years, however, Diamond has steadfastly denied any connection.

"Have you tried contacting Country Mike?"
Diamond asks during an interview one after-
noon in a combination art gallery and café on a
SoHo side street. "It'd be great if you could talk
to him for your book, but it'd be hard."[2] He men-
tions that Nathanial Hörnblowér, the Beasties'
lederhosen-wearing, longtime video director—
who reportedly bears a remarkable resemblance
to Adam Yauch—has already attempted to
reach out to Country Mike, and failed.

"So if Hörnblowér couldn't do it, then . . ."
Mike D concludes, shrugging his shoulders as
his voice trails off. He looks around the café, lost
in thought, before concluding, "Country Mike
has gone underground."

Until now. Two of the many goals of this
book are to settle the story of White House, *once*
and for all, and to bring one reclusive country
star in from the cold. So, Country Mike, if you're
reading the news, please phone home.

Perhaps the best way of describing *White House* is that it was a threat, not a promise. But it was a threat that carried more prom-ise than most commentators have afforded it over the years, and it opens one of the most fascinating "what if?" windows of any album discussed in this book.

The origins of *White House* stem from the dispute that arose in the fall of 1987 between Def Jam impresario Russell Simmons and the Beastie Boys, following the trio's No. 1 debut, *Licensed to Ill*. Simmons understandably expected the group to return to the studio to create a follow-up to that unexpected success; the Beasties, just as understandably, wanted nothing more than to take some time off. They had toured in each of the last three years, and were trying to cope with the backlash that was rising in response to their beer-drenched, frat-boy image. It seemed incredible that three upper-middle-class Jewish boys from New York had suddenly become both the most popular group in hip-hop, and the scourge of Middle America. And the Beasties themselves were as surprised, and ultimately disheartened, as anyone by this strange turn of events.

"You haven't even gotten off the roller coaster, and the record company says, 'Okay, here's your ticket for Round Two. Give us more of the same right now,'" remembers Mike D. "And you say, 'Wait a minute, I'm dizzy and sick. I'm taking a break and getting some popcorn.'"

Actually, the Beasties wanted more than just popcorn. They wanted the estimated $2 million in royalties they'd earned from the multiplatinum sales of *Licensed to Ill*. Those close to Simmons at the time, like former Beasties road manager Sean "The Captain" Carasov, believed the withheld payments were largely a result of the unfavorable distribution deal Def Jam had struck with Columbia. "[Simmons] wasn't trying to rip anybody off," says Carasov. "They would have gotten paid eventually."[3] But the fact that the Beasties had, to that point, received less than $100,000 in royalties for *Licensed to Ill* was a sore spot.

Besides the money, they also wanted creative freedom. *Licensed to Ill* had been largely produced by Rick Rubin, Def Jam's metal-loving cofounder. But the Beasties, who had produced the single "Hold It Now, Hit It," themselves and had been more involved in the making of their debut than most people realized, were unhappy being perceived as Rubin's creations.

The trio's list of grievances could have broken up the group, and by most accounts, this very nearly happened. But instead, having a common enemy—Simmons and Def Jam—ultimately pulled the three Beasties back together. Contending that Def Jam had breached its contract, they began seeking a new label.[4] The Beasties would sign with Capitol Records in mid-1988, triggering lawsuits from Def Jam and its corporate parent, Sony. As the dispute dragged through the courts, the Beasties moved to Los Angeles to begin working with producers Matt Dike, Mike Simpson, and John King, and engineer Mario Caldato Jr. on the album that would become *Paul's Boutique*. Russell Simmons, however, was not about to let what he saw as the betrayal of his biggest-selling act go unpunished.

As the release date of *Paul's Boutique* drew nearer, Simmons began telling interviewers he planned to release his own package of Beasties material, a story broken in the U.K.'s *New Musical Express* in June 1989. First described as "a collection of previously unreleased raps to which new musical backing is being added,"[5] this album would become known as *White House*.

It was a story that seemed plausible at the time; after all, releasing a new Beasties album on Def Jam to steal sales from *Paul's Boutique* would have been the sweetest sort of payback for Simmons. But the tales grew sillier as time passed. By the autumn, rumors were flying that the "House" in the album's proposed title was a reference to house music—over which the Beasties' rhymes would purportedly be placed.

Publicly, the Beasties scoffed at the idea that the album would ever come to pass. It was a revenge fantasy, they thought, that had little grounding in reality. "It's not like he has huge vaults filled with master tapes of us," Mike D pointed out to *LA Weekly*. Yet he knew his old boss well: if Russell Simmons couldn't have the Beastie Boys, he might try to humiliate them instead. "It's just every musician's nightmare," Diamond would add. "Not only your past coming back to haunt you, but your past in songs you know you won't like."[6]

Years after the fact, Diamond can be more candid about those fears. "It was Def Jam threatening us, saying, 'If you guys leave, we're gonna release this really terrible Beastie Boys album that'll, like, ruin your lives,'" he recalls, shaking his head. " 'This terrible, terrible remix Beastie Boys album. You'll have nothing to do with it, and it'll make you look ridiculous.' "

At the time, however, the band could only meet one threat with another. "If he puts it out," Adam Yauch would say of Simmons, "we've got a video of him getting boned in the ass, and we're gonna put that out."[7] In the event, it turned out that alleged videotape would not be necessary.

The man who had been charged with overseeing the *White House* project, rapper Chuck D of Public Enemy, had been following the story in the press, and had noted the Beasties' unhappy reactions. The Beasties might have been derided in some quarters as white hijackers of hip-hop, but Chuck D had a genuine affection and respect for the trio. One legend has it that Chuck decided against working on *White House* after hearing the mind-blowing brilliance of *Paul's Boutique*. However, Chuck says today that he and the rest of Public Enemy's production team, the Bomb Squad—Hank and

Keith Shocklee, and Eric "Vietnam" Sadler—chose not to work on *White House* out of professional courtesy.

"We didn't know the Beasties were coming out with anything,[8] so we thought it'd be a wise idea to get into those old tracks and make something. But that didn't happen," Chuck recalls. "We didn't realize that the Beasties were so adamant against it. That's kinda why it didn't go any further. In the end, it was nothin' but a thought."[9]

That doesn't mean, however, that creating *White House* would have been an impossible dream. To the contrary: there was enough extra, unreleased material to have assembled an album, Mike D's comments notwithstanding. And when it's further considered that *White House* would have been produced by the Bomb Squad—which had just completed Public Enemy's masterpiece, *It Takes a Nation of Millions to Hold Us Back*, and was at the peak of its power and popularity—it's not completely out of line to imagine the results as a minor hip-hop classic.

Thinking back on his "peek at the tapes" in Def Jam's vaults, Chuck D remembers that the material in question would have been "many of their songs that were rejected from *Licensed to Ill*. Also, stuff from '84 to '87, when Rick [Rubin] was still with Def Jam, before he split." Former Def Jam publicist Bill Adler—one insider who has never dismissed the idea of *White House*—recalls the possibilities in more detail.

"There were at least two tracks left that Rick wanted to use on the first album," Adler says.[10] Those were the single "She's On It," the centerpiece of the group's sets during the 1985 odd-couple arena tour with Madonna, and a shambolic rap version of the Beatles "I'm Down," pitched somewhere between *Licensed to Ill*'s "Fight for Your Right" and "Girls."

Although it reportedly got some airplay on Los Angeles radio station KROQ, the latter song was kiboshed by one Michael Jackson, who had recently purchased the Fab Four's publishing rights. This earned the gloved one the ire of the Beasties, and of Mike D in particular. "I gotta say this—if I ever see Michael Jackson, I'm gonna light his Jheri curls on fire. I'm gonna sneak up on him with a can of lighter and go to work," he insisted in a 1987 interview. "I think if they had a 3-D movie in Disney World of Ad-Rock punching Michael Jackson's face, they'd get a good draw."[11]

In addition, another pair of unreleased songs was available for *White House* consideration. "Desperado" was a Clint Eastwood–style dry run of sorts for "High Plains Drifter," an outlaw favorite that appeared on *Paul's Boutique.* And "The Scenario" was an even more starkly violent fantasy, which CBS higher-ups had ordered pulled from the Beasties' debut because of the line "Shot homeboy in the motherfucking face."[12]

Beyond those four contenders, the Beasties had left behind three more tracks that appeared on a 1985 twelve-inch single. The B-sides, "Beastie Groove" and "Party's Gettin' Rough," shared the same beat and spartan production, with Rubin—a.k.a. DJ Double R—scratching in metal riffs atop the massive drum machine rhythm. The flip, "Rock Hard," used the same formula to more controversial results. Again the Beasties would be foiled by a copyright holder: in this case, the band AC/DC, from whom Rubin and the band had pilfered the unforgettable riff to "Back in Black."[13]

One additional item, which has become a Beastie rarity, was on hand as well. In 1985, before the Beasties became household names, Def Jam had released a solo single from Adam Yauch. Credited to MCA and Burzootie,[14] Yauch's stripped-down ode to his "Drum

Machine" would likely have been another candidate for inclusion on *White House.*

Those eight tracks represent only the known material available for a second Beastie Boys album on Def Jam; while no one interviewed specifically recalls more, it's probable that other, unfinished tracks existed. "There was enough stuff to do something with," Adler says, "if Russell wanted." Def Jam might even have been able to negotiate the use of "Cooky Puss" and "Beastie Revolution," the A- and B-sides of the Beasties' 1983 independent single, which marked the trio's first brush with hip-hop.

Now imagine that material given the full Bomb Squad treatment. Or at least the partial Bomb Squad treatment, since Chuck D remembers that the goal was "that we would have gone in and enhanced them, in the directions they were already going. That was the thought process."

Regardless, it's worth noting that one of the reasons *Paul's Boutique* initially failed so miserably in the marketplace was that its Dust Brothers–produced sound—dense, psychedelic collages of samples—was nothing like the rock-rapping *Licensed to Ill, Part II* that Beastie fans were expecting. Under the ultimate direction of Russell Simmons, who was the most prominent supporter demanding such an album, it seems safe to assume that *White House* would have filled that brief.

Unleashed on the public before, or concurrently with, *Paul's Boutique, White House* can easily be envisioned as handily winning the sales competition. What that might have meant to the trio's career, which went into decline even after releasing *Paul's Boutique* with no Def Jam counterpart, is impossible to say. But it is unquestionable that *White House* would have radically changed the Beasties; that it might have finished them requires no stretch of imagination, either.

Which is why, when Adam Yauch concludes simply, "I'm just glad it never happened,"[15] he may be happier than anyone realizes.

As it turned out, a little more than half a decade later, the group's career arc had reached its zenith. The Beasties had rebounded from the initial debacle of *Paul's Boutique* by holing up in a newly purchased compound in Atwater Village, picking up their instruments once again, and playing short, funky instrumentals that paid homage to all the vintage R&B records sampled on their last album. The result, 1992's *Check Your Head*, was a surprise hit; two years later, the Beasties reprised that sound with even jazzier undertones—and more commercial success—on *Ill Communication*. The band was back at No. 1, this time completely on its own terms. It was a stunning resurrection, capped off by a co-headlining slot at Lollapalooza and a sold-out 1995 arena tour. When the shows ended, the Beasties still had plenty to keep them busy, including the maintenance of their new Grand Royal label. But for the moment, it seemed there were no new musical worlds to conquer. That might be why Adam Yauch confessed to an interviewer that, by the year 2000, "I'm gonna become a cowboy." Mike D would jokingly respond, "So, are you gonna be a cowboy for real, or are you gonna be like the cowboy in the Village People?"[16] Unlike most of the Beasties' predictions, though, this one had an element of truth to it.

First, however, the band turned its collective attention to making a film. It was in no sense a new interest for the Beasties: as early as 1986, there had been talk of various cinematic endeavors, including plans for them to star in a comedy called *Scared Stupid.* Those projects were all a casualty of the dispute that would lead the Beastie Boys to leave Def Jam, and some insiders believed they were a cause of that departure as well. Reportedly unhappy with the level of control Rick Rubin wanted to exercise over the movie projects, the Beasties would wait until they could take matters into their own hands.

They got that opportunity after signing to Capitol Records and directing several videos for songs from *Paul's Boutique.* This period would see the unveiling of Yauch's alter ego (and purported Swiss uncle), Nathanial Hörnblowér, who began receiving the bulk of the group's video production credits. However, it would be the director Adam Spiegel—better known as Spike Jonze—who created the Beasties' most memorable promo. "Sabotage," a 1994 parody of '70s cop shows, put the group in big sunglasses and bad wigs to general hilarity, and is now considered one of the all-time great music videos.

So it was natural that the group would seek out Jonze for its second crack at the big screen. Since his early days filming skateboarders, Jonze had become a hot property. He had signed on to direct a cinematic version of the popular children's book *Harold and the Purple Crayon,*[17] and was also in the early stages of overseeing what would become *Being John Malkovich*, the film that would net him an Oscar nomination for Best Director.

In the spring of 1997, Jonze formalized his new partnership with the Beasties by agreeing to direct a film with the working title *We Can Do This.* He and the band had worked on the script, which,

Adam Yauch now recalls with a chuckle, "kinda jumped around a lot." However, it became apparent early on that one element of the film was beginning to take on a life of its own.

"One of the characters in this script was this crazy country singer, played by Mike," Yauch remembers. "The storyline was that he was this young country singer who became a big star, and then his life went down in the dumps, because of drugs and stuff. And then later he comes back and gets his own TV show. So that was the story of Country Mike."

When comic relief was needed, Diamond had come to serve as the band's go-to guy. For all the Beasties' collective antics over the years, both Ad-Rock (Adam Horovitz) and Yauch still maintained a veneer of conventional cool. Mike D, on the other hand, had unhesitatingly placed himself at the center of the band's biggest goofs. Some of them had been B-sides that allowed him to play the role of the group's Barry White, like 1989's "Some Dumb Cop Gave Me Two Tickets Already," and "Netty's Girl," a 1992 love song whose video featured Diamond in a velour tracksuit, lip-synching aboard a paddleboat. Now he was ready to create his most memorably ridiculous persona yet.

It soon became a story that required more background, which the Beasties were only too happy to provide. "During the course of writing the script, we were mentioning all these songs," says Yauch. "Spike might've helped us come up with song titles, because we were all just kicking them around while we were working on the script. And at one point, we decided to just write the songs so we'd have 'em for the movie."

That was a jump that seemed more radical at the time than it appears in hindsight. Ad-Rock, Yauch, and Mike D had by that point been playing regularly for the better part of five years, and had become accomplished enough players to shift from funk to hardcore to jazz with skill, if not clinical precision. Mike D now jokes self-deprecatingly that the Beasties became "Nashville studio pros. Oh yeah. Very high-end. Studio chops," but knocking off a dozen blues-based country songs was certainly not beyond them—especially not when they could summon a genuine studio pro to sweeten the finished product.

The first job, however, was to turn promising titles like "Sloppy Drunks" and "Sally Was a Half-Wit" into actual tunes. "It was a group thing. I think I might've had to write probably the lion's share of the lyrics, somehow," says Mike D. "But Spike Jonze was involved, also, in some of it. He was a coconspirator." After fleshing out the songs, the Beastie Boys entered their studio of choice to lay down the results on an old eight-track machine.

The Dungeon was a facility that lived up to its name. Located at 262 Mott Street, along the main thoroughfare of Chinatown in Lower Manhattan, it was in fact little more than a musty old concrete sub-cellar that, recalls Beasties producer Mario Caldato Jr. fondly, "smelled really funky."[18] Recording for the band's fifth album, *Hello Nasty*, had already started at the Dungeon; the Beasties decided to rent it out for a few more days to provide Country Mike with the soundtrack of his life. "We recorded 'em really fast," remembers Yauch. "They were kinda like demos."

Among the cuts recorded were "We Can Do This," which would have become the movie's title tune. It featured hilarious, high-pitched backing vocals from Horovitz supporting Mike D's admission that "Drinkin' whiskey and playin' music, that was always my wife." But Country Mike was ready now to settle down, and this mid-tempo love song was touching in its goofy way. Later, a "live" version of "We Can Do This" was appended to the album; slowed down and with greater emphasis on the melody, it revealed itself as a remarkably well-crafted track.

Opening with train noises and yee-haws that hadn't been heard by the Beasties since "Five-Piece Chicken Dinner" off *Paul's Boutique*, "Railroad Blues" told the story of Johnny, a nineteenth-century railway worker who broke his mother's heart by leaving home. Set to a more traditional rhythm and with a minimum of tomfoolery, it could almost have passed for some obscure country single from the '50s.

The same couldn't be said for "Country Delight," an adaptation of the Sugar Hill Gang's pioneering hip-hop classic "Rapper's Delight." "That was Country Mike's big crossover attempt. I don't know if you knew that, but that was where he tried to sell out," says a barely smirking Mike D. "But it didn't go over too good for him. In terms of the Country Mike arc, that was his moment, where he tried to go for it. But the country community turned its back on him. I'd even go further: they stabbed him in the back. They were mad at Country Mike after that."

Slightly more seriously, Mike D recalls that Yauch came up with the idea for the song: "I kinda remember him playing the bass line, of course, but after that I'm not remembering who carried the joke any farther." Whoever did, it was a pretty good one; there were even scratched-in chicken noises from the Beasties' DJ, Mix Master Mike, but at under two minutes, the spoof managed not to outstay its punch line. So did the brief "Country Mike's Theme," which was to have been the music for Country Mike's TV show. It found Mike promising to "read them boys the news," a declaration that would become his character's trademark threat.

Once the basic tracks were completed, they were set aside. Other projects were demanding the group's time by this point, including the completion of *Hello Nasty*. Diamond admits that working on Country Mike had been a welcome diversion from trying to finish a follow-up to the hugely successful *Ill Communication*. "It was a case of where we really should've been making a record, y'know?" he says.

In fact, some of the material from the Country Mike sessions was briefly considered for inclusion on *Hello Nasty*, according to Mario Caldato Jr.[19] "But it didn't fit," he adds. The Beasties' next task would be to make Country Mike's songs fit a little more closely with the traditional sound of country music.

Adam Yauch had been mulling over the Country Mike tracks the band had recorded, and had decided on the perfect use for them. "At some point, I thought it'd be funny to finish the album," he says, "and press some copies to give to our friends for Christmas."

However, he felt the songs needed some extra polish before they would be suitable for gift-giving. And in one of the strange cases of synchronicity that mark so many musical careers—Country Mike's included—Yauch soon happened onto a man who was perfect for the job.

An avid skier and snowboarder for years, Yauch was vacationing in Utah when he met a girl on the slopes who was a close friend of the musician William "Bucky" Baxter. It was a name that would have been familiar to Bob Dylan fans. A Florida native raised in Virginia, Baxter was a multi-instrumentalist who had met Dylan in 1989, as a part of Steve Earle's band. Impressed with the curly-haired player in his opening act, Dylan soon contacted Baxter, who began giving the music legend lessons on the pedal steel. And in 1992, Baxter began what would turn out to be a series of more than 700 concerts with Dylan.

It was an impressive run, but, even more significantly, Baxter would also receive credit for Dylan's mid-'90s renaissance. His pedal steel, mandolin, and Dobro parts brought Dylan back to the old-fashioned country music that had informed some of his best work and were integral parts of his new "thin, wild mercury" sound, described by author Paul Williams.[20]

Yauch told Baxter about his group's dormant country album, and the latter was intrigued enough to offer his help. "So when Bucky was in town next, we had him come in [to the Dungeon] for a couple of days, and he just overdubbed all his parts," says Yauch.[21]

"It was spur-of-the-moment. The whole Country Mike's thing came together very fast. But without Bucky, I don't think we could have pulled off," Mike D says, adding with a grin, "Not that we really pulled anything off with our Country Mike's recordings, but I don't think we could have even got as far as we did."

One of the songs that most benefited from Baxter's liquid pedal-steel runs was "Sloppy Drunks," a stern admonition to those who imbibe, smell up the room "like a stinky skunk," and later throw up in their bunks. Another Baxter showcase was the unforgettably titled "Don't Let the Air Out My Tires," a talking blues where his tougher playing fell somewhere between steel and slide guitar.

Baxter's pedal steel sat out "How Do You Mend an Achin' Heart," a nearly straight acoustic ballad that Mike D again managed to talk his way through—that is, before the anguished yodeling that closed out the track. But Baxter was all over the jaunty shuffle "One Song a Night," an ode to Country Mike's creative muse that found him in full twang and declaring modestly, "With me, writin' songs just ain't that hard."

Baxter also contributed soaring steel-guitar swells to the choruses of "Kenny Jones (Country Knows Best)," dedicated to Country Mike's old Tennessee friend, who left Music City to play rock 'n' roll but saw the error of his ways. And pedal steel figured prominently in "On Your Way Up Again (The Fowl Song)"; without Baxter's playing as an anchor, the tune's gentle Tex-Mex fusion wouldn't have been possible—and Country Mike's spoken intro, crammed with as many bird- and egg-related clichés as possible, would have been lost as well.

On the track "Country Christmas," the Beasties decided they needed even more help. Besides Baxter's contributions, Country Mike and the Boys were augmented by mandolin from Yauch's friend William Meyer and whistling by Bill McMullen, a graphic artist who had once worked for Def Jam and was later immortalized as "Sweet Cheeks." That a trio of Jewish New Yorkers would open a Christmas song with a deep-voiced dedication to "the Lord Jesus Christ" made the satirical intent obvious, but surprisingly, the tune never quite descended to outright parody. Except for Mike D's comically bad singing, it shared the peculiar charm found on the rest of the album, with its clip-clop rhythm augmented by sleigh bells and images of a biscuit-baking Kris Kringle.

Now the Beastie Boys were ready to give their families, friends, and some Grand Royal employees a country Christmas of their own. An unspecified number of vinyl copies of *Country Mike's Greatest Hits* were pressed up and distributed amongst Beasties intimates as gifts.[22] It was an inside joke that had worked to perfection—or so it seemed.

"We didn't really think about it getting passed around and boot-legged and put on the Internet. None of us had really figured on that," admitted Mike D years later. "I guess we just kinda miscalc-ed."

The general public would not learn of Country Mike's existence until the summer of 1998, around the time that *Hello Nasty* received its long-awaited release. In interviews, the band began dropping hints about its country surprise; that August, Mike D would joke with a MuchMusic interviewer that the band was recording with Garth Brooks, whose new live album threatened to knock the Beasties from the Canadian chart summit. "That's why we're working on this country record with Garth. Because we figure inevitably, this can only last but so long," Diamond said, straight-faced. Teaming up with Brooks, he explained, could help the Beasties "regain our status."[23]

Because the Beasties would also suggest, at various times, that their country album was part of a trilogy that was to include *Hello Nasty* and an album called *Submarine*, created aboard one and fea-turing recordings of whales, Country Mike received little attention initially. However, more substantive reports of his existence were also surfacing. One came from the band's new DJ, Mix Master Mike, who claimed his new employers had "made this whole country album and Mike D's the singer on it, and I swear, those guys are off the hook. It sounds really good; they're good at all that shit."[24]

In an interview with the BBC, meanwhile, Jill Cuniff and Gabby Glaser of the band Luscious Jackson—who were then recording for Grand Royal—had divulged some tantalizing details about Country Mike that made it appear less likely that the project was merely a joke. While the idea of Yauch and Mike D emerging from the Dungeon clad in full cowboy gear and visiting a nearby pizza parlor might have seemed far-fetched,[25] Glaser's description of the recording process—"Adam would sit there mixing with the country outfit on—Mike's in the booth, and they're out there going, 'Sing lower! Sing lower!'"[26]—was somewhat more plausible.

During the same BBC special, Mike D checked in with the claim that the Beasties had actually recorded a half-dozen new albums—"among them a record we worked on with a fella by the name of "Country Mike." He named five songs, all of which would eventually surface: "Sloppy Drunks," "Country Christmas," "Country Delight," "Country Mike's TV Theme," and "Sally Was a Half-Wit" (later called simply "The Half-Wit"), which turned out to be the spoken tale, less than thirty seconds long, of a girl who "just didn't like to speak."[27]

"It's like, the funniest thing you've ever heard," Glaser concluded of the album. "They should just put this stuff out—you know—Grand Royal, on a small level," added Cuniff. "It is classic."[28] In an interview for Portuguese TV, Adam Yauch sounded as though the Beasties had decided to do just that. "Well, there is the country album. It is pretty much done. There's actually one song that needs to be mixed. It was out but we recalled it," he said. "There was one song . . . there were no sleigh bells on this one song . . . so we need to record those sleigh bells and remix that."[29]

Whether that remix—presumably of the song "Country Christmas"—actually happened is unknown, but it is certain that more concrete evidence of the accompanying album had begun to find its way into the hands of collectors. Beastie Boys expert Mark Laudenschlager recalls "almost falling off my chair"[30] when he was contacted in July of 1998 by a trader who was offering copies of "Sloppy Drunks," "Country Mike's Theme," and "Country Delight." The trader later reneged, but someone in the Beasties' inner circle had evidently leaked tracks at that early stage.

It would be more than a year, however, before the rest of the fan base got proof that Country Mike was no hoax. The Beasties had decided to include two songs from the album on their double-disc anthology, *The Sounds of Science*. The sound on "Country Mike's Theme" and "Railroad Blues," both remixed by Mario Caldato, was a lot clearer than the explanations that appeared in the accompanying book. "At some point after *Ill Communication* came out, Mike got hit in the head by a large foreign object and lost all of his memory," Yauch was quoted as saying. "As it started coming back he believed that he was a country singer named Country Mike. The psychologists told us that if we didn't play along with Mike's fantasy, he could be in grave danger. Finally, he came back to his senses. This song is one of the many that we made during that tragic period of time."[31]

With the knowledge that more tracks—specifically, "Sloppy Drunks"—probably existed, the curiosity of Beasties fans had been piqued. It would take a little longer to be sated, however. In 2000, vinyl copies of the full album—some of them pressed on red vinyl, and with a guitar-toting Country Mike on the cover—began appearing on the online auction site eBay. The bidding quickly reached into the hundreds of dollars for each. Within six months, the price was driven down by vinyl bootlegs, but it wasn't until two years later that high-quality CD copies became readily available.

The feverish demand for *Country Mike's Greatest Hits* both surprised and amused the Beasties themselves, who had considered carrying out their own bootlegging scheme. "At one point we decided we'd take some copies and drag them around in the street and scuff 'em all up, and then smuggle 'em into record stores, and put them in the cut-out bin," says Yauch. "You know, break out some 25-cent stickers and put those on 'em.

"Instead of stealing records, we'd smuggle records in," he adds with a laugh. "But we never got around to that, unfortunately."

What the Beasties would do instead was to continue to deny all involvement with the album, keeping the story of Country Mike alive, even when they could barely keep straight faces. In a 2002 interview with MTV2, Mike D was asked again about Country Mike, and demurred. "A lot of people seem to have me confused. I'm an MC. I don't know anything about country music," he said earnestly. About Country Mike, he would admit, "I've known the man. He's a bit of a lone, loose cannon. He's actually even been violent at times—only because he comes from an abused background himself."[32]

After Adam Yauch warned that the subject was one of Diamond's "triggers," his mock-grateful bandmate responded, "I can get very emotional on the topic. I keep a lot kept inside. Y'know, there's a lot of controversy surrounding Country Mike. And it hurts sometimes inside."[33]

It evidently didn't hurt enough to keep Country Mike and "reading the news" out of the lyrics and video for "Alive," a single that had first appeared on *The Sounds of Science*. Along with "Country Mike's Theme" and "Railroad Blues," it was official proof of Mike's existence, for those unwilling or unable to pony up hundreds of dollars for a bootleg of the album.

The film that had launched Country Mike to stardom, unfortunately, would never get made. "We Can Do This" was abandoned—according to one seemingly tongue-in-cheek report, because Mike D had watched *Disorderlies*, the 1987 hospital comedy starring the Fat Boys, and realized the Beasties might be making the same sort of movie as those rotund rappers.

With no cinematic vehicle, Country Mike would end up disregarding Neil Young's advice and just fading away. He was a brilliant joke that had served its purpose, and references to him grew fewer as the years passed. The singer from Tennessee would join imaginary figures like the homeless rockabilly star Johnny Ryall and Nathanial Hörnblowér—as well as flesh-and-blood characters like Sean "The Captain" Carasov and photographer Ricky Powell—in the Beastie Hall of Fame.

Will Country Mike ever be called back into action with a belated, official release? Mike D seems nearly stumped by the question before answering, "Who knows? I would say I can't imagine, but whatever." He considers the prospect again for a moment, then adds, with a smile beginning to steal across his face, "At some point we'll all be old enough . . . where who knows what'll be safe? I just don't know."

If it's up to Adam Yauch, however, Country Mike will remain in the land of imagination whence he came, with his ten-gallon hat and his tales of lovers, fighters, and sloppy drunks. "I think it's good for it to be a little underground," Yauch says of the album. "If people find it and get a laugh out of it, that's great. But I don't think we need to be out there hawking it."

"Without Country Mike / What would you do?" the man himself once sang, in a more innocent time. Those who have followed Yauch's advice and tracked down a copy of *Country Mike's Greatest Hits* will thankfully never have to answer that question.

The Beastie Boys: *Country Mike's Greatest Hits*
Recorded for: *Grand Royal Records (private release)*
Scheduled release date: *1998*
Recorded at: *The Dungeon, New York, NY; 1997–98?*

TRACK LISTING:

1. Sloppy Drunks
2. Railroad Blues*
3. We Can Do This
4. Country Delight
5. Don't Let the Air Out My Tires
6. How Do You Mend an Achin' Heart
7. One Song a Night
8. Country Christmas
9. Kenny Jones (Country Knows Best)
10. Country Mike's Theme
11. On Your Way Up Again (The Fowl Song)
12. We Can Do This (Live)
13. The Half-Wit

All songs by: *Country Mike and the Boys*
Produced by: *the Beastie Boys*
Mixed by: *Adam Yauch (except for *, remixed by Mario Caldato Jr.)*
Mastered by: *Howie Weinberg at Masterdisk, New York City*

Credits:
Adam Horovitz—*guitar, backing vocals*
Adam Yauch—*bass*
Mike D—*drums, vocals*

Bucky Baxter—*pedal steel*

Guest artists:
Mix Master Mike—*chicken fiddle on "Country Delight"*
William Meyer—*mandolin on "Country Christmas"*
Bill "Sweet Cheeks" McMullen—*whistling on "Country Christmas"*

Ray Davies

Thank You for the Days

*I*t's an irony worthy of the songwriter as responsible as anyone for making rock 'n' roll ironic. During the '60s, it was Ray Davies of the Kinks who became rock's first great storyteller, creating sharp and occasionally cynical little vignettes that laid the groundwork for what we now know as the "rock opera." Yet it would be Pete Townshend whom history would hail as an innovator instead; the Who's Tommy, released in 1969, would become a defining moment in popular music, as its tale of a deaf, mute, and blind pinball wizard generated millions of record sales and a major Hollywood film. Lost in the shuffle was Arthur, an album touted as Davies's own masterwork. Released later that year in Tommy's massive wake, Davies's fable about postwar England was ignored by the *press and buried in the marketplace. The television show that* Arthur *had been written to score was canceled at the eleventh hour, and the Kinks limped off to America, where they would enjoy the occasional hit, but would forevermore exist on a different plane from the stadium-filling, larger-than-life Who.*

That part of the story is well documented; it is twenty years later, via a lesser-known sequence of events, that the irony kicks in. Davies had continued his theatrical interests and was approached by director Des McAnuff about scoring a new stage version of Jules Verne's novel Around the World in Eighty Days. *He agreed, and the result, staged in the summer of 1988, seemed Broadway bound. But, despite a grandiose production in California, the show would never make it east, and yet another deserved honor would elude Davies.*

The first rock star to conquer the Great White Way would instead be Pete Townshend; the show that did the trick was a retooled version of Tommy. *And, in a final twist, the man who oversaw it all was none other than Des McAnuff.*

"I've never had that conversation with Ray, but I guess there's a certain amount of irony in all that," admits McAnuff, who won one of his several Tony awards in 1993 for his direction of Tommy. *"But the world's full of irony. And*

from where I sit, Tommy *was coming from a completely different place."*[1]

Its music ended up in a completely different place, as well. Hundreds of thousands would purchase Tommy's *original-cast recording, which was overseen by famed Beatles producer George Martin and won a Grammy. Almost no one, meanwhile, would even know about the songs Ray Davies had written for* 80 Days; *his hastily recorded demos were shelved along with the failed musical, which McAnuff now describes as "the one that got away."*

This qualifies as one of the great tragedies chronicled in this book, since those demos represent some of Ray Davies's most brilliant work since his '60s heyday. Davies had spent the Reagan years in his usual uneasy alliance with his brother Dave in the Kinks, sometimes transcending arena rock clichés and sometimes bowing under their weight. But on 80 Days *he returned to the subjects and songwriting style of his most fertile period. How could an album of Ray Davies tunes about Victorian England and the decline and fall of the British Empire fail? It couldn't, and these demos are proof; discovering them is a little like unearthing an '80s version of* Arthur.

It's disappointing, though unsurprising, that Davies has chosen not to speak about these songs. Though he expressed early interest in this book—because "He is very fond of the score he wrote for 80 Days," wrote Linda McBride, from Davies's Konk Studios in London[2]—Davies ultimately decided not to participate. It could have been the pressures of his first proper solo album, Other People's Lives—*a project almost forty years in the making—or it could have been that the bitter end of* 80 Days *was a wound Davies felt wasn't worth reopening.*

In any event, one thing agreed upon by McAnuff, and the collaborators who did consent to be interviewed, is the quality of Davies's score. "Ray's songs in the Kinks always seemed as if they were going to jump off the record at any minute and become a stage show," recalls arranger Robby Merkin, who orchestrated 80 Days. *"And here we had one, and it was brilliant." McAnuff concurs: "The music was absolutely fantastic."[3]*

It exists now only on bootlegs, instead of the original-cast album it deserves, circulating around the world electronically, infrequently, and illegally. The seventeen songs are demos, occasionally sung by Davies in a different voice to match their intended character. They are also "monochromatic," as Merkin observes, with their drum-machine rhythms and block synthesizer chords or acoustic strumming. "He wasn't layering things in to give you a hint of what the color was supposed to be. It was like he just said, 'Here are the songs.'" And Davies himself would confess, "My demos have to be the worst in the world. They'll never be released as bonus tracks on my records!"[4] But, as is sometimes the case, the simplicity is part of the charm; so is Davies's return to a gentler, more Anglophilic idiom, away from the stadium rock for which the Kinks had become standard-bearers.

"There was something emotional in every single track," notes Merkin. A couple of cassette generations and the absence of its accompanying show can't obscure the emotion, or the magic, of 80 Days—which in many ways defines the overused term "great lost album."

When director Des McAnuff and playwright Snoo Wilson stepped into the woods that California evening in 1988, breezes from the nearby Pacific Ocean muting the August heat, they were creative partners. The two disagree on the substance of what was said during their short walk among the pines, but both concur that after they emerged, their partnership was, for all intents, over.

That conversation would help spell the end of *80 Days*, the musical they had collaborated upon, which was just about to open at La Jolla Playhouse. And it would profoundly affect a third man not present: Ray Davies, whose score for *80 Days* would be lost along with the show, effectively abandoned in the sandy pine groves behind the Mandel Weiss Theater.

To casual observers, *80 Days* appeared bound for Broadway, and was awaiting only confirmation from its financial backers before heading east. Even Wilson wryly admits that "at that point . . . a blood test would probably have turned up traces of hubris in everyone involved." Yet behind the scenes there were concerns about the length of the musical and its complicated plot. Wilson now says he expected his discussion with McAnuff to concern some last-minute fine-tuning. Instead, he alleges, what he got was a demand for a writer's credit. "Des's purpose with me, it transpired, was not further cuts to the script or scenery," claims Wilson, "but the appropriation of some of the writer's future percentage in the work, because 'Some of the words on the page are mine!'"[5]

Standing there among the trees, in sight of the accumulated London scenery of the show, Wilson remembers

> being too shocked to speak at first. I finally said something to the effect that if Des felt like that, he should raise the matter with my agent rather than cornering me on my own amongst the pines. It did not bode well for our future working partnership. But it rapidly transpired there would be, alas, no royalties to dispute.

The conversation, Wilson thought, was an ill omen—one that seemingly manifested itself in the lukewarm reviews and audience response that helped spell an early end for *80 Days*. "It was as if some gods must have overheard Des's greed for gold—either Neptune, whose realms were traversed by our adventurers, or possibly great Jove himself," Wilson wrote in an e-mail, "and decided to punish us all, by sinking the show in a sea of faint praise."

However, McAnuff's memory of the conversation differs in several crucial details. Even before *80 Days* opened, he asserts, there was dissatisfaction with the book Wilson had created. "Frankly, I felt Snoo was in denial. His job was in jeopardy," McAnuff says, insisting that he had been trying to save it.

McAnuff knew that a new script would have to be created to satisfy the show's prospective financial backers; he says he simply wanted credit for the work he knew he would be doing to prepare it. "I wasn't willing to sit in a hotel room for the next year," McAnuff asserts, "without getting credit for the writing I was inevitably going to be doing. But I was very anxious to try to keep the collaboration going."[6]

The real purpose of the conversation, he adds, was to plead with Wilson not to return to London before an important meeting with the show's money men. "But Snoo decided to get on that plane. He missed very important meetings, and he ultimately decided to submit his own book to the producers," says McAnuff. The book was rejected, McAnuff adds, and Wilson would eventually be replaced. "I think," concludes McAnuff, "I gave him good advice."[7]

It wasn't the first difficult collaboration *80 Days* had inspired since its beginning earlier in the decade. But this final dispute placed Ray Davies in a very unfamiliar position. As the leader of the Kinks, he had spent the past quarter-century intermittently feuding with his brother Dave, the group's guitarist. However, over the years, Ray Davies had won most of the important battles, turning the Kinks into his own creative autocracy. All of a sudden, he was on the sidelines as others squabbled, watching some of the best music he'd composed in ages slip increasingly beyond his control.

McAnuff and the British playwright Barrie Keeffe had originally teamed up to work on a theatrical piece contracted by Radio City Music Hall in the early '80s. When those plans fell through, and Radio City's rights to the project expired, McAnuff and Keeffe decided to continue, and began looking for a musician to join the creative team. Davies was an obvious choice: he had already worked with Keeffe on a modern-day adaptation of a play by the ancient Greek dramatist Aristophanes. *Chorus Girls* opened at the Theatre Royal, Stratford East, in April 1981; reviews were mixed, but Davies "thoroughly enjoyed" the experience. "It got panned because it was political. It was about Prince Charles going to open a job centre in Stratford and being kidnapped," Davies would say in 1984. However, he added, "I loved working with Barrie. It was great . . . really my first taste of freedom as a writer."[8]

And of course, it would have been difficult to imagine a songwriter better suited to tackle the Victorian setting of *80 Days*. Since the mid-'60s, many of Davies's finest songs had reflected the music hall sounds and nostalgic themes that characterized an era of slowly eroding empire; the album many consider his greatest, 1968's *The Kinks Are the Village Green Preservation Society*, was filled with a then-unfashionable longing for a Britain that existed only in memory. The following year, Davies and the Kinks would celebrate the matriarch who had presided during the sunset of

England's worldwide dominance. "Victoria" was an exuberant rocker that was only partly facetious; Davies presumably did not want to revisit the days when sex was "bad and obscene," but there was a wistful undercurrent running through this ode to a simpler time, nonetheless.

That wistfulness suffused the accompanying album, *Arthur, or The Decline and Fall of the British Empire.* Written to accompany a Granada TV show, the songs charted the life of Arthur Morgan, a suburban London everyman based on Davies's brother-in-law. The themes of postwar disillusionment and yearning for the green and pleasant England of memory and myth were beautifully rendered, and in 1984 Dave Davies would call *Arthur* the "highlight" of his Kinks career. "Ray was writing about real things," he said, "and I felt this was what we should be doing."[9]

But, as Kinks biographer Jon Savage pointed out, *Arthur* was a bit too real for a pop audience high on peace, love, and Woodstock. "Its concern for the old was desperately unfashionable," Savage wrote, even though concern for the old was one of the things Ray Davies did best, one of the things that separated him from his peers. Davies might well have believed it when he said, years later, that "I never really considered *Tommy* any sort of threat. I'd heard it."[10] Yet, in 1969, the hard-rocking, forward-looking Who were, as Savage put it, doing everything right that the quaint and nostalgic Kinks were doing wrong. Without its accompanying TV special, shelved in part because of last-minute cost cutting at Granada, *Arthur* tanked, barely cracking the British Top 100. "They had made their best shot," said Savage of Davies and the Kinks, "and it had been met with indifference and incomprehension."[11]

Nearly two decades later, Ray Davies would get a second chance, of sorts, to right that wrong. McAnuff now reveals that he and

Barrie Keeffe "talked about a couple of other people initially" whom they might approach to score *80 Days*. "I remember that we talked about Elvis Costello at one point, but at that time, Elvis didn't seem to be interested in that sort of thing." But Davies seemed the man for the job. "I had just worked very successfully with Roger Miller on *Big River*," adds McAnuff, mentioning the breakthrough 1985 Broadway musical that won him his first Tony Award, "so when we finally approached Ray, I think he could see himself writing this kind of score." He continued,

> You have to remember, he'd shown an interest; even before Pete [Townshend] wrote *Tommy*, Ray had demonstrated an interest in, and a talent for, writing concept albums. He was able to write story songs. He'd demonstrated an ability to write program music. He clearly had a sense of characterization in his repertoire. And those sorts of Victorian music hall roots definitely lent themselves to Phileas Fogg and his journey. And Ray's kind of ironic lyrics were also appropriate.

McAnuff remembers first approaching Davies (who may already have known about the planned musical from Keeffe) after a Kinks show somewhere in New York.[12] But Davies would later claim that when the opportunity to work on *80 Days* was first presented, he wasn't interested. "I didn't like the novel. It was a bit of a travelogue," he said.[13] That was the underlying theme behind most previous stage adaptations of Jules Verne's book about the gentleman adventurer Phileas Fogg, who makes a £20,000 wager with fellow members of

London's Reform Club that he and his valet can circumnavigate the world in eighty days.

Verne's own theatrical version, which featured real elephants and ran in his native France for more than fifty years, played up the sensational aspects of the book's globetrotting. More recently, Orson Welles had overseen a disastrously received 1946 Broadway adaptation;[14] ten years later, director Mike Todd had made a similarly over-the-top film that starred David Niven as Fogg. But when Davies gave *Around the World in Eighty Days* a second read, he began to recognize some familiar themes, including English imperialism. "I've always," he admitted, "had a passion for that."[15]

Passions evidently ran higher than expected. Early on, Keeffe left the project, "pretty mysteriously," as McAnuff recalls it. "I never really understood what had happened." What he remembers is that there was apparently some dispute between Davies and Keeffe. "I think frankly Barrie gave us an 'It's him or me' ultimatum," says McAnuff. "Which was the equivalent of withdrawing, in my opinion, because the three of us were all partners."

McAnuff and Davies would settle on another British playwright to round out the team. Andrew "Snoo" Wilson, who had made a name for himself in the '70s with surrealistic dramas like *The Glad Hand*, flew to New York from London around Christmas 1986 and began working on the book, discarding any script work done by his predecessor. As the collaborators huddled in a midtown Manhattan apartment,[16] there was no clue what had happened to Keeffe. "Ray didn't talk a lot at the early meetings, and I got the impression that the break with Barrie—whom I also knew—had been quite painful for everyone," Wilson says, "so I trod carefully as I could."

McAnuff and Wilson agree that at this point Davies had come up with an initial batch of songs, including "On the Map"—a bouncy number in the classic music-hall style, to have been sung, in part, by Queen Victoria herself[17]—and perhaps "Members of the Club." The latter was a stately march that included synth horns on the demo, and was to have been primarily voiced by the British Prime Minister William Gladstone and members of the Reform Club. The line "I must comply / to satisfy the club" carries echoes of Kinks songs all the way back to "A Well-Respected Man," and was an extension of a theme—the gap between public expectations and private realities—that Davies had grappled with frequently over the years, in song and in his sometimes troubled personal life.

But the real keeper among those first songs was "Be Rational," a duet between Fogg and his creator, Jules Verne. Exactly who was responsible for making Verne a character in his own story has been debated; Davies would claim it was his idea, saying he wanted the show "to be about Verne, rather than the sort of travelogue like the Mike Todd movie."[18] Snoo Wilson, meanwhile, recalls bringing the "idea of Verne-as-instigator into the initial discussion to show what I could do," although he adds, "It's also perfectly possible that Ray had the idea separately, and had discussed it earlier with Des." Regardless, Wilson thought including Verne was a necessity. "The novel is a brilliant sleight of hand," he argues, "but—to modern eyes—the characters only make sense from the point of view of their creator."

Having Verne involved—he replaced Fogg's French valet, Passepartout, a "twerpish" character Wilson was only too glad to write out of the script—would complicate the show, and would inspire perhaps the weakest song in the score. "Let It Be Written," which began with the sound of a clattering typewriter, outlined in too-clear detail Verne's dilemma: his publisher wants his latest book, which he's struggling to finish in eighty days. The dual deadlines faced by Verne and his character, Fogg, may have been intended to tie the plot together, and staring down a drop-dead date for a piece of art is a dilemma with which Ray Davies doubtless had plenty of experience. However, the song suffers from the occasional clumsy line ("Staring at the empty page / fills me with anger and with rage / it gives me chills, it makes me age") and a static melody.[19]

"Be Rational," however, was an entirely different story, a gentle piano ballad that found Fogg struggling to acknowledge a love that threatened to crack his stiff and sober demeanor. It was one of Davies's finest and purest love songs, and "arrived on my doorstep from a conversation Ray had with Barrie, I believe," recalls McAnuff. Robby Merkin, who would orchestrate the show when it reached La Jolla, recalls that this song convinced him to undertake the project. "I felt like Ray, with the words and the music, and very little under him, so effectively created characters, and put me inside their hearts. And I thought, 'Man, if the whole thing is gonna be like that, this will be tremendous.'"

It's possible that the title track was also part of this early batch of songs. The tune, which appears in demo version as a straight-ahead rocker with synth backing, outlines the dilemmas faced by various characters—among them Verne, Fogg, and the Indian princess Aouda and her young child, both of whom Fogg rescues on his travels. Deadlines weigh heavily on many of the participants, although not Aouda ("What's eighty days? / Time has no meaning . . . floating endlessly in space"), who has "betrayed" her faith—by not allowing herself to be cremated along with her dead husband—and is living in limbo. Verne, meanwhile, frets about his book having no "hook," a complaint Ray Davies had doubtless heard about certain of his songs over the years. "I remember having a very strong idea of that one being a pivotal number to close the act," says McAnuff, and it did indeed round out Act One.

Davies still had the Kinks to guide, and the first months of 1987 were spent on tour in support of the album *Think Visual*. The band's initial recording for a new label, MCA, *Think Visual* was distinguished by its leadoff single, "Rock 'n' Roll Cities," which marked the only time a Dave Davies composition would be the first A-side drawn from a Kinks LP. That novelty aside, the disc received a decidedly ho-hum response from critics and in the marketplace. But Ray Davies had his own project to distract him from that increasingly glum reality. "I've got to do these things," he would say later of *80 Days*, "otherwise I won't be happy playing with the band."[20]

Sometime after finishing a second leg of the *Think Visual* tour in July, Davies entered Calliope Studios in New York City to demo songs for *80 Days*.[21] The producer was Calliope owner Chris Julian; according to Kinks scholar extraordinaire Doug Hinman, Davies was probably accompanied by Kinks keyboardist Ian Gibbons, and perhaps by bassist Jim Rodford. In any event, the sessions produced a collection of songs proving that, away from his band and his perpetual dramas with his brother, Ray Davies's muse was functioning as well as ever.

Perhaps the most overtly Kinksian pair of tunes included "The Empire Song," a rousing sing-along for several characters (including Gladstone and the Scotland Yard detective, Fix) that declared the sun would never set on "our world," Britain's colonial empire. Over just two chords, Davies constructed a melody that conveyed the sweep of England's nineteenth-century holdings and ambition. "Well-Bred Englishman," a number for Fogg and his fellow club members, was less than two minutes long but carried even more of a satirical sting. A Drury Lane knee-slapper led by jaunty pub piano, it found Davies laconically reciting a list of foreign nations that might conceivably send a representative to best Fogg on his errand, and pointing out the alleged faults that would prevent it ("The Japanese are competent but much too petite / The Germans are competitors but are bound to defeat"). The song's bridges underscore the superiority of Anglo-Saxon breeding with a laundry list of notable Englishmen, a device Davies would use again years later on his "London Song."

Snoo Wilson, like many of his collaborators, had grown up on the Kinks' '60s hits. And he was genuinely curious about his world-famous new partner, who seemed ambivalent at best about his own legendary status. "When on our way to one of many Mexican meals, I asked Ray once if he was not proud of having produced such world-famous favorites. He said no," Wilson recalls. "I don't think he was faking modesty. He is a tireless worker, and the next thing he is doing is always the most important one."

Wilson also noted a tendency any of the long-suffering members of the Kinks might have seconded: Davies was "a very particular performer of his own work. It was clear from the start that he didn't like anyone messing with his lyrics." Coming from a musician who had been the undisputed leader of the Kinks since at least the late '60s—as well as one of rock's greatest songwriters—this was an understandable preference, but it would cause friction as the play progressed. It might also have explained why, shortly before the show went up, Davies publicly entertained the notion of using some of the score on the Kinks' next album, the then-untitled *UK Jive*.[22]

Much of the show was created with the three collaborators working in Manhattan hotel rooms during 1987, side by side when schedules synchronized, and alone when McAnuff's increasingly busy professional life kept him away or glued to a phone in another room. At those times, Wilson found himself working solo on the book, at "a ludicrously expensive rented Mac word processor, in various uptown hotels," with a dot-matrix printer slowly churning out copies of his work through the night. "A nocturnal hornet," he jokes, "at a hundred decibels."

When McAnuff was present, Wilson realized, he "usually had an opinion about my every line—well, he was going to have to direct it, so that was okay with me. I didn't realize this would become an issue between us." Wilson, however, had his own issues. He found Verne's novel lacking in character development, especially the part of Aouda, which he believed to be sorely in need of a rewrite. "I wanted Princess Aouda . . . to be more than a pretty doll tagging along in the wake of the boys," Wilson says. At one point, he took his argument directly to Davies.

> When Ray once came to my house in London with his teenage daughter Tor, she played on my early Mac while I played Ray a track of Maria Callas singing a Gounod classic—melodramatically pleading with the Judges of Hades. I asked Ray, couldn't we have a *big* crisis number for our female lead? Sadly, that never happened.

There would, however, be plenty of characters. Besides Verne, the script received several additions from outside the novel, including Mrs. Fix, the oversexed mother of the Scotland Yard detective mistakenly on Fogg's trail; the real-life Nellie Bly, the pioneering female journalist who traveled the globe in just seventy-two days in 1890; and even Verne's fictional Captain Nemo, from his novel *20,000 Leagues Under the Sea*. Most of these characters would have singing parts; Mrs. Fix would take the lead on "It Could Have Been Him," which had some of the melodrama Wilson was seeking. Perhaps the closest thing to a conventional show tune in the score, with its rhythmic shifts, its dialogue-heavy construction, and its crescendoing melody, the song was an ode to Mrs. Fix's missing husband, one of several subplots in the script.[23]

In addition, Mrs. Fix would get a vocal turn on "Tell Him, Tell Her," which also featured Fogg, Verne, and Aouda. Despite its complex romantic narrative, it was one of the simplest songs on the demo, a sweet, folky waltz played on Davies's acoustic guitar.[24] And there was even "Ladies of the Night," a number for the streetwalkers tempting the prim and proper Fogg on his travels. More two-dimensional than Davies's "Monica," a song from *Village Green Preservation Society* commonly believed to be a portrait of the local prostitute, "Ladies" is still a charming romp, with up-and-down piano and bass runs, and the euphemistic admonition, "Be a little continental."

The ranks of the cast were swelled further by the use of masks, which allowed the eighteen supporting actors to play more than seventy parts. But the crowded stage would cause confusion, even among those who were working on the show. By the time the production had made its way to La Jolla in the summer of 1988, Robby Merkin sometimes found himself scratching his head as he watched rehearsals. "In rehearsal, Des has a particular way of working," Merkin explains.

> I don't know if he still does, but what he was doing then was, if he felt a scene wasn't quite clicking, rather than trim it, and say, "Let's get to the essence," he

would say, "Let's add something." And we would add and add and add until it became clear to him what we needed, and then he would cut. And so we had these incredibly inflated scenes, and everyone was working feverishly—Snoo was writing more dialogue, and I was adding more music, or Ray was. So throughout the rehearsal process, it felt like, "This show is gonna be goddamn *epic*. It's gonna be four hours long!"[25]

Merkin had been a former member of the '60s psychedelic folk act Pearls Before Swine, before going on to a distinguished career in TV, movies, and Broadway. In early 1988, he had been drafted to arrange the score by Danny Troob, a Broadway veteran charged with the initial task of making Davies's demos stageworthy. Troob's revisions surprised Merkin, and apparently Davies as well. "I had questions in my own mind about how like the Kinks they wanted it to end up sounding. And I was looking forward to the idea of being able to orchestrate things that were homages to Ray in the approach," says Merkin. However, the results bore little resemblance to the Kinks, or to rock in general. "They were very transformed in certain ways," Merkin says of the songs.

In places they'd been expanded to allow for dance or movement or whatever, but the feel had also been changed . . . no chords or melodies, but feels had been changed.

Here and there, I admit I felt that the ways the music had been transformed were unnecessary. There were certain songs that worked so well on the demo, and told me everything I needed to know about the

story and the character, that I thought, "Why do we
need to change it?" But it wasn't my job to ask that, it
was my job to orchestrate what I was given. But here
and there, I regretted that I wasn't given the chance
to orchestrate what Ray had done instead![26]

I wasn't privy to the initial discussions . . . and I
happen to think Danny Troob is supremely gifted, and
the work that he did was superb. But my only insight
into the way it might have gone done was that during previews, I was sitting at back at the soundboard.
And Ray came over and pulled me aside, and said to
me, "Is there anything you can do to make that song
more rock 'n' roll? I've given up the others, but I want
that song to be rock 'n' roll. Anything you can do, I'll
be grateful."

Merkin has forgotten the song in question, but it is apparent
that Ray Davies had found himself in a system far removed from
the Kinks' single-party rule. That point would be underscored after
Davies wrote "Against the Tide," one of his classic paeans to misfits
and underdogs. Another vehicle for Fogg and Verne, and perhaps
the finest of the score's several music-hall pastiches, it stunned
Snoo Wilson upon first listening. "It had that classic 'click' feeling
you get when you hear 'Waterloo Sunset,' " Wilson thought, "but it
was in the way of the juggernaut of narrative and out it went, to
Ray's intense sorrow. It was a lot better than many of the numbers
that stayed in. I remember him leaving an emotional message on
everyone's answerphones saying it should go back in."[27]

However, Davies impressed his coworkers—especially given the
difficulties of his personal life during this period. His mother had

passed away at the end of 1987, and in early 1988 he suffered from health problems that were alternately reported as bronchitis or even a heart attack, and left him hospitalized at the start of the new year. Nevertheless, "I found Ray to be a man of elegance and kindness and patience, and very willing to collaborate. He went about his business quite quietly, and I was so impressed with that," remembers Merkin. "So it became very personal to me, that I wanted this to be terrific for Ray." Snoo Wilson is less effusive, but agrees: "We had some silly moments over the two years' collaboration, but [Davies] was always there for the important stuff."

In Merkin's view, there were several successes in the adapted score. One was "Just Passing Through,"[28] a number that found Davies returning to fertile creative ground. In the '60s, songs like "See My Friends" and "Fancy" had introduced the Indian drone to pop music. For a number that marked Fogg and Verne's entry to India, Davies drew once again on those drones, with a deliberate, percussion-assisted rhythm and backing vocals that may have resembled the chanting fishermen who inspired "See My Friends." Even on the demo, the tune made eerily visible the beggars, squalor, and stifling heat mentioned in its lyrics. Another triumph was "A Place in Your Heart,"[29] a buoyant ensemble piece sung from a speeding "prairie schooner."[30] "That song, I remember feeling like . . . as I listened to it, I got this incredible feeling of transcendence, that even though the wheels were on the ground, you really felt as though you were sailing," recalls Merkin. "And I remember feeling really pleased when I heard that back, that I'd done it—that I'd captured this feeling of transcendence in some way."

The band that would perform Davies's reworked compositions included a pianist and synthesist, who also played the string parts; a percussionist; a small saxophone section that doubled on flutes; a pair of trumpeters; and—unusually for this sort of small orchestra—a French horn player, as well as the standard rock rhythm section of guitar, bass, and drums. Meanwhile, a cast that included Timothy Landfield as Fogg, Stephen Bogardus as Verne, and Brooks Almy as Mrs. Fix would bring Davies's songs to life.

But it was the scenery, created by designer Douglas Schmidt, that got everyone's attention. "La Jolla has a good budget, but not like Broadway. And we were trying to do something that was like a very expensive Broadway show," says Merkin. "Douglas Schmidt got my respect in a way that no other set designer has, for the work he did on that show. All of us were sort of genuflecting to him. He worked *magic*! The elephant comes out, and you just gasp. It was just two-dimensional, but it looked so real."

Besides the prop pachyderm, the dazzling scenery included ships, rickshaws, the prairie schooner, and even a huge typewriter that followed Verne onstage—a visual reminder of his own writer's block and pressing deadline. Wilson recalls one of McAnuff's most sage pieces of advice, "which is worth any number of 'Teach Yourself Writing' books": in a show, " 'You can make it rain, once.' Meaning, everything that happens onstage has to have an appropriate singularity. I've passed that handy tip out whenever I have taught creative writing subsequently."

There was the open question, however, of whether *80 Days*, which would run a final price tag of more than $700,000, contained too many cloudbursts. Wilson acknowledges that the show was becoming reminiscent of the kitchen-sink spectacle Orson Welles had created on Broadway, and Robby Merkin shared those concerns. "Scene by scene, it was brilliant theater," he says. "All together, you'd have to ask yourself, 'Was all this really necessary?'"

The critics would pose that very question after the show opened on August 23. The hometown reviewer, The *San Diego Union*'s Welton Jones, called *80 Days* "a dizzy, complex, glittering pageant of stagecraft, an encyclopedia of tricks and gimmicks, a fancy mechanical marvel in the spirit of Verne's own baroque sense of technology." That acknowledged, Jones would add, "The trouble is there's no soul in the show. When sentiment threatens, everything goes stiff and formal. Lack of coherence is one thing. A quick dance routine or some moving scenery distracts from minor plot details. But a musical unable to take sentiment seriously is in trouble."[31]

This fault Jones would place at the feet of Snoo Wilson, who he complained "never comes close to generating genuine human emotion. Instead, he dwells at length on the same matched set of leather-bound British idiosyncrasies that have served satirists from Gilbert and Sullivan to Monty Python."[32]

More specifically, Jones pointed to Fogg's failure to generate believable feelings of affection towards Aouda and her infant. That, McAnuff now acknowledges, was the central weakness onstage. "It's a shame we couldn't have seen that when it was in workshop," he says, "but it was ever thus." And the song Davies wrote to convey this budding romance, "Who Is This Man," was received unenthusiastically. "Davies's best shot at a ballad," Jones wrote, "starts vague and meanders."[33]

However, reviewers would find little fault overall with Davies's score. "[Davies] demonstrates a definite flair for this type of work," *Variety*'s critic wrote. "He uses an appropriate variety of styles and rhythms to capture moods and locales."[34] Even Welton Jones agreed.

"Ray Davies's seventeen songs never hurt the show and often help. Obviously, he must be encouraged to keep writing show scores," Jones opined. "This time, though, there's a feeling that Davies has tried too hard to be part of a package and help push the plot."[35]

That would be the least of the problems faced by the creators of *80 Days*. The numerous representatives from back east who had come to see the show responded with deafening silence. Broadway producer Rocco Landesman, who would years later lead *The Producers* to a dozen Tony awards, was to have bankrolled the transfer from La Jolla to New York. But after the lukewarm reviews of *80 Days* appeared, Landesman instead "spent longer and longer at the Kentucky Derby," recalls Wilson wryly.

Ultimately, the show would run for a little more than a month at La Jolla, closing on October 9. Even after its disappointing reception, however, there was still the belief among many involved that the show was Broadway-bound. "I don't think that idea ever changed, really," says Merkin, adding,

> Rocco Landesman came and said he wanted to do it, but he felt that certain things needed to be changed. And it then lay in the laps of Snoo, Des, and Ray to make the necessary changes. When I left La Jolla, I thought, "There's gonna be a layoff while they do the creative work, and then we're gonna come together and we're gonna put it on Broadway."

What happened next is not entirely clear. Wilson remembers returning to England, where he rewrote and shortened "the sluggish second act" at the suggestion of producer David Singer. "I've talked to Ray subsequently, about rumors of revival," he adds, "but heard nothing more." Doug Hinman's research shows that Davies spent December reworking the show for possible runs in Portland and San Francisco, with an eye toward Broadway in the spring of 1989. That projection was later pushed back until summer, and ultimately nothing would come of it.[36]

As Robby Merkin recalls it, a long period of inactivity was followed by rumors that the show's three creators

> were fighting, that they weren't able to agree. And then the rumors stopped—I didn't hear anything at all for a really long time. But then about a year and a half later, I got a letter from Ray, and he said, "Get ready, we're gonna start it up again, and we're gonna go to New York!" And then I never heard another word. I don't know why he thought that.

"I didn't get the feeling that Ray was really fighting," adds Merkin. "But I don't think his songs were ever in question." Some time later, Merkin remembers hearing "that Des was talking to Ray about the possibility of getting a new writer. And I remember talking to Danny [Troob] at that point, and both of us thinking, 'There's no way that's ever gonna happen! That's desperation talking.'"

In fact, says McAnuff, there were not one but two people later approached to rework the book. Twice in 1990, Davies reportedly spent time in Santa Monica, California, revising the script with an unidentified female writer, and as late as February 1991, he was in Los Angeles, still working on the show, according to Doug Hinman.[37] Since then, however, there has been only silence surrounding the project.

McAnuff now believes the show's failure rested primarily with David Singer. "Really I think it fell apart on the production side as opposed to . . . well, it wasn't the art that went wrong in this case. The producer . . . just at a certain point didn't seem to be able to move the project forward, and by that point I was on to other things, and Ray had taken up with other things as well."

So had Snoo Wilson, who would return to the theater, both musical and non-musical, and would also undertake the creation of a new book and lyrics for *80 Days*—"a cleaner version of Verne's adventure story which includes the author as adventurer, but without the clutter of construction that also brought down Orson Welles, forty years before."

Des McAnuff, meanwhile, would take the lessons of *80 Days* and turn them into box office gold with Pete Townshend and *Tommy*—although he insists that the two shows had little, if anything, in common. "I remember listening to *Tommy* during a band break when I was seventeen," recalls McAnuff. "And honestly, I don't think my conception of it changed much since that day. I'm convinced that a lot of the ideas I had for the show were ideas that were formed that day.

"In fact," he insists, "working on *80 Days* would probably have been viewed as a detriment" by Dodger Productions, the company that paired him with Townshend. "I had done three musicals since *80 Days*, and I had a better sense of what I was doing, and I was just on a creative high during *Tommy*."

In the years that followed *80 Days*, Ray Davies would discover his own creative high. Finally jettisoning the Kinks, Davies would spend most of the '90s on the solo career he had so often postponed. He wrote a well-received "fictional autobiography," *X-Ray*, and followed it with an acoustic tour that laid claim to his often forgotten role as rock's original storyteller. Reprising Kinks hits and relating the tunes' origins, Davies took audiences on a nostalgia trip that was soon copied by any number of artists with less interesting tales to tell, and less interesting songs to deliver them.

At some point after the show had closed, a cassette of Davies's demos slowly began to circulate. Doug Hinman remembers receiving a copy around 1990; he obtained it from a friend who had in turn gotten the tape from an actor auditioning for *80 Days*. Hinman, like many admirers, preferred Davies's work with the Kinks, and realized all too well the pitfalls of a rock musician writing for Broadway. Still, he says, "it was clear this was [Davies'] dream musical."

Davies's own beliefs about the failure of *80 Days* remain among his many secrets. In a 1993 *Pulse* magazine interview to promote the Kinks' new release, *Phobia*, Davies revealed to writer Harold DeMuir that, among other projects, he was still "hoping to mount a new production of his *80 Days* stage musical."[38] Three years later, however, he tartly dismissed the entire idea of the show. "I was a hired gun. I don't think I would've come up with that silly notion," he told the *Philadelphia City Paper*. "Very ambitious. Even Orson Welles tried to stage it and failed."[39]

Be that as it may, *80 Days* left some with a sense of unfinished business. "There was so much that was brilliant in that show," laments Merkin. "Once you saw it up [onstage], for all its flaws, you saw its potential. This show should have been gigantic. It should have out–*Les Mis*-ed *Les Miserables*.

"It really felt like we were inches away, instead of miles," he adds. "But ultimately, I guess it was the creators who were miles apart."

Whether McAnuff, who ended our interview to return to a rehearsal of *Dr. Zhivago*, will ever have time to entertain a revival of *80 Days* is a dubious proposition at best. But the thought frequently crosses his mind—and the minds of others, as well. "Not a month goes by that someone doesn't tell me, 'You ought to do *80 Days* again,'" he says. "Of all the productions I've ever worked on, this is the one that really ended before its time. In all honesty, I would love to revive it.

"Hey, I'm alive, and Ray's alive," McAnuff adds. "So the door hasn't shut on this yet." Whether or not a revival actually occurs, and whether or not Ray Davies's songs get the original-cast album they so richly deserve, the door remains open to Davies's lost masterpiece as well.

Ray Davies: *80 Days*
Recorded for: *N/A*
Scheduled release date: *N/A*
Recorded at: *Calliope Studios, New York, NY; probably July–August 1987*

TRACK LISTING:

1. Let It Be Written
2. The Empire Song (Our World)
3. Well-Bred Englishman
4. Against the Tide
5. Ladies of the Night
6. On the Map

7. a) It Could Have Been Him
   b) Mongolia Song
   c) No Surprises
8. Welcome to India
9. Just Passing Through
10. Who Do You Think You Are?
11. Eighty Days
12. Members of the Club
13. Conspiracy
14. Tell Him, Tell Her
15. Be Rational

The following songs were also written for the show, but were not on the demo: *"A Place in Your Heart," "Who Is This Man," "Here!"*

All songs by: *Ray Davies*

Produced by: *Chris Julian*

Credits (where known):
Ray Davies—*vocals, acoustic and electric guitar, keyboards, programming*
Ian Gibbons—*keyboards?*
Jim Rodford—*bass?*

8 Adam Ant

The Power of *Persuasion*

*R*arely, if ever, does an album go unreleased strictly on its musical merits, or lack thereof. For a star at the major-label level, a new release is surrounded by layer upon layer of variables, any of which might derail an otherwise worthy collection of songs. The list includes the problems of coordinating a coterie of producers on different continents, management struggles, turnover at the label, and the sometimes-fragile psyche of the star himself.

All of these factors played a role in the ultimate rejection of Adam Ant's 1993 release Persuasion; if it falls somewhat short of legendary status as a work of art, its history provides a textbook example of the conflicting pressures that can consign a perfectly fine album—one that even boasts several flashes of brilliance—to the proverbial dustbin of history.

"It was a strange kind of dancey rock-pop album," recalls guitarist Marco Pirroni, Ant's longtime musical partner. *"But that was one of the ideas behind it, and I thought we'd achieved that."*[1] Adam Ant himself would later call it *"the best album I'd made in a long time."*[2]

The Music Corporation of America—a.k.a. the major label MCA, Ant's employer at the time—did not agree. In the years since that decision, Pirroni has spent little energy obsessing over the reasons why. "I think it's just all about money. The balance sheet doesn't balance at the end of the quarter. I mean, it's the music business," he points out. "People moan about it, but I always say, 'Would you? Would you put your own money out for someone else's art?' I wouldn't."

Still, Pirroni acknowledges that the subsequent fate of Persuasion *has been baffling, to say the least. Over the years, acting on behalf of his old friend, he has made numerous attempts to gain the release of the album, or even a few tracks. In each case, the efforts have been fruitless. "It's confusing," he says with a sigh. "It's really confusing."*

So is the fact that an entire tour was played to promote songs that would never officially exist. However, those few weeks spent in small clubs across America would contain the seeds of Wonderful, *the album that would grow into Adam Ant's comeback hit.*

It's conceivable that Persuasion *could have performed equally well, had it ever reached the public. What effect such a success might have had on Ant's subsequent, well-documented struggles with mental illness is impossible to imagine and ultimately not worth the speculation. Happily in good health at the time of this writing, and busily promoting a well-received autobiography,* Stand and Deliver, *Ant is presumably focused on larger issues than the fate of an album almost two decades old.*

Yet the part of his past left behind on these songs deserves re-examination. Until MCA agrees to provide a listen officially, this look at Persuasion *will hopefully suffice.*

As he walked into EMI Music Studios in Soho on a sticky August morning in 1991, Leigh Roy Gorman felt the butterflies stirring. It had been more than a decade since he'd stabbed Adam Ant in the back, but Gorman was still apprehensive about their forthcoming reunion—even though it had been proposed by his old boss himself.

The split between them had become one of the most famous in British music history. On a January day eleven years earlier, Gorman, drummer Dave Barbe (né Barbarossa), and guitarist Matthew Ashman had ceased to be Adam's Ants. The trio had been talked into abandoning Adam by Malcolm McLaren, the impresario who had become infamous while overseeing the Sex Pistols' roughshod ride over Britain.

McLaren had next signed on as the manager of Adam and the Ants, a second-wave punk act that seemed destined for success. He had given the fledgling Ants tapes of African Burundi music, which the group had begun to translate into a percussive, instantly identifiable sound under the tutelage of Simon Jeffes, leader of the avant-garde ensemble the Penguin Café Orchestra. But McLaren soon became fascinated with the prospect of replacing Adam Ant and finding a singer more malleable to his own, singular vision.

The young Ants, barely out of their twenties, were certainly under McLaren's spell. "I was so under the euphoria of his personality," remembered Barbe, years later, "I would have gone out and fucking shot someone if he told me."[3] Thus it was that Adam was sacked by his Ants at their rehearsal space in the basement of a Camden Town pub, as McLaren looked on in amusement. Never one to pass up giving the knife an extra twist, he would reportedly chase after a tearful Adam and offer him a job—as the group's hairdresser.[4]

This was one instance, at least, where McLaren's instincts backfired spectacularly. He would replace Ant with fourteen-year-old Annabella Lwin, a half-Burmese girl he'd seen at a West End dry cleaners,[5] and she and the ex-Ants would generate several Burundi-inspired hits (and even more outrage, thanks to McLaren's stunts) as Bow Wow Wow. But that success would pale next to the global fame of the reborn Adam Ant. With a new colony of Ants, including guitarist and songwriting partner Marco Pirroni, Adam's makeup-smeared visage became the MTV era's most recognizable face. He strode through promo clips in fanciful getups that seemed half-pirate, half-Elizabethan highwayman, offering his own pop-friendly version of the Burundi beat and looking down on his old bandmates from the summit of the charts.

One of those bandmates, at least, had always felt guilty. And those feelings came to the fore as Leigh Gorman prepared to come face to face with his past in 1991, "with irony hanging heavy in the air. Out of all the Ants, Adam had treated me really well. He'd always championed me and my ideas, and here I was betraying him?" Gorman now recalls. "So I really didn't feel good about the split. Not good at all."[6]

But he was here at the invitation of Ant, issued via Marco Pirroni. The two were working on what was to become Adam's fifth solo album, and, Gorman's checkered personal history with Ant aside, the summons made sense. After the breakup of Bow Wow Wow, Gorman had turned his attention to production, and the previous year he'd scored a huge hit with a British act called Soho, with whom he also toured. Led by twin sisters from Wolverhampton, Soho enjoyed a Top 20 single on both sides of the Atlantic with "Hippychick," a dance track notable for its sample of the tremolo guitar riff from the Smiths' "How Soon Is Now?"

According to Marco Pirroni, that hit wasn't the reason Gorman got the call. "I hadn't really heard what Leigh was doing, but I didn't really need to hear," he says. "You know if you can work together . . . you can tell if someone's all right."[7]

Whatever the impetus, Gorman was immediately put at ease by his former employer. "Adam was extremely gracious. He made a joke of the whole thing," Gorman says.

In fact, when we got into the vocal booth, it was hard to shut him up. He was doing this standup routine, and doing all these impressions of British comic actors.

So his joke to me was, "Oh yeah, Leigh. You got the cred, but I got the cash. Did you get one of those checks with six zeroes on it? Or was it seven? I can't really remember. That's right, you didn't. Funny, that, eh?"

It was all really good-humored. That was probably my biggest problem during those sessions, just getting him to knuckle down and do a vocal.

The sessions were held at a small studio EMI owned in Soho, and were used to demo material for Ant's new album, the follow-up to his 1990 surprise hit *Manners and Physique*. Gorman recalls four or five tracks being cut at EMI. When the recording moved to Swanyard Studios in Islington, he was joined by a team that included studio drummer Dave Ruffy, programmer Marcus Bush, and backing vocalist Tracey Ackerman, a session whiz whom Gorman remembers as "almost not human. She'll sit there with a cigarette and a cup of coffee, and you'll say, 'Could you take it up a third?' And she'll say, 'Do you really mean a third?' And it's spot-on. One take and she's out of there."

With Pirroni adding his signature guitar licks, and Gorman on bass, the sessions produced a pair of songs that would perfectly bridge the gap between the old, glam-meets-rockabilly sound of early-'80s Antmusic, and the electronic soul that had given him a club-driven comeback with "Room at the Top" in 1990. "Persuasion" had all the swagger of classic Adam, marrying a colossal riff to an equally big beat, while "Headgear," addressed to an alluring "soul pirate," repeated the trick, once again combining programmed swing with Ruffy's live fills. "I was obsessed with loops at the time, and in particular with getting snares bang-on. I think I drove Dave Ruffy crazy," Gorman explains with a laugh. "We just tried to make everything sound as massive as possible."

However, these London sessions yielded only a small part of what would become *Persuasion*. It had been decided that the album was to be a multi-producer affair, a trend that was gaining cachet within the music business. By the time Adam and Pirroni joined Gorman in London, there were already collaborations with two well-known Americans—Bernard Edwards, the bassist in disco legends Chic, and Larry Blackmon, the front man and mastermind of the R&B group Cameo—in the can. Gorman remembers that Adam and Pirroni "weren't keen on playing" finished tracks, "and I wasn't clear why."

It might simply have been because those sessions had been fraught with difficulty. Hiring American producers best known for their work with urban artists wasn't exactly foreign ground for Adam, of course. He had relocated from London to Los Angeles in 1987, pursuing an acting career as his chart success began to wane. And his previous album, *Manners and Physique*, had been overseen by André Cymone, Prince's childhood friend and former bandmate.

That connection was made via Adam's new manager, Bennett Freed. Freed's management company, dubbed Loot and run with partner Ron Weisman, also handled Cymone and his girlfriend, ex-Shalamar singer Jody Watley. In the summer of 1987, Watley's "Looking for a New Love" had been the hottest sound in R&B, thanks to Cymone's aggressive, big-beat production, and by the time he began work with Adam two years later, the magic had not yet worn off. Driven by a shuffling rhythm and chattering electronics, "Room at the Top" lodged inside the U.S. Top 20 in the spring of 1990. The accompanying album, as Adam noted in his autobiography, was "a three-man job," completed by himself, Cymone, and Marco Pirroni. "All of us," he claimed, "were more than happy with the finished product."

The third man in that equation, however, harbored some understandable doubts. *Manners and Physique* was the first record since Adam's Marco-less debut, *Dirk Wears White Sox*, that had been penned with only minimal contribution from Pirroni. "For *Manners*, Adam and André Cymone had done about five or six demos which I'd heard. André's a bass player and Adam plays a bit of guitar, so they weren't guitar-led songs. It wouldn't be, because they're not guitarists," says Pirroni. "And they kind of presented them to me and said, 'Can you put stuff on it?' And so I put some stuff over the top."

"Which is a lot different," Pirroni adds significantly, "from actually starting at that point."

Besides being left out of the songwriting process (except for "Room at the Top," which he penned with Adam), Pirroni was also not part of the deal negotiated with Adam's new label, MCA,[8] an omission that must have smarted.

"I just had this problem with Adam's management at the time, who were American and really trying to make him work with American artists," says Pirroni. "Which was fine, but I didn't think them the right people. Just because someone's a great producer doesn't mean you can work with them. It's about personalities, y'know.

"Who's Michael Jackson's producer? Right, because Quincy Jones is the most successful producer on Earth doesn't mean he can make a hit single with everybody. He's not God!" adds Pirroni with a laugh.

Neither were the two Americans chosen to work on *Persuasion*, Pirroni believed. At one point[9] during the recording of the album, he had been summoned to Miami, where Adam was to collaborate with Larry Blackmon. But Pirroni had other plans. In the late '80s, while his old friend was trading London for the California lifestyle and trying to get his acting career off the ground, Pirroni had begun to pursue other interests as well. He made an attractive collaborator: besides his role in crafting so many Ant hits, he'd been a punk legend before ever setting eyes on Adam. That was thanks in large part to his 1976 appearance at the 100 Club alongside Siouxsie Sioux and Sid Vicious, at a fabled gig that consisted of a twenty-minute disembowelment of "The Lord's Prayer." "I guess," Pirroni would say years later, "it was as pure as punk could get."[10]

One artist suitably impressed by Pirroni's pedigree had been the Irish singer Sinead O'Connor, no stranger to controversy herself. Pirroni had worked on O'Connor's first two albums, and when her cover of Prince's "Nothing Compares 2 U" became a breakthrough hit in 1990, Pirroni found himself involved in a worldwide tour.

Busy and a bit annoyed at the dictates of Adam's new management, Pirroni declined to participate in the Larry Blackmon sessions. "I just got this call that said, 'You're going to Miami to work with Larry Blackmon.' And I said, 'I am not going.' No one asked me if I wanted to work with Larry Blackmon. Nothing against him, but I was just like, 'What's this got to do with me?'"

Very little, as it turned out. Blackmon and Ant would produce a pair of songs for *Persuasion* with no writing input from Marco. "Little Devil" was a swinging, funk-rock festival of the libido, a workable midpoint between the well-documented sexual obsessions of both Ant and Blackmon. It boasted a quote from the Doors and a silly mid-song rap that managed to rhyme "barstool" with "rascal." "Brain Candy," however, was probably the album's weakest track. A belated echo of Cameo's hugely influential 1986 hit "Word Up"—as well as its follow-up, also titled "Candy"—it retained the rhythm, explosive snares, and drawled vocals of those songs, but lacked their melody, originality, and charm.

"I didn't want to be ungracious to someone like Larry Blackmon," recalls Leigh Gorman,

> but I wasn't sure about that big, heavy snare drum sound. That had already been here and gone, years ago. But Adam had this theory: he said, "The way Larry gets that big drum sound is that he hits the drum machine really hard!" And we all knew that with MIDI, it has nothing to do with that. But we were all standing around, being polite, going, "Er, yeah. Wow!"

In the spring of 1991, Pirroni and Adam would reunite at New York's City's famed Power Station studio to work with Bernard Edwards.[11] Since the dissolution of Chic, both of the group's principals had enjoyed great success as producers; guitarist Nile Rodgers had scored the most massive smashes, with the likes of David Bowie, Duran Duran, and Madonna, but Edwards had also acquitted himself well, creating hits for ABC, Robert Palmer, and Rod Stewart, and guiding the Palmer-fronted supergroup the Power Station.

That resume was somewhat lost on Pirroni, who found the two weeks in New York unsatisfying.

I never thought it was a good idea. Not that I had anything against [Bernard] or anything like that . . . I just didn't understand what it had to do with Adam Ant, really. Y'know, Bernard was great, we worked fine with him . . . but there was this big void between our musical backgrounds. That's sometimes good, it sometimes works well . . . but we just really didn't have time to get to know each other. So I just did my parts, but there wasn't much development of the demos.

Adam Ant would admit to his own frustrations with the process. "Bernard Edwards turned out to be a painstaking producer," he recalled, "and took weeks over each track before handing over the tapes."[12]

Nevertheless, four songs would ultimately emerge from the sessions. Adam would call the music "Bad Company meets Chic," and the description wasn't a bad one, if the reference was to Chic's heavily programmed '90s reincarnation, and not its better-known (and more organically grooving) '70s hits. Three of the songs—"Charge of the Heavy Brigade," "Sexatise You," and "Don't Knock It Till You Got It"—were built around tough, blues-based riffing balanced atop a funky (albeit programmed) bottom end.

The lyrics didn't stray far from matters of the groin; "Don't ever let your private life / Get in the way of your sex life" was the rather direct message imparted by the female protagonist of "Sexatise You," and that was advice Adam had already been following faithfully for many years. However, there were a few intriguing twists. "Charge of the Heavy Brigade" contained a disavowal of Adam's face-painted past—"New romantic, very twee / I'd rather that not include me"—while "Don't Knock It" took a decidedly cynical look at a "Beverly

Hills star" of the sort Adam had been rubbing elbows with for the past couple of years.

The former track was evidently completed by Adam and Pirroni in the studio near the end of the sessions. "There was always a song that we would leave undone, always a song that we would just write in the studio," recalls Pirroni. "I can't really say why, it's just something we always did." The fourth song completed with Edwards, "Obsession," was more reliant on synthesizers, and reminiscent of the adult rock-funk he had created on Rod Stewart's *Out of Order* the previous year.

All the work with other producers, however, seems to have convinced Adam and Pirroni that their own collaboration was as viable as ever. The duo would write and produce a trio of songs for *Persuasion* by themselves, and the tunes affirmed the strength of a partnership then entering its second decade.

"All Girl Action" offered clear glimpses of both the roots and the future of Antmusic; the live rhythm section, twanging guitar, and cheeky sentiment were reminiscent of any number of Ant classics, and the song laid out the blueprint for Adam's reclamation of his own sound later in the decade, on *Wonderful*. Leigh Gorman would play bass on this track and at least one other, and couldn't help feeling that the work he'd done on "Persuasion" and "Headgear" had proven inspirational. "I suppose they were trying to copy my style on the other two tracks," he says with a laugh.

The punning "Survival of the Fetish," meanwhile, was awash in keyboards, but represented perhaps the most successful experiment in pure synth-pop Ant had ever attempted, the big hit "Room at the Top" notwithstanding. Referencing Prince Charles and boxer Joe Louis—a natural name to drop for Adam, a huge boxing fan—the tune and its brooding melody were a welcome change of pace;

amidst the hard rock and R&B rhythms, "Survival" was the closest thing to a ballad *Persuasion* had to offer.

Surprisingly, the best of these three songs would be left off the final track list. "Seems to Me" seemed to have it all: a killer Marco riff; a soaring, poppy chorus; funky drumming; and an impassioned Adam vocal with several great lines ("And it seems to me / we got a new aristocracy") that reflected the old punky, one-for-all spirit.

Yet according to Pirroni, "We were never happy with 'Seems to Me,' either as a track or a song . . . it would have been released as a spare track somewhere."[13] The tune would be bumped in favor of "Charge of the Heavy Brigade," eventually becoming the most obscure song from the sessions.

The omission of "Seems to Me" aside, *Persuasion* had, as Pirroni noted, fulfilled its brief. Despite the abundance of chefs stirring the broth, the album had achieved a cohesive sound,[14] which was a marked improvement on the sterile electronic R&B of *Manners and Physique.* Pirroni's return to the songwriting process had given the new songs a welcome rock edge that contrasted nicely with the club-inspired rhythms, and the result was an always defensible, and often inspired, update of Adam Ant's signature style.

That would prove to be not nearly enough to guarantee *Persuasion* its deserved release, thanks to the series of unfortunate events that next unfolded.

In November of 1990, MCA and its theatrical division, Universal Studios, were sold to Matsushita Electric, a Japanese electronics giant and the parent company of Panasonic. The $6.1 billion purchase followed Sony's 1988 acquisition of Columbia Records, and came at a time when Americans were beginning to express fears that Japanese investors were trying to take over the country from within.

Those fears would prove laughable as the decade progressed and Japan began to struggle with an economic recession. But those afraid that MCA's takeover portended big changes on its music roster were right on the money.

The company had been run for the past thirty years by Lew Wasserman, a Hollywood legend who had worked his way up through the ranks to become one of the most influential studio executives in movie history. Wasserman had engineered the sale to generate cash for planned expansions into cable, home entertainment systems, and the developing global market; one of the interested parties was mogul David Geffen, who had sold his own Geffen Records to MCA just months earlier, becoming the biggest shareholder in the newly expanded company.

Wasserman would stay in charge of MCA after selling out, signing a five-year employment contract, but the power structure beneath him would inevitably shift. And despite public assurances by Matsushita executives that they would never interfere with the creative aspects of MCA, new faces meant new priorities.

Several acts would be dropped, including ex–Men at Work singer Colin Hay and a quirky new artist named Jill Sobule, who would later achieve fame with the song "I Kissed a Girl." Given that *Manners and Physique* had provided Adam Ant a comeback hit and had sold respectably, conventional wisdom would have suggested that he was one of the label's assets, and thus safe from the purge.

The first hint of trouble came in the summer of 1991, when the label refused to fund a final mix of the album, reportedly because executives had not heard all the tracks. According to Adam, this dispute was settled by Bennett Freed, and plans continued to prepare *Persuasion* for release in the first quarter of 1992.

Within weeks, those plans had changed. Adam was abruptly informed that MCA "was dropping me from the label and the album wouldn't be released." He was "gutted by the decision," although he claimed years later that it had not come as a complete surprise. "The company had new Japanese owners who seemed to be releasing any non-gold-status artists from their contracts," he wrote in his autobiography, "and my first album hadn't quite made it." With sales just short of the 500,000 units needed to achieve gold status, *Manners and Physique* had come close, but Adam was assured by Bennett Freed that "he'd be able to sell [*Persuasion*] to someone else, so I set him on doing that."[15]

Not only would Freed not find a suitable taker, but within months he would also no longer be representing Adam Ant. In early 1992 he resigned his post, and was replaced by the legendary Miles Copeland, who had brusquely—and brilliantly—guided the career of the Police, and later of Sting. In the long run, this switch would pay off handsomely for Adam, but the remainder of 1992 would prove to be discouraging.

His acting career was progressing in fits and starts. That year, Adam landed roles on the TV shows *Tales from the Crypt* and *Northern Exposure*, and also produced a rockabilly-themed play called *Be Bop a Lula*. But, as Copeland sought a new American deal for his client and *Persuasion*, musical activity was largely on hold. A London writing session with Pirroni that spring would produce the first draft of "Wonderful," the song that would ultimately resuscitate Adam's career. Yet back in Los Angeles things were far from wonderful—especially when a stalker named Ruth Marie Torres began paying regular visits to her idol's home in Meadow Valley Terrace.

Torres would ultimately be jailed and prevented from making contact with Adam, after a series of bizarre incidents that included breaking into his house and leaving him a cake with an accompanying note that read, "Get the whores out of the house." But Torres's visits would resonate long after she was gone. They had triggered the mental instability that had actually created Adam Ant in 1976, when an unhappy twenty-one-year-old student named Stuart Goddard took a deliberate overdose of pills at his in-laws' Muswell Hill home. When he recovered, he renamed himself, declaring Goddard dead. And all his subsequent wealth, success, and sexual conquest as Adam Ant could not eradicate his periodic attacks of depression. By late 1992, the illness had become pronounced enough that the .38 special Adam had bought for protection became a source of fear instead. "I lay in my bed sweating, terrified and hearing the gun call to me, 'Go on, load me. Squeeze the trigger and it'll all be over,'" he would later remember. "If I wasn't such a coward, I told myself, I would get it out, load it, and blow my brains out."[16]

By year's end, Adam would feel well enough to participate in the third "Almost Acoustic Xmas" concert staged by legendary L.A. radio station KROQ. He was joined by Pirroni, and his first live appearance in five years—which featured old favorites like "Desperate but Not Serious" and "Goody Two Shoes" in its five-song setlist—was enthusiastically received and reviewed. *The Los Angeles Times*'s J. Martin McOmber noted the "wild response" of the surprisingly young audience,[17] and Adam would later write that the experience "filled me with optimism for the new year and new album."[18]

Which new album is a question muddied somewhat in his autobiography. In *Stand and Deliver*, Adam claimed that by mid-1992 he had given up on *Persuasion* and decided to record a new album. It is certain that he and Pirroni had already come up with an early version of "Wonderful"—which had debuted at the KROQ show—and that he had also developed a rapport with guitarist Boz Boorer, who had actually engineered his London demo sessions the previous year. Boorer had entered the public eye as a member of the Polecats, an early-'80s rockabilly outfit with decided glam tendencies; the group's 1981 debut featured covers of Bowie and Bolan and was produced by Tony Visconti, as well as Dave Edmunds. However, it would be another rockabilly band of felines produced by Edmunds, the Stray Cats, that would capture the public's fancy that same year. Boorer would resurface a decade later in Morrissey's band, beginning a long-running partnership with the ex-Smiths singer on *Your Arsenal*, a fusion of rockabilly and glam with clear roots in Boorer's past—as well as Adam's.

Adam, Pirroni, and Boorer plotted a short American tour for the first quarter of 1993. In a throwback to the heavily percussive sound of Antmusic, they would be joined by a pair of drummers—Daves Ruffy and Barbe—as well as American bassist Bruce Witkin. A recording of a February 1 rehearsal at the Henry Fonda Theatre in Los Angeles documents a tight and lively group running confidently through Adam's back catalog, adding a cover of the Johnny Kidd and the Pirates oldie "Shakin' All Over" and remaking the electronic "Room at the Top" as a guitar-heavy Ant stomper.

But the concerts that followed were dubbed "The Persuasion Tour," which certainly indicated that Adam had not abandoned hope of releasing the album. So did the consistent presence of at least three songs from the disc—the title track, "Obsession," and "Headgear," which was often introduced with the guitar riff from Bowie's "Ziggy Stardust"—as well as radio ads for the tour that touted *Persuasion* as "his upcoming album," atop the opening riff from the song itself. And in a pre-tour interview with the *Los Angeles Times*'s Bill Locey, Adam noted that "my new [album] is really only eighteen months old, and that's due to different producers. I've been in London, New York, Miami and Los Angeles."[19]

The tour, reportedly financed by Adam himself, kicked off on February 22 in Redondo Beach, California, and ran through the end of March. A *Los Angeles Times* review of a show at San Juan Capistrano's Coach House was not encouraging: it described the new songs as "a vague mixture of pop and big-beat dance music, not far afield from the style of Ant's previous album," and concluded, "If Tuesday night's performance is the best he can muster, we don't really need another chapter of his New Romance."[20] Yet spirits evidently remained high; a band introduction from the Trenton, New Jersey date found Ruffy delivering an obscene, rapid-fire rap, later translated by Adam to general hilarity. "Joni Mitchell wrote those lyrics," he insisted.

Excluded from the hijinks was Leigh Gorman, who had been the first choice as bassist. In a near-perfect bit of irony, what got him bumped from the tour was the re-emergence of Adam's old nemesis. At the least opportune moment, Malcolm McLaren was about to make his grand reappearance.

The last time Leigh Gorman had spoken to his former manager, he'd been standing outside a New York City subway station, giving McLaren the sack via collect call. By 1982, Gorman and his bandmates had become unhappy that McLaren was perpetually distracted with other projects. The band was especially unamused to find that McLaren had taken plans for the next Bow Wow Wow album and used them to jumpstart his own solo career. "We'd talked about going to Africa and getting the real beats" behind the Burundi sound, Gorman recalls, "and using the new technology." Instead, McLaren made the trip alone, and producer Trevor Horn and engineer Gary Langan would organize the results into *Duck Rock*, which crunched hip-hop, Zulu music, and Appalachian folk into an unclassifiable new hybrid. McLaren finally had the rock star client he'd always dreamed of—himself—and there was simply no more time for Bow Wow Wow. "We had a huge row," says Gorman, "and that was it."

McLaren had continued to test boundaries—on albums like 1984's rap-opera *Fans* and 1987's classical-meets-funk *Waltz Darling*—and the patience of nearly everyone around him. By the early '90s, after an unsuccessful stint in Hollywood, he was working on commercials. Hearing "Hippychick," he got Gorman's number and had his assistant, Nils Stevenson, ring him up. "Nils said, 'I hear you're a bit of a producer these days,'" remembers Gorman. "'Malcolm wants to know if you'd be interested in turning up tomorrow and working on a Coca-Cola commercial.' So I said, 'Sure.' "

When this news reached Adam Ant, however, Gorman found himself on the outside looking in. "Adam still had a whole beef with Malcolm. And as soon as Adam found out I was speaking to Malcolm again, that was it—he didn't wanna know," Gorman says. McLaren, as might be expected, was delighted by the turn of events. "Malcolm was like, 'Ah, you're stuck with me, now, aren't ya?!' " says Gorman, imitating McLaren's high-pitched cackle.

Besides being left out of the tour, Gorman believes he also lost a chance to produce "Wonderful," which he had already worked up in a demo version. The song—and the accompanying album of the same name—would be overseen by veteran David Tickle at London's famed Abbey Road studios, and the result was Adam's most successful release in more than a decade.

Yet even then *Persuasion* had not been forgotten. At the turn of the millennium, Marco Pirroni was charged with assembling a box set of Adam Ant material for his old label, Sony.

> I went to MCA to try to get two or three tracks from *Persuasion* to put on our box set. Y'know, people should hear 'em somewhere, and it's nice to have these unreleased tracks. And first of all, they claimed they didn't own them, right? So we went to Sony and we had a meeting, and I said, "I know they're claiming they don't own them, but I know they do own them." And Sony's saying, "We're a multinational corporation, and we can't risk getting involved in a dispute with another corporation."

So we thought the best solution was for me to go back to MCA and say, "Pretend you *do* own them. We'd like to give you some money for them! How much money would you like? We wanna give you money." And they came back and said, "Well, we can't license just two or three tracks, we have to license the whole album. And I said, "We don't want the whole album, we just want two or three tracks." And they said, "In which case, you'll still have to pay the cost for the entire album." That's bollocks, innit?

It doesn't make sense to me. It's like, you're in the hole for $150,000, or whatever it is. That money's already gone. You can kiss it goodbye. But them someone comes along and says, Look, okay, I wanna give you $25,000 for three tracks, or whatever. That's gotta be better! But no, not according to them.

MCA also turned down a request for material from the officially released *Manners and Physique*, which necessitated the use of demos of those songs instead. However, Pirroni would return to MCA a few years later, offering to take the label up on its offer to license the entire disc of *Persuasion*. The thinking went, "If we can get it cheap enough, we can put it as an additional album with one of the Sony releases, or somewhere," Pirroni says. There was, he claims, an unwillingness by MCA to compromise on the price, which sank this deal as well.

As late as 2004, Pirroni was still attempting to negotiate with MCA, which had become part of Geffen Records the previous year. Pirroni's proposal this time was different.

We said, well, why don't you just release this album? And we'll put special artwork on it, we'll put the remixes on it, we'll make it the whole great lost album thing. You've spent the money anyway, so put it out for a budget price. And you don't have to do any-thing—just let me do it! I'm asking for no money to do this, just whatever royalties I get on it. But they didn't wanna know, so I just stopped chasing them.

Despite his struggles with MCA, Pirroni can see things from the label's perspective:

On the face of it, it looks insane. But if you were to work at a record company, it makes sense. The record business is now trying to achieve the same targets with a third of the staff. And they just don't have the time to spend on smaller projects. They have to spend all their time with the projects that make the most money. You have to prioritize. That's just how it is.

Still, the potential of the album remains intriguing. "Can you imagine all the licensing opportunities of *Persuasion*, in movies or commercials or whatever? It's enormous," says Gorman, who has since done work in television and film, and has included the album's title song on his show reel.[21] "But one of the things I've learned over the years is that when you're out of the limelight for a while, no one wants to know."

That problem has been solved, at least for the time being. Adam Ant would return to the limelight in the new millennium, although not exactly in a manner of his choosing. In 2002, he was arrested after throwing a car alternator through the window of a London pub and threatening patrons with a starter's pistol. Diagnosed with bipolar disorder, he was "sectioned" to the Royal Free Hospital. The following June, he made headlines again after another bizarre incident, in which he smashed the patio door of a Primrose Hill neighbor and then entered a local pub, where he removed his trousers and fell asleep in the basement.

Adam would have an opportunity to explain those occurrences, as well as his long battle with depression, in his 2006 autobiography. Slimmed down and healthier than he'd been in years, he promoted the book with a series of jam-packed signings throughout the U.K., and after ten years of near-inactivity, he even spoke of making music once again. "There was a time when I thought that was all finished," he would tell the music magazine *Uncut*. "Now I know there's some more great music left in me."[22]

There is also some great music left in his past, waiting to be rediscovered by a new generation of Ant fanatics. Despite his lack of success in negotiating with MCA, Pirroni remains optimistic that he may yet persuade the label to relinquish its grip on *Persuasion*.

"There's a lot of people in their twenties who work for record companies, who just don't know what the label actually owns," he says. "It just doesn't occur to people . . . until one day you're in an office, and someone says, 'Yeah, what about that?'"

Adam Ant: *Persuasion*
Recorded for: *MCA Records*
Scheduled release date: *Early 1992*
Recorded at: *Swanyard Recording Studios, London; The Power Station, New York, NY; Unknown studio, Miami, FL; 1991*

TRACK LISTING:

1. Persuasion (Ant/Marco)**
2. Headgear (Ant/Marco)**
3. All Girl Action (Ant/Marco)#
4. Brain Candy (Ant/Larry Blackmon)*
5. Obsession (Ant/Marco/Bernard Edwards)
6. Little Devil (Ant/Larry Blackmon)*
7. Sexatise You (Ant/Marco/Bernard Edwards)
8. Survival of the Fetish (Ant/Marco)#
9. Charge of the Heavy Brigade (Ant/Marco)
10. Don't Knock It Till You Got It (Ant/Marco/Bernard Edwards)

Also recorded: *"Seems to Me" (Ant/Marco)#*

Produced by: *Bernard Edwards; Larry Blackmon *; Leigh Gorman **; Ant/Pirroni #*
Mixed by: *Brian Malouf, except "Persuasion" and "Headgear" (Leigh Gorman) and "Survival of the Fetish" (Marco Pirroni)*

Credits:

Adam Ant—*vocals*

Marco Pirroni—*guitars*

Leigh Gorman—*bass, programming on "Persuasion" and "Headgear"*

Dave Ruffy—*drums on "Persuasion" and "Headgear"*

Tracey Ackerman—*backing vocals on "Persuasion" and "Headgear"*

Marcus Bush—*programming on "Persuasion" and "Headgear"*

Tim Wiedener—*engineer on "Persuasion" and "Headgear"*

Larry Blackmon—*programming*

⑨ Juliana Hatfield

You Can't Put Your Arms Around a Melody

Viewed from afar, Juliana Hatfield's unreleased God's Foot *seems to be as much an illustration of principles like the Butterfly Theory or the Tipping Point—which trace large events back to small, apparently unrelated causes—as it is the story of a dozen or so unheard songs.*

That is, until you consider the personal cost of its failure. No other album discussed in this book offers a better example of the effect such unreleased recordings can have on a career. The psyche of an artist can be a fragile thing at the best of times; for one who struggles with depression, the rejection of an album can truly be a life-altering event.

Especially when the album in question happens to be her best ever. It is little wonder that Juliana Hatfield says today about God's Foot, *"I don't listen to this stuff anymore. Because if*

I listened to it, I would probably cry. I just have such fond feelings for it."[1]

Working largely on her own to create God's Foot, Hatfield delivered a collection of songs that fulfilled all the promise others had seen in her since she debuted in the late '80s as the singer of Boston's Blake Babies. Going solo in the early '90s, she had enjoyed a spell as the alt-rock goddess of choice, her unusual combination of pop hooks, good looks, and soul-baring confessionals synchronizing perfectly with the zeitgeist. But God's Foot was a deeper and wider work, the music of a woman who had given up on stardom, but not on the sound that had helped make it possible. Playful and wise, heartbreakingly bitter and exhilaratingly sweet, it would have been one of the best albums of the decade.

Atlantic Records' rejection of the album in 1996 was a crushing blow that Hatfield now admits was a turning point in her life. "Juliana got really, really depressed," recalls her longtime drummer, Todd Phillips, "and it wasn't until we made Bed—this very aggressive, lo-fi record—that she really came out of it."[2]

That album appeared in 1998, yet the aftereffects of God's Foot would manifest themselves for years afterward. The second-guessing that sent Hatfield back into the studio repeatedly, trying to capture that elusive hit single, took some time to overcome. And while her personal life and career have both returned to a more even keel, the latter development is not entirely positive. Hatfield has taken control of her art, starting her own label, Ye Olde Records, and releasing her own albums. Yet, as is the case with most independent musicians, that control also involves the sacrifice of the larger audience Hatfield once commanded—an audience God's Foot conclusively proved she deserved.

Emerging from beneath God's Foot, however, has been a job as big as its title suggests. "We lived under that shadow for the rest of her career," says Gary Smith, who served as Hatfield's manager for almost two decades. "I don't think we ever got out from under it."[3]

Painful an experience as it was, the music on the album is so good that Hatfield later acknowledges she couldn't keep it at arm's length forever.

"Actually, I went back and listened to it about three months ago. I dug it up. It had been years since I listened to it, and it was great to hear it. But it did make me cry. A couple of tears," she says, fighting back a couple more. "It was like, I just felt so much compassion for my old self."

If you get nothing else from this book, you will hopefully leave with some compassion for God's Foot.

The first thing Juliana Hatfield wants to make clear is that, contrary to persistent rumor, she never went on a hunger strike to force Atlantic Records to release *God's Foot*—or to release her from her contract.

"That was a joke!" she says—a joke she started herself, in the liner notes of her 2002 greatest-hits album, *Gold Stars*. "It was funny to me to say I was on a hunger strike, because they were really eager to let me go, and I wouldn't have had to do that."

But Hatfield's description of her meeting with Atlantic's co-CEO, Val Azzoli, sometime in 1997, gives some indication as to her troubled mindset at the time. *God's Foot*, the album she rightly considered her masterpiece, had been in limbo for months. And it had finally dawned on Hatfield that Atlantic—where Azzoli, the former manager of AOR (album-oriented rock) icons Rush, was now sharing power with the label's founder, Ahmet Ertegun—had no intention of putting it out.

"So I went to see the new president. And I made a point not to shower for a couple of days, and I didn't brush my hair. And I went in and I tried to look . . . ugly and dirty, so the guy would let me go, and I basically begged him to let me go," she recalls. "So of course, he did, and they let me out of my contract. But I probably didn't have to beg . . . they were probably planning to drop me anyway."

At the time, being dumped by Atlantic didn't seem the worst fate in the world. Though Hatfield had called it home since her old imprint, Mammoth Records, had become part of Atlantic in 1992, she had never had any particular allegiance to the label, and owed even less to its new regime. So Hatfield was ready to entertain some new suitors.

"Well, I think that . . . part of my thinking was that I had this great bunch of songs, and I wanted somebody to get behind them who really liked them. And I thought, 'I'll leave Atlantic, and go to someone else who will like them and appreciate them, and let them put them out,'" she says. "If my relationship with Atlantic was like a boyfriend and girlfriend, then it was time to break up. And I was gonna move on and find the cooler boyfriend.

"But . . . I couldn't find him," adds Hatfield with a sardonic laugh. "No one liked me. So my plan didn't work."

The story of *God's Foot* really begins in the autumn of 1994, when Danny Goldberg's brief tenure as president of Atlantic Records came to an end. Goldberg was not the first domino to fall in the chain that would eventually topple Juliana Hatfield, but he was probably the most important one.

"I think that was kind of the beginning of the end. When he left, we all knew I was doomed. We just accepted it," Hatfield says now. "Danny was a cool guy, and he had signed me . . . and I knew that without him on my side, I would be lost and forgotten at the label, which is exactly what happened."

Goldberg, who had made his name in the music business by founding the powerful management company Gold Mountain Entertainment in the early '80s, had been Hatfield's biggest champion during his two years at Atlantic. But when he departed that October to take over the chairmanship at the company's parent label, Warner Brothers, he seemed to be leaving Hatfield in a strong position.

She had come to Atlantic at about the same time as Goldberg. Her old band, the Blake Babies, had made three albums for the North

Carolina indie label Mammoth; after the group's split, Hatfield had recorded a well-received 1992 solo debut, *Hey Babe*, for Mammoth as well. The disc sold more than 75,000 copies, making it one of the top-selling independent releases that year.

However, waves from the tsunami set in motion by Nirvana's shocking success that same year would sweep over Hatfield in short order. Major labels realized that the crop of alternative rock acts nurtured on small imprints over the past decade was ripe to be harvested, and began partnering with independents, or purchasing them outright.

In September 1992, Hatfield, along with the rest of Mammoth's roster, became part of a "joint venture" with Atlantic Records. Goldberg now recalls making the deal "because when I got here Atlantic was not too successful in 'alternative' music. They had the Lemonheads and a couple of other acts but that was about it."[4] However, at Gold Mountain, Goldberg and his partner John Silva had managed some of the most important alternative acts, including Nirvana, Hole, and Sonic Youth. So Goldberg understood the rapidly changing musical landscape better than most of his contemporaries.

"My feeling was that the best way to accelerate Atlantic's presence in 'alternative'—which was rapidly becoming the most successful rock—was to invest in indie labels," Goldberg says. He would later make such investments in indies Beggars Banquet and Matador, but Goldberg's first choice was Mammoth. The label boasted other notable acts, like folk singer Victoria Williams and alternative country pioneer Joe Henry. Based on the sales of *Hey Babe*, though, Hatfield was the prize.

"I picked Mammoth because its owner, Jay Faires, was actively looking for a deal—and of the artists he had at the time the one I was most aware of was Juliana Hatfield," explains Goldberg. "I knew Gary Smith because my wife, Rosemary Carroll, was the lawyer for Juliana. And I also knew of [Hatfield] through Evan Dando of the Lemonheads, who was a friend of hers. And I knew she had a great reputation as an artist in the rock press."

That reputation would receive a further boost from the release of Hatfield's first album for Mammoth/Atlantic, 1993's *Become What You Are*, under the name the Juliana Hatfield Three. In fact, she became a minor media sensation. There were multiple angles for the press to work: her provocative friendship with Evan Dando; her musical independence (she wrote her own songs and had studied voice at Boston's prestigious Berklee School of Music); and the claim that she remained a virgin. Meanwhile, her sultry pout made her a natural choice as the female pinup of the grunge generation, even as quotes like, "I'll never be a slut. I can tell you that much. I can tell you that will never happen,"[5] promised fame would happen strictly on her own terms.

In sum, Hatfield seemed like an artist on the cusp of superstardom, one who could easily weather the departure of her patron at Atlantic. "There was a lot going on. She was a cultural figure. She was hot, although her record sales didn't show it," says Gary Smith, who had produced Hatfield for years and now served as her manager. "It seemed she was on her way somewhere." Yet, as is so often the case in the music industry, the picture was far less rosy when examined closely.

No one knew that better than Smith, a Rhode Island native who had built an alternative rock empire from his Fort Apache Studios in Cambridge, Massachusetts. During the '80s, Smith had helped two seminal bands—Throwing Muses and the Pixies—get their careers off the ground, and he had since worked with a virtual who's who of alt-rock royalty. With years of experience in the industry, Smith was already wary of Hatfield's marriage to Atlantic.

For one thing, there were the aforementioned record sales. All the press coverage Hatfield had received hadn't helped *Become What You Are* get past No. 119 on the Billboard album chart. And while she did enjoy her first Top 40 hit in 1994 with "Spin the Bottle," Smith felt the tune had clearly succeeded thanks to its inclusion on the *Reality Bites* soundtrack. Featuring songs from U2 and Lenny Kravitz, and the huge Lisa Loeb hit "Stay," the collection of tunes from the slacker drama went quintuple-platinum, giving Hatfield's career a boost as well.

Goldberg defends the label's work on Hatfield's behalf during the *Become What You Are* period:

> I know I loved Juliana's first record that came out via Atlantic—the song I remember that we worked very hard on was "My Sister." I guess a manager always thinks a label could have done a better job, and Gary always was irritated that she didn't do as well as Belly had on Warner Brothers. All I can tell you is that it was a priority and that I pressured the company as much as I could to work very hard on it. But honestly the details of what we did or didn't do have faded from my memory.

In an ominous sign, however, "For the Birds," the third single from *Become What You Are*, failed to make a dent in the charts. It was released after Goldberg's departure for Warner's, a move about which he expresses mixed feelings:

I would have preferred to stay at one company for twenty years, or even for ten, or even five—but that just wasn't my destiny. The Warner Music execs wanted me to move to Warner Brothers Records and they were my bosses. When execs leave, sometimes the artists they championed aren't treated as well. I think that the Mammoth, Matador, and Beggars deals all suffered somewhat from my departure.

On that point, he was in agreement with Smith, who saw an old industry truism about to repeat itself. "When your person leaves, it's very hard to drag that inspiration to a new person," he says. "People wanna have their own new thing."

By the time Hatfield's *Only Everything* appeared in March 1995, it was clear there was a new thing at Atlantic. Not yet twenty-one, Jewel Kilcher was a Utah native whose debut, *Pieces of You*, had been released just a month earlier. Known only by her first name, Jewel was presented to the public as a poetry-writing, freshly scrubbed folkie so earnest it made one's teeth hurt, an image her delicate first single, "You Belong to Me," perfectly reinforced.

Behind the scenes, Jewel was a bit savvier than her wide-eyed public persona, as Hatfield and Smith would discover when the two artists played some dates together that year. "Juliana didn't want to wear a push-up bra and sit on people's laps, but Jewel was a trollop," says Smith with a chuckle.

She'd come around and we'd be whispering, "What the fuck is she wearing?" I mean, not to be moralizing, but she'd have on some little slip and tell us, "The record company's coming today!" So it was like, "Tits out!" you know? But it's not Jewel's fault.

Neither was it Hatfield's, but the contrast between her brooding, uncompromising stance and the eager-to-please Jewel was pronounced. "That didn't work to Juliana's advantage," Smith acknowledges. "I'm willing to bet, if you charted sales for the two of them on SoundScan, that you'd see Jewel going up as Juliana was going down. And credit to [Atlantic executive] Ron Shapiro—he sat on Jewel's record, and sat on it, until it sold a squillion copies."

Hatfield's *Only Everything*, meanwhile, would top out at less than 150,000, and its lone single, "Universal Heartbeat," barely made it inside the Billboard Top 100. That disappointment would have an effect on the power vacuum at Atlantic. It meant Hatfield would have to work more closely than ever with the man she least wanted to see—making allies of strange bedfellows, with her career in the balance.

Not that things seemed quite so ominous at first. At least, not to Hatfield, who admits to not losing much sleep over the machinations at her label. "I knew I was kinda screwed. I had my little supporters here and there at the label, but not people in power. But it wasn't something I was too concerned with," she says. "At the time, I was still in la-la land, you know, 'makin' my music, makin' my records,' not really strategizing. I was just doing my thing.'"

However, a person who was probably more worried about Hatfield's decline was Jay Faires, cofounder of Mammoth Records. Hatfield had been the centerpiece of the deal he'd signed with Atlantic in 1992, and while she'd generated plenty of ink, her record sales hadn't backed it up. Other Mammoth acts, like the Australian quartet Frente! and the industrial act Machines of Loving Grace, had not picked up the slack, while Faires's biggest success stories—the Carolina retro-swing band Squirrel Nut Zippers, and Pearl Jam–indebted alt-rockers Seven Mary Three—were still developing.

"Jay's deal was a big deal. He had gotten a lot of money from Atlantic," says Gary Smith, "and the deal was not bearing fruit." Which was why, as preparations began for Hatfield's fourth solo album, Faires took an unprecedented step that reflected his personal stake in the album. He would serve as Atlantic's A&R for the project, a decision that couldn't have been more unwelcome for Smith and Hatfield.

When Hatfield had come to Atlantic in 1992, Smith recalls, he had asked Danny Goldberg for one condition to seal the deal: "We never wanted to talk to Jay again." Hatfield remembers, "That guy was born with a silver spoon up his ass, that's what I always used to say." And Smith adds, "I never found him to be the most creative thinker; we all thought of him as an artless boob, frankly. But things had gotten so desperate that Jay was now an ally, which was a revolting concept."

It was revolting for reasons beyond working with Faires. In all Smith's years in the industry, he had managed to avoid ever dealing with an A&R man, turning in albums by the likes of the Pixies and Dinosaur Jr. without ever being second-guessed by a label's representative. "We'd never had anyone *dare* to tell us what to do," Smith says, becoming indignant at the thought. "And if they had, I'd have told them, 'Get the fuck out of my studio!' It was all about the artist. That was part of our shtick at Fort Apache."

But the business was changing, and instances of artists having complete creative control were becoming less and less frequent—at least for those artists who recorded for the multinational conglomerates beginning to dominate the industry. And Smith is candid enough to admit that complete control could create its own problems. "Frankly, I think Juliana had been spoiled by this environment," he says. "It compromised her ability to work in this sort of Brill Building manner, where you have to take suggestions and compromise."

Still, given all the attendant pressures, Atlantic made two curious decisions prior to the recording of what would become *God's Foot*. One was agreeing to let Hatfield produce herself, for the first time. The other was signing an agreement with the singer stating that if album sales of *God's Foot* did not exceed 350,000 copies, she would be free to leave the label.

Gary Smith cannot recall the reasoning behind the first decision, except to speculate,

> This was a battle I assumed I had won as a manager—maybe not to my client's advantage. I have to assume the thought was to keep more money [from the record company advance] in Juliana's pocket. Bringing in a high-priced producer didn't always guarantee you were going to sell more records. And Juliana was having trouble figuring out who she wanted to work with anyway.

The fact that Atlantic did not insist on a "name" producer to help create the hit Hatfield was still seeking, however, contrasts sharply with the sales agreement. One way to view that document is as a not-so-subtle reminder from the label of its expectations for *God's Foot*; another is that if Hatfield failed to meet those expectations, Atlantic could rid itself of a performer already considered "difficult." Either way, the agreement set an ominous tone for the sessions. "It's a lot like a pre-nup," says Smith with a sigh.

Hatfield herself viewed the developments with some suspicion. "I produced *God's Foot* myself, which is pretty amazing," she says. "Maybe that was a sign that [Atlantic] didn't really care."

But Hatfield cared, and cared deeply—something that would become painfully apparent as the songs for *God's Foot* began to come to life.

During Hatfield's 1995 tour, drummer Todd Phillips became aware of what he felt was a troubling phenomenon. "The thing that I remember was, there were no label people around whatsoever. I mean, we were doing some of the biggest shows we'd ever done—we had Jeff Buckley opening up for us, and then John Doe, but the label people were conspicuous by their absence," he says. "It was strange."

However, the presence of Doe and Buckley would soon become conspicuous in Hatfield's new music. Both Doe, who had co-led country-punk pioneers X, and Buckley, touring in support of his acclaimed debut, *Grace*, were old-fashioned songwriters who paid keen attention to detail. "That had a big effect on Juliana's writing, I think," Phillips offers.

As Phillips remembers it, he and Hatfield recorded basic tracks at Fort Apache in the winter of 1995–96. With no producer on hand, the pair went about making the album in their usual, low-key way; they would later be joined, on some songs, by bassist Tony Marsico, a veteran of Bob Dylan's '80s band. "Basically, the way Juliana likes to make records is that she records her guitar and vocals onto a really shitty cassette player," says Phillips. "And she would give me the cassette of that, and I would listen to it, and then we would go into the studio and figure out how we were gonna do it."

The rough sketches for *God's Foot*—a title Hatfield discovered in a line from Herman Melville's *Moby Dick*—were then taken to Dreamland Studios in Woodstock, New York,[6] sometime early in 1996. At Dreamland, Hatfield would work with "an amazing engineer" named Dave Cook, who helped her polish her most personal batch of songs yet.

However insulated she felt from the struggles taking place at Atlantic, it was clear that the apparent decline of her career was weighing heavily on Hatfield's mind. The two best-known songs from *God's Foot*—the only two, in fact, to ever receive an official release—both dealt with this topic. The heavy-riffing "Fade Away" tackled the ephemeral nature of fame directly, with a chorus that declared "Thank God today / Is gonna fade away." Years afterward, however, Hatfield can admit she was "putting on a front" with those words.

> It's like always knowing that [success] is not gonna last. Because nothing lasts. But when I write a song like that, I think it's a way for me to save face, or keep some dignity. "Oh, it's great to be popular now, but when it ends, I won't really care."

> But really . . . it hurts me. It hurts to be forgotten.
> It hurts not to be appreciated. So a song like "Fade
> Away" . . . the sentiment isn't entirely honest. I mean,
> it is, in a way . . . I know the commercial success I had
> was a fluke. But at the same time it felt good to be
> acknowledged, and it hurts when people just . . . turn
> away.

"Mountains of Love," meanwhile, was the more wistful and melodic flip side of that coin, a lump-in-the-throat farewell to precious things, liked a loved one—or perhaps a career. "[It's about] making a good effort to leave things behind, to move on," Hatfield says quietly. "But it's hard." The yearning was underscored by a lovely string arrangement from violinist Joan Wasser, of the Boston-based group the Dambuilders.

"What Have I Done to You" opened with an arresting, gender-bending couplet—"Waking up, hitting myself / With a headache and a hard-on"—that Hatfield now laughingly dismisses as "just me trying to be funny. Dorky humor." But the tune, another melancholy gem, was far more serious, finding Hatfield repentant for all the heartache she'd caused. "I know I need to get some help," she sang. "You say I'm crazy, inconsistent and confusing, selfish too / And I know that it's all true." Thinking back now, she muses, "It was probably written about someone, but I really can't remember who I was thinking about. It just seems like you're hurting somebody, or you're being hurt by somebody. You find yourself in one position or the other, and that was where I was the hurter, instead of the hurt-ee, I guess."

Even more heartbreaking was a ballad that swiped its title from the old Johnny Thunders classic "You Can't Put Your Arms Around a Memory." It was "a song that I had never heard, at the time, just the title. And I just stole it, changed it," Hatfield says. A dreamy number that featured Hatfield on piano and steel guitar from Greg "Smokey" Hormel, "You Can't Put Your Arms Around a Melody" featured a tune as beautiful, and hard to hold, as its title suggested. When a multitracked Hatfield sang, "Look real close and you'll see / There is something wrong with everyone," the sadness was tangible enough to have been listed as an instrument. "That one's pretty self-explanatory, isn't it?" Hatfield asks. "I remember working really hard on the piano. It was such a pain, such a headache. I remember being so stressed trying to get the piano done. But it was so worth it."

Although it contained one of the most forthright dilemmas Hatfield ever committed to tape—"Oh me, can I be / True to you, until we sleep / Together again? And if I can / It's gonna be so sweet!" she insists that the eroticized rocker "Chance Is Waiting" was about "no one in particular. Chance wasn't a real person." Reciting more of the lyrics to herself, including the opening lines "Chance is waiting over with the boys / He's really, really stoned and he's playing with his toys," she adds, "I think that was just a song about temptation. A lot of the songs are about, like, just feeling . . . anxious about hurting someone—not wanting to hurt someone, but fearing that I'm going to. Because that's what happened."

Alienation had been a theme of Hatfield's work since the early days of her career, but she had never expressed it as simply, or as devastatingly, as she did on "How Would You Know." At one level, it was dedicated to all the people who had ever walked home alone from a party, kicking themselves for not talking to that certain person, for not letting them know "that's my favorite song." "I think it's just a song about being really shy. And about getting down on myself for being too shy, and too scared," says Hatfield. "It's pretty universal." But the soaring chorus, erupting in slow motion in the best alt-rock tradition, suggested a deeper disconnect: "How would you know / What I feel / I never give you anything / That you can call real."

"Yeah, I love that one," Hatfield adds with a sigh.

Hatfield's brother, Jason, would provide some sibling harmony to "Don't Need a Reason," a shimmering, soulful mid-tempo track that Todd Phillips thought was "just an incredible song. It's sublime." Hatfield considers it "really one of the most hopeful songs in my repertoire. It's kind of about faith, I think." That sentiment might have thrown some listeners, had they been able to hear the lines, "I don't know how / To pull out of this" and "Depression's always asking me / Why I keep on trying / But I . . . / I don't need a reason." However, Hatfield explains the apparent contradiction.

"I think that's just my . . . general attitude. I used to call myself a depressed optimist. In my twenties especially, I was pretty miserable, but I also had a lot of faith in something I couldn't name. It was wrapped up in music.

"It's guess it's like . . . " she continues, singing softly to herself, "yeah, things are shitty, and I'm really depressed and I don't know why. But life is pretty wonderful, too. It's kind of like 'Fade Away' and 'Mountains of Love,' about accepting it. It's no reason to be depressed."

The acoustic version of "Charity" that survives sounds demo-rough, with Hatfield solo and complaining, "I know you / But you don't know shit about me." But in this instance, the failure was clearly the fault of the other party, and it's no stretch to place Atlantic Records on the receiving end of this broadside—especially when Hatfield sang about keeping her "baby" safe from harm. Meanwhile, the subject of the countrified "Eye to Eye," one of the most gorgeous songs of Hatfield's career, was a significant other she can no longer remember.

"Isn't it weird that I can't remember who I was thinking of?" she asks, singing the song's opening lines—"I / Love your eyes / Your diamond eyes / That cut me up"—to refresh her memory. "In that period, there was one guy I was thinking of a lot. But there was also a general sense of the hopelessness of love, that people hurt each other."

That hopelessness was submerged beneath layers of twinkling guitar arpeggiation, pedal steel solos, and more harmony vocals from Jason Hatfield, making "Eye to Eye" the sweetest possible vehicle for its bitter message. "I really like 'Eye to Eye.' I remember playing that one live," says Hatfield. "I really thought Jay Faires would like that one, I thought it was catchy. But he didn't appreciate it."

Yet hope would emerge, albeit in muted fashion, on "Jake's," a mood piece about a neighborhood bar that offered the flip side of the emotionally distant "How Could You Know?" "More than drunk," Hatfield was finally ready to commit. "I wanna give you all that I never did," she sang. "Makes me think that up 'til now / Maybe I haven't really lived."

Todd Phillips thought Hatfield had never written and performed better. "That original batch of ten songs was just mature, it was ... just a huge step up for her," he says. But Hatfield's bosses and corporate minders were about to illustrate the unfortunate truth of one of her new songs: that none of us "can ever really see eye to eye."

Jay Faires would ensure that *God's Foot* did not survive long in its first incarnation. Hatfield recalls,

> Jay was paying attention to the recording. He would listen to what I would do, but he would always come back and say, "I don't hear a hit. Go write some more and record some more." And I was like, "Cool." So I would write some more and record some more. And he'd be like, "I still don't hear a hit."
>
> At some point it just became clear that I wasn't gonna be able to satisfy this person. I wasn't gonna be able to write a smash hit because that wasn't who I was. And when Jay Faires said, "Go write a hit," I would just go write more songs I liked. Because I was still naïve enough to believe that what made songs hits was that they were good.

Gary Smith recalls that Hatfield was sent back into the studio no fewer than three times, beginning in the latter half of 1996, to create that elusive hit. Even though most of those trips appear to have been made to Fort Apache, a cost-effective environment for Hatfield, they were still eating away at the profits from her advance.

However, in Faires's defense, the extra sessions were not entirely unproductive. In fact, they produced at least one song that ranks with Hatfield's all-time best. And if Faires was beginning to put pressure on Hatfield to deliver a hit, it was most likely a response to pressure he was feeling from within Atlantic.

Once the hottest rising star connected with the label, Faires had been surpassed on the company totem pole, says Gary Smith, by other former indie kids now operating under Atlantic's umbrella.

One of them was Craig Kallman, the former owner of the dance music label Big Beat. Kallman, a New Yorker who had bluffed his way into the city's top DJ booths as a teenager, had built Big Beat into an underground success, and then sold it to Atlantic in 1991. He had a definite ear for what was hot—an ear that would later help bring singers like Aaliyah, Brandy, and Lil' Kim to the label—and his bosses were beginning to listen.

In short, he was exactly the right guy to have on board supporting *God's Foot*. Except, unfortunately, that he didn't. "He didn't like it," Gary Smith alleges, "and he had clout." While Kallman might have been beneath Faires in title, "it was clear that the politics of it were more than someone's rank," says Smith.

The amazing thing about the extra sessions is not that they were demanded of Hatfield, but that they so clearly produced the desired result—a result that was rejected, just like the first version of *God's Foot*. Yet it's hard to imagine that anyone in 1996 wrote a better pop song than "Perfection," a tune that somehow managed to live up to its title. Set to an ebullient riff that could have melted the hardest heart, the track was gloriously, almost unbearably, bittersweet—the musical embodiment of something too good to be true.

When he first heard the acoustic demo of the song, Todd Phillips was reminded of another Massachusetts alt-rock icon. Dinosaur Jr's J. Mascis had brought his love of '70s sounds—including multiple guitar overdubs and walloping drums—to the indie scene, and Phillips and Hatfield appropriated those elements for "Perfection." "It just felt like it should have that *You're Living All Over Me* drum feel," Phillips says. "So I asked Juliana if that'd be all right, and it wasn't the way she had pictured it, but it's the way we ended up doing it. And it ended up really cool. It's a really strong song."

Talking about "Perfection" seems to strike an even deeper chord in Hatfield. "I know, right? Right?" she agrees, when the song's standout qualities are mentioned.

> I know, my God . . . I thought that album was full of hits! I mean, it's got my quirks but . . . I was so proud of "Perfection," and a lot of those songs. And to have it just hit this . . . wall of blankness . . . I mean, what can I do? These people knew who I was, right? They knew my shtick, right? And then all of a sudden, it wasn't right anymore.

"I loved that one. There's *so much* feeling in it," she adds. "And I just love all the little guitar parts. I put so much work into it, just all the little parts and voices. I'm very fond of that one. The solo on it."

Unfortunately, the lyrics to "Perfection" could also be viewed as Atlantic's response to Hatfield's efforts. "Would perfection be enough?" Apparently not.

The other two songs recorded during this session weren't as perfect as "Perfection," although they weren't without their charms. The blunt-spoken, straight-ahead power-pop of "Losing Your Looks," Hatfield now says, would never have made the final album. "I decided that song was too annoying, and stupid. It was too mean, or something."

It was certainly a curt dismissal of an ex-lover whose "two greatest qualities" were his face and his body. And if it sounded like Hatfield had a specific target in mind, "Yeah. Yeah, I did," she admits, laughingly. "I'm not gonna name 'im. A pretty boy. A pretty boy who's rotten on the inside."

"I Didn't Know," meanwhile, featured Hatfield's friend Lisa Mednick on keyboards, and somehow went unclaimed by Hatfield's label. "That was definitely part of the sessions. That was one that slipped through the cracks somewhere. The label doesn't own that one—it's not on their list. There's this list of songs that they paid for and owned, and 'I Didn't Know' wasn't on it, for some reason." Because of that apparent oversight, Hatfield would make the song available for download from her website for a limited time in 2005 and 2006.

When these songs were rejected, Hatfield and Phillips returned to the studio for a second go-round. It may been during these sessions that "Takin' It Easy" was recorded; it's another remarkable track that showed Hatfield was still able to compose under duress, drawing on elements of her own troubled past.

Featuring one of Hatfield's breeziest, most winsome melodies, given life by electric piano comping and shimmering guitar lines, "Takin' It Easy" was about selective serotonin reuptake inhibitors—antidepressants like Prozac and Zoloft, which Hatfield had been prescribed earlier in her career. "It's about a depressed boyfriend who gets on Prozac or something. And . . . it helps. Except then he has some . . . sexual dysfunction problems. But it's okay, because it makes him more pleasant to hang around," she says, adding with genuine curiosity, "Did you get that from it?"

In its theme of "loving a depressed guy, loving him in his depression," there were echoes of Lou Reed's 1972 classic "Perfect Day," another song about trying to live and love normally in the shadow of what are implied to be serious obstacles. "Yeah, it's definitely about having an appreciation for the dark side of people," Hatfield agrees.

> But at the same time, you know . . . I think in the song I'm actually giving the guy his pills. Because at the time, I think I was pro-Prozac. I was on Zoloft for

a year. And it was working. It was like, "Wow, this is great! The drug works!" So I was pro-SSRIs at the time. I was an advocate, like telling people, "You gotta try these drugs, they really work."

After a year, I stopped doing it. Because I didn't like the idea of being on a drug every day of my life. Because no one knows what the long-term effects are gonna be. Now I would say . . . I would try other avenues of therapy and healing and diet first. I actually recommended Prozac to a friend of mine who was just hitting the wall. I was told that when the drugs work, they change the chemistry in your brain, so that when you stop taking them, you're happier. Or else they can help you see things from a different perspective. If you know you can feel better, then it's gonna make your depression shorter. Because you know it's not gonna last.

I used it as a tool at a time when I was wanting to jump out a window. I did a lot of things, including therapy and getting a dog and a whole lot of other stuff, while I was taking Zoloft. And all that stuff helps me. And then I didn't need Zoloft any more. It's a crutch, a tool or a crutch, that you gotta get off of eventually.

Even so, those closest to Hatfield were becoming concerned about the effects of so much rejection on her self-confidence. Jay Faires still hadn't heard a hit, and by the time a third round of rewrites had been ordered, "I think we'd really reached the point of diminishing returns," says Gary Smith. Hatfield was already a natural second-guesser—"Juliana always hated everything within minutes of finishing it. It was impossible to keep her interested"— and Smith thought the additional sessions were exacerbating that problem.

"Can't Kill Myself" was a song Hatfield now reveals was directed to her dog; the idea that her pet's well-being was all that was stopping her from committing suicide was either jet-black humor or a fairly troubling admission. But "Number One," the other new song to emerge from the third rewrite session, was troubling for different reasons.

"That was one of the last attempts to write a catchy single. One of the last attempts to give Jay Faires what he wanted," Hatfield explains. "That was literally my attempt to write a No. 1 hit. And it's a song about the label telling me to go record a hit. And that was the last I did, that was the end of the sessions."

Today, she can admit that the song, a gentle mid-tempo shuffle that begins addressed directly to Faires—"I wrote this song for you / Because you asked me to / You said you don't hear a hit / So here it is here it is / You asked for it," was "kind of a wiseass move. Jay Faires was probably not amused by that song," Hatfield says, chuckling as she recalls the line she used to defend herself: *"But my job as a songwriter is to take my life experiences and write about them!"*

But despite her recollection that "After I left Atlantic, there was another label that was really into that song, that almost signed me because of that song, because they thought it could be a hit," Todd Phillips was not convinced. "By that point, things had really started to disintegrate," he says. "It was like, 'Why is she *doing* this?'"

As a new year dawned, the answer to that question was about to get even less clear.

When he surveys his correspondence with Atlantic Records regarding Juliana Hatfield—a series of letters that he has archived, like all his other important papers, on old-fashioned microfilm—Gary Smith notices a recurrent theme. "The phrase 'Kafka-esque' came up a lot,'" he notes with a laugh. "Which I thought was very telling."

By the early part of 1997, official communiqués about Hatfield had gotten ugly. She and Atlantic had reached a stalemate, since it was becoming clearer and clearer that the label had no intention of releasing *God's Foot*. Although she owed Atlantic one more album, Gary Smith had begun to petition for her release. As is always the case in the music industry, things wouldn't be that simple.

Smith's plan was straightforward: Hatfield's new label would pay an override—giving Atlantic back its money for the recording costs of *God's Foot*—and "then we'd waltz in somewhere else with the record in hand." It seemed like a foolproof scheme. Hatfield was still one of the most notable female artists around, and her stock remained high. Her lawyer, Rosemary Carroll, was taking calls from labels that had heard Hatfield might soon be a free agent, and "everyone we talked to had interest," Smith says.[7]

"But at some point, Atlantic started saying they had helped launch her," adds Smith, who didn't believe that assertion. "In fact," he contends, "they had done damage." However, the company now wanted a payment of $175,000, plus an unspecified number of points on her first album for a new label. "We finally got so fed up, we just said, 'Oh, fuck it. We'll just take the hit on the first record,'" Smith says.

While Hatfield struggled to get free of Atlantic—making her now-infamous trip to see Val Azzoli at some point in the process—it was clear she hadn't given up on *God's Foot*. In April, she visited the show "The Open Road," at Santa Monica radio station KCRW, with her acoustic guitar, offering versions of "Eye to Eye"—which, somewhat surprisingly, she said was not a lock for inclusion on the new album—and "What Have I Done to You." Sounding taken aback at host Gary Calamar's knowledge of the turmoil at Atlantic and Mammoth, she insisted, "It's a complicated situation. It's gonna work out." But when questioned, she offered a somewhat revealing explanation of the title *God's Foot*. "Sometimes," Hatfield said, "it steps on your head."[8]

That summer, Hatfield would join the first Lilith Fair tour for several dates, playing a rocked-up second stage set that included "Fade Away" and "Perfection." However, it was clear she felt out of place amidst the more mellow pop that dominated the event. "We got invited to do this Lilith Fair thing, and I just thought it would be fun to go out and remind people that I still exist. I'm still making music—it's just not out there now. And I wanted to try out some new songs," she told *Flagpole*. "I sort of feel like an outsider on this tour, but, you know, I'm just doing what I always do. A mixture of rock stuff and some mellow stuff. But it's going well."[9]

Hatfield may have been expressing more optimism than she felt. A hint of what was happening behind the scenes would surface during a caustic cover of X's "The Unheard Music"—a song choice that was certainly no accident. Even within Hatfield's own band, there was marked unease. "I was getting really nervous," admits Todd Phillips, "because I'd staked my whole future on playing with Juliana Hatfield." Phillips would continue to turn down other gigs, but his future was becoming cloudier by the month.

By that autumn, Hatfield was finally off Atlantic, a move that mirrored the end of the partnership between the label and Mammoth. Smith had signed her to a one-off deal with independent label Bar None, and she recorded an EP titled *Please Do Not Disturb* that was released in October. Once again, reviewers searching for clues to Hatfield's tumultuous professional life didn't have to look far. Hatfield would later say of the first song, "Sellout," "I hope people don't think it's about me, because it's not,"[10] but with lines like "It's not a sellout if nobody buys it / I can't be blamed if nobody likes it," that would have been an easy mistake to make.

The Bar None arrangement, Gary Smith now says, was simply a stopgap designed to buy time for what was still viewed as the inevitable major-label return. "It just didn't seem possible that we couldn't walk into a deal," he says. The negotiations with Atlantic, however, had dragged on for the better part of a year. And during that time, Smith now realizes, "the world changed."

Part of the change involved fallout from the landmark Telecommunications Act of 1996, Congress's first change in telecommunications law in more than sixty years. The act's elimination of ownership restrictions on media companies led to the growth of the ClearChannel radio empire, which made it even more difficult for acts like Hatfield to get airplay. Just as significantly, the wave of mergers that soon swept the music industry created giant conglomerate record labels more sales-obsessed than ever before. The worth of a critically acclaimed but underselling performer like Hatfield had changed, as well—and not for the better. "A lot of these people at labels realized their jobs were different, and harder now," acknowledges Smith. "And Juliana wasn't making pop music."

Thus it was that meetings with Al Cafaro at A&M Records, and Tom Whalley at Interscope, turned up sincere interest, but no offers. "People weren't sure where she was in her career," says Smith. "Maybe she was besmirched by her reputation, by being so tough to deal with at Atlantic." Smith would turn his attention to other possibilities: independent labels, even a Japanese-only release. "But the wind had just gone out of our sails," says Smith, who would continue to manage Hatfield for the next decade, and remains a close friend. "That came as a terrible shock to everyone."

The reality of the situation would not sink in, for Hatfield, until the new year. As late as December 1997, she was playing songs from *God's Foot* on tour, still expecting they would soon appear in some form. Yet when she finally came to grips with the fact that no label was willing to pay Atlantic what it would take to free, and then release, *God's Foot*, "that's when I really realized my . . . position in the world. I realized I was gonna have to start over in a way.

"It was really, really difficult when I realized that this album wasn't gonna come out. It was a very hard, hard blow for me to take," she says. "Because the whole time, I never thought it wouldn't come out . . . somewhere." Even as she acknowledges the defensibility of Atlantic's position—"they paid for it, so they want to keep it"—she finds it hard to reconcile, considering the label's rejection of *God's Foot*. "The idea of that . . . it's so *greedy*. And it's also so random. Because I know people who, when they left their label, the label said, 'Here, take your stupid album. Go put it out.' But I just wasn't lucky that way.

"I was pretty naïve, I guess," she says finally. "That was sort of a turning point in my life, when I realized this record wasn't coming out. That was when I really had to grow up, and realize that the world isn't fair, and that . . . your hard work comes to nothing, you know? It was really harsh for me . . . but it was a good lesson to learn."

The lessons Hatfield learned would first send her to her bed in a state of depression. She would rouse herself to create an album named after that experience, and *Bed*, recorded for just $3,000 at a converted Providence, Rhode Island firehouse, sounded as raw as Hatfield felt. "This album's very, very personal to me, and very inspired by what was happening in my life at the time," she told Reuters. "It's the first record where there are actual real villains that exist. All my other stuff is about how I hate myself and I screw everything up."[11]

That might have been a necessary moment of catharsis, but *God's Foot* was not so easily escaped. When Hatfield assembled her greatest-hits album, *Gold Stars 1992–2002: The Juliana Hatfield Collection*, she included "Mountains of Love" and "Fade Away." Even then, the specter of possible chart success haunted the proceedings. The latter song appeared in remixed form, she says, because "we remixed it to try to give the label something that was a hit. Something hit-y," she says, laughing. "So we did this remix with a drum loop."

That decision did not provide Hatfield's new label, the Rounder imprint Zoë, with a hit, but it did mark the first official release of *God's Foot* material. The problem was that by that point some fans had already been able to hear the entire album—or at least, some version of it. The rise of Napster, and other digital file-sharing services, at the turn of the century meant bootlegs that had previously circulated amongst a small network of traders could now be sent around the world with a mouse click. And one of those bootlegs was a series of songs from Hatfield's lost masterpiece.

Her response was an understandably tortured ambivalence that continues to this day. During an online chat with Launch.com in 2001, she reacted angrily to a question about the bootlegging of *God's Foot*. "Screw Napster! Screw them, it's not fair! It's not what I want on there! It could be bad mixes, it could be songs I don't want on the album, and I'm offended deeply by this," she said.[12] But, talking to the Boston Phoenix's Brett Milano that same year, she offered a more measured view:

> I have mixed feelings about that. I feel offended by what I see is a violation of my rights and my property. The version on there has a completely random sequence, and there's songs on it that I didn't want people to hear. But there's a thin line between right and wrong. After Jeff Buckley died and the record [*Sketches for My Sweetheart, the Drunk*] came out, I knew Jeff wouldn't have wanted that—but I bought it anyway.[13]

Looking back now, Hatfield says, "It's all so bizarre to me, because when you say 'it,' 'it' doesn't really exist. It was never officially completed and compiled. I just had this bunch of songs and a title. And someone out there put together sequences, with songs I may not have wanted on there." However, it's also clear she still wants the songs to be heard. "I should finally put together . . . I should just leak a version onto the Internet," she says.

It's an idea she's discussed with Todd Phillips, who has counseled her against it. "If she could find someone to put it out now, it'd be an event. Not to mention," he adds, "the possibility of a lawsuit if the album were leaked." The first idea has occurred to Hatfield, who admits she's considered approaching Hollywood Records—the Walt

Disney–owned label that acquired Mammoth in 2003—about buying back the album. So has the second possibility, although Hatfield notes bitterly—and perhaps correctly—that "if I did release a version, I doubt if anyone at Disney would even notice."

But she laughs when she considers the idea of "lighting a fire under Mickey Mouse's ass," and generating renewed interest in her great lost work. It's a good laugh, an infectious laugh—a laugh that suggests one day we might all be able to put our arms, or at least our headphones, around some of Juliana Hatfield's finest melodies. A laugh that suggests one day, she'll be out from under *God's Foot* at last.

Juliana Hatfield: *God's Foot*
Recorded for: *Mammoth/Atlantic Records*
Scheduled release date: *1997*
Recorded at: *Dreamland, Woodstock, NY; Fort Apache Studios, Cambridge, MA; 1995–97*

TRACK LISTING (original version, according to Todd Phillips):

1. Fade Away
2. Mountains of Love
3. What Have I Done to You
4. You Can't Put Your Arms Around a Melody
5. Chance Is Waiting

6. How Would You Know
7. Don't Need a Reason
8. Charity
9. Eye to Eye
10. Jake's

Also recorded: *"Perfection," "Losing Your Looks," "I Didn't Know,"*
"Takin' It Easy," "Can't Kill Myself," "Number One"

Produced by: *Juliana Hatfield*
Engineered by: *Dave Cook*

Credits:
Juliana Hatfield—*vocals, guitars, bass, piano*
Todd Phillips—*drums*

Guest artists:
Tony Marsico—*bass*
Greg "Smokey" Hormel—*guitar, pedal steel*
Lisa Mednick—*keyboards on "I Didn't Know"*
Joan Wasser—*violin on "Mountains of Love"*
Jason Hatfield—*backing vocals on "Don't Need a Reason" and*
"Eye to Eye"
Rick Gilbert—*pedal steel?*

⑩ Should've-Beens, Never-Weres, and Still-Might-Bes

*D*espite our natural tendency to overrate them, not all unreleased albums are created equal. Some of them have stayed lost for very good reasons (especially the ones that never existed in the first place). Still others never became mythic because only a handful of fans ever realized they had been committed to tape.

And many other unreleased albums, when one has the chance to hear them, are not dissimilar from the vast majority of recorded music put out each week: they are equal parts the good, the bad, and the mediocre. Perhaps they have not earned legendary, or even great, status;

still, they may boast some interesting anecdote that has been buried and deserves retelling.

During my research for this book, I came across lost albums of all types, including albums that fit into one (or more) of the categories mentioned above. In this chapter, I have tried to tell as many of their stories as possible. If one or two might have been more fun left as legend, I hope that what is revealed about the others will make up for it.

Kraftwerk
There's No Pop Like Techno Pop

So many "great lost albums" exist in the realm of pop music myth that the law of averages dictates that at least a few must be imposters, faux Bigfoots in gorilla suits. The Beastie Boys' *White House*, mentioned in Chapter 6, is one example. Another is *Techno Pop*. This mid-'80s release from German electronic music pioneers Kraftwerk has become part of the group's legend—thanks in part to their also-legendary secrecy.

Author Pascal Bussy did his best to tackle *Techno Pop* head-on in his excellent 1993 biography of the band, *Kraftwerk: Man, Machine and Music.* However, two years later he admitted he had found Kraftwerk "more mysterious than ever" on the subject. "So mysterious that at one point I had the feeling that this album never really existed!"[1]

It was a prescient observation. "I must say it very clearly: There was never a *Techno Pop* album," declares Kraftwerk's former drummer and percussionist, Wolfgang Flür. "There was just a song with this title."[2]

In fact, founding band member Ralf Hütter had suggested as much in 2004. Speaking to *The Scotsman*'s Stephen Dalton while doing a rare interview, in support of Kraftwerk's first new album in almost two decades, Hütter remarked in passing that *Techno Pop* was much ado about nothing.

"We were working on an album concept *Techno Pop*, but the composition was developed and we just changed the titles," he explained.[3] The material developed for this project, he continued, was simply absorbed into the group's album *Electric Café*, which saw official release in 1986.

That should have been the end of the story. But, given the group's less-than-forthright release of information over the years, doubt persisted. After all, fans have been searching Düsseldorf for the location of Kraftwerk's Kling Klang Studio for decades, and mechanical doppelgangers are occasionally sent to fill in for the band at press conferences and concerts. Was Hütter's confession just another Kraftwerkian cover-up?

According to Flür, it was not. If little has been revealed about *Techno Pop* over the years, the reason may be found in the other details he relates about this troubled era in Kraftwerk history. It was a period that began with the group returning to Germany, exhausted but triumphant, after a global tour in support of the 1981 album *Computer World*.

Kraftwerk was more popular then ever, but Hütter and cofounder Florian Schneider were increasingly protective of the all-electronic sound they had developed. It had become massively influential, especially in the U.K., where synth-pop groups like Depeche Mode, Soft Cell, and the Human League had successfully adapted Kraftwerk's guitarless aesthetic. Yet when potential collaborators, including David Bowie and Michael Jackson, approached Hütter and Schneider about the possibility of a partnership, they were turned away. "Ralf and Florian didn't want to mix different styles and images," explains Flür, via e-mail. "They wanted to stay as unique, as German as possible." That was a disappointment to Flür and the quartet's fourth member, electronic percussionist Karl Bartos. "Karl and I were not so much amused," Flür admits. "Additional fun we surely would have had."

Instead of fun, according to Flür, there was an increasing state of paralysis within the group. Following the *Computer World* tour, the members of Kraftwerk had understandably gone their separate ways for a time, and Flür enjoyed the holiday, leisurely touring Europe in his new, blue Daimler Benz 220b. However, Hütter and Schneider had developed a passion for bicycling that became more than just a hobby: it shoved all thoughts of the group out of the picture. Hütter especially began to exhibit signs of obsession, shaving and waxing his legs like a professional cyclist and spending increasing amounts of time on the mountain passes of the Alps. Maxime Schmitt, a longtime friend and head of Kraftwerk's French label, remembered, "Ralf had a tendency to go too far with the bicycle. Sometimes we were riding in the mountains for 200 kilometers, having done two or three passes in the Dolomites, I would stop but he would carry on doing some more passes, and he wouldn't get back until well after sunset."[4]

This new pursuit was reflected in "Tour de France," the lone song Kraftwerk worked on during 1982 at the mysterious Kling Klang. However, Flür recalls that during this period he and Bartos "were waiting thousands of times in the studio after dark—waiting for Ralf and Florian. I claim that Ralf and Florian had lost interest in their own musical project then.

"From my view, with the *Computer World* album and tour we were over the peak of our creativity. And passion. A very important point!" he adds. "Florian had annoyed Karl, Ralf, and me during the extended tour all too often with his craziness and listlessness. . . . Circumstances inside the group had changed, furthermore, and led to very strenuous and half-hearted meetings."

Circumstances weren't improved when Hütter, riding without a helmet, suffered a serious cycling accident in 1982, fracturing his skull and lapsing briefly into a coma. When all four members of Kraftwerk were finally able to regroup at Kling Klang, they had another problem to address. A new keyboard called the Emulator was helping usher in the era of digital sampling, which allowed musicians to manipulate sound with unprecedented ease. The computer world Kraftwerk had sung about just a couple of years earlier was here, and a group that had built its career on a futuristic, cutting-edge image could hardly afford to ignore this advance. They would have to master this technology before showing their faces (or at least, their robots' faces) to the world again.

"No one today can feel with us what it meant to us then recognizing the range and future which a music sampler could open us," says Flür. "We had to learn new technique and try the magic device for a long time. We then used it for diverse songs on our new album for natural sounds—a process which was absolutely new in Kraftwerk music." The song "Tour de France," which had been nearly completed before Hütter's accident, would be reworked, with sampled bicycle noises and breathing added to its rhythm track.

But, as the group began experimenting with sampled sound, another complication arose. Hütter and Schneider might have turned down a chance to collaborate with Michael Jackson, and they might have taken a dim view of the unauthorized samples of Kraftwerk's "Numbers" and "Trans-Europe Express" used in Afrika Bambaataa's 1982 hip-hop classic "Planet Rock."[5] But they were still periodic club-goers with a fascination for American funk and soul. "The Isley Brothers; James Brown; Earth, Wind and Fire; the Commodores; George Clinton—all such artists and bands had a pretty good funk in their rhythms which we admired and which we used to dance to in discotheques," says Flür. "And we wanted to have similar funk in our music too. We could consume it, but weren't able to produce funk. It was, for example, one reason why we engaged coproducers and mixers for the first time in Kraftwerk music."

The insular Hütter and Schneider would turn to producer and remixer Francois Kevorkian, a French-born New Yorker who had DJed in legendary disco clubs like the Paradise Garage and Studio 54. Kevorkian did a remix of "Tour de France," which was released as a single in 1983 and was even featured during a memorable dance sequence in the film "Breakin'" the following year. Afterward, Kevorkian would play an even greater role, Flür says, creating sounds and rhythms for Kraftwerk's next album.

It was a release Hütter believed should carry some conceptual weight.

I remember that we often listened to the Eagles' *Hotel California*. Similar to the Beach Boys[6]—Ralf was very impressed by U.S. groups who brought the real

American sound and lifestyle. Ralf's idea and hope was having a record equipped with an image, a word, a slogan or title like *Hotel California*, for instance, or anything similar to the Beach Boys' image.

Coming up with such an evocative title took some time. "For a new album there were different names in all members' mouths," recalls Flür. "First it was *Technicolour*. This name was rejected because of the same-sounding name of an U.S. film company, and it surely would have given legal problems with the company. *Techno Pop* was the next title, which I preferred."

Hütter, however, was not so sure. "What Ralf didn't like on it was the syllable *pop*," contends Flür. "'Pop' sounded too average to a group's image like Kraftwerk. Too much general!" It was a moment of indecision that was mirrored in the fate of the music. Album artwork and even a catalog number for *Techno Pop* had been prepared by the band's label, EMI, as early as 1983, but Hütter's accident and convalescence—which took as long as a year, according to Flür and Bartos—made that schedule impossible to meet. Analog versions of the songs "Techno Pop" and "Sex Object" had apparently been recorded in Düsseldorf; however, when this material was taken to New York's Power Station for mixing sometime in 1984 or 1985, Hütter lost his nerve when faced with the new digital technology that was becoming standard issue.

Karl Bartos would claim that an entire version of the album was abandoned at this point and redone digitally, although to date no further evidence of this has come to light via bootleg.[7] The two, presumably analog recordings that have surfaced are the proverbial mixed bag. A shorter version of "Techno Pop," which clocks in at four and a half minutes instead of nearly eight, is far punchier, bearing a marked similarity to "Tour de France," with its cycling rhythm and pastoral melody. But the reworked "Sex Object" that wound up on *Electric Café* is a vast improvement; the original is missing its faux string arrangement and pop polish, spotlighting an awkward, synthesized slap bass instead.

The most important point, according to Flür, is that there were no lost songs. "I can tell you that there was and is no other material," he says, "for a *Techno Pop* album." The new songs that were written—including "Boing Boom Tschak" and "Musique Non Stop"—were created to replace "Tour de France," which Hütter and Schneider had already decided not to include. Those two tracks would join another new composition, which would embody the album concept for which Hütter had been searching.

The origin of the name "Electric Café" is uncertain, but when it emerged, Flür says, it was immediately adopted as the new album's title, a proud declaration of the group's Teutonic techno-wizardry.

> We knew what we had delivered the world, against this all-American sound and style—technology and electronics! This was special German. The spirit of researching and inventing. It was in Kraftwerk. We were whol[ly] electric! We had to have this word on our album then, in any way or form. These thoughts were the birth of the *Electric Café* album and song.

Years of relative inactivity, however, had worn on Bartos and Flür, the latter in particular. "I will say that from my view it was especially Karl who was most responsible that actually anything came out of Kling Klang those years. Karl had his own home studio, and he often brought themes and parts from there to the Kling Klang [in the] evenings to convince Ralf and Florian for further work.

"I myself went to the studio more and more rarely. I didn't like the new themes too much," Flür adds. "For me the new songs were 'cold coffee,' as we say in Germany, nothing for 'moving the world.'"

Many reviewers would agree when *Electric Café*, barely half an hour in length, finally appeared in 1986. The group's previous belief that it could consume, but not produce, funk, seemed ironic now: by attempting to assimilate trends like digital recording and hip-hop-influenced rhythms, Kraftwerk was not only imitating its imitators, it had sacrificed the singular Germanic groove that had attracted those imitators in the first place. "Even Kraftwerk fans," wrote Ira Robbins in the *Trouser Press Record Guide*, "will find this brief album disappointingly short on ideas and content."[8]

Now that the album was completed and an even more pronounced inactivity loomed, Wolfgang Flür realized there was no longer any point in living as one of Hütter and Schneider's showroom dummies. It was a point driven home when he watched the band mime in the shadows of the noir-style video for the album's single, "The Telephone Call." "Karl sings in the song. 'You're so close but far away.' How true he was then!" The distance between Bartos and Flür, and Kraftwerk's founders, had become an unbridgeable gulf.

"I myself did not write music or lyrics then, and—as an electric drummer—I had to admit that there was no further work and perspective in the group for me," Flür says. "No future at all.

"I had to rescue myself from the robots and find the power and courage to do it. I was very hesitating, believe me. The time was horrible. I had lots of nightmares about it because I had no idea what to do right afterwards. I fell into a sort of vacuum."

It was a space that later would be filled with Flür's 2001 autobiography, *I Was a Robot*, which detailed the surprising sexcapades of his old, buttoned-down band, and by an even more surprising resumption of his musical career. Pursuing a warm, electronic sound reminiscent of classic Kraftwerk, Flür's Yamo scored several successes on the German club charts. The time would also be filled with continued disagreements with his old bandmates; an angry Flür told Hütter and Schneider he felt their digital reworking of Kraftwerk hits on 1991's *The Mix* was an abomination, and he was in turn sued by the duo for allegations made in his autobiography. He claims no regrets: "I had no other chance but leaving the band and paving a new path. Any path!"

Meanwhile, the album that never was may at last become a reality. In 2004, it was reported that Kraftwerk would issue a limited-edition box set containing remastered versions of its eight studio albums; *Electric Café*, it was claimed, would revert to its original title of *Techno Pop*.

That historical rethink has not yet emerged from behind the hidden cloister of Kling Klang. However, that *Techno Pop*'s resurrection has been considered at all is proof, perhaps, that even robots aren't immune to the seductive myth of the great lost album.

Beck
Scraps the Vultures Left Behind

"When you're on a major label, you put out albums on the two- or three-year plan. But it's not like it takes three years to write ten songs," says singer, songwriter, and pop provocateur Beck. "I can write 200 songs in three years. And I've never really reconciled what to do with all the extra music."[9]

Which is why Beck says he has no fewer than five full albums reposing in his archives. And that doesn't count homemade folk and blues efforts from early in his career—like 1988's *Banjo Story*, or *Fresh Meat + Old Slabs*, a collection recorded as a gift for his mother—which have never seen official release.

One disc from that lost quintet is a moody 1994 album of orchestral folk, created as a response to those who believed Beck's ramshackle hip-hop hit "Loser" pegged him as a mere slacker novelty.[10] But perhaps the most intriguing of the five missing discs is a scrapped companion piece to the 1999 outing *Midnite Vultures*.

Vultures was slated to be the official successor[11] to 1996's *Odelay*, on which Beck and the Dust Brothers created a sample-strewn soundscape that drew from nearly every musical style and won its creators rave reviews. It was a tough act to follow, and the hedonistic '70s and '80s dance music of *Vultures*—even though it won a "Best Album" Grammy nomination—didn't strike quite the same chord with reviewers or fans. The disc would eventually go gold, a far cry from the double-platinum success of *Odelay*.

Meanwhile, Beck did himself no favors when he described the new album, prior to its release, as "a party record with dumb sounds and dumb songs and dumb lyrics," leaving himself an easy target for those who still believed he was the cynical poster boy for Generation X. *Vultures* drew heavily from Prince's textbook of falsetto soul, but it also included his sly sense of humor—something a lot of listeners missed amidst the apparently rampant, and remorseless, libido.

"I just thought people hated that record. It was so misunderstood," laments Beck. But one of the reasons for its rocky reception, he believes, is that it did not appear in the form he had intended. *Vultures*, he reveals, was supposed to have been a double album, but his label, Geffen—with whom he'd clashed the year before—balked, forcing Beck to leave a full disc of fifteen songs on the cutting room floor. "I think one of the problems with [*Vultures*]," he offers, "was that it didn't have all those extra songs to explain the whole picture."

And that full picture, as Beck describes it now, would have been an intriguing one, to say the least. "We had songs with Johnny Marr [of the Smiths] playing guitar on them," he recalls. "There's all this electronic stuff. There's two songs with [rapper] Kool Keith. There's just a whole world of stuff on there."

The material was so strong, in fact, that Beck planned to release the second disc the following year as a follow-up to *Midnite Vultures*, "kind of like what Radiohead ended up doing with *Kid A*." The muted reaction to *Vultures*, however, dampened his enthusiasm for the project.

"I was gonna get it out, but I ended up after that just taking a year or two off and traveling. I'd been on tour for about seven years straight, so the idea of jumping back in and releasing the album at that point was just kind of . . . " he says, his voice trailing off. "And after that . . . I was just more in the mood to do *Sea Change*, you know?"

It proved to be the right move, as that 2002 collection earned Beck back any respect he'd lost with *Midnite Vultures*, and became his first Top 10 album to boot. But as he talks about his missing, turn-of-the-century musical treasures, he warms to the subject. "All those [unreleased] albums are not quite finished or a little bit flawed, but there's just all this extra stuff, and I don't know what to do with it," he sighs. "It's just one of the predicaments with the way the music business is set up. So I now really wanna read this book!"

Brian Wilson
Sheer Insanity

"You know who Brian Wilson is, right?" Matt Dike asks.[12] If that seems like an odd question, you have to consider that Dike may still be wondering who Brian Wilson really is, himself.

When the former producer of the Beastie Boys came face-to-face with the former leader of the Beach Boys in 1988, the man who wrote "Surf's Up" was in many ways at low tide. After years of well-documented drug abuse, crippling ailments, and flat-out insanity, Wilson had apparently cleaned up his act. No longer a morbidly obese 350 pounds, Wilson was now a health nut. The creator of the most famous unreleased album in history, who had simply abandoned his masterpiece, *Smile*, had just released his official solo debut and was at work on the follow-up to that well-received effort.

But all the activity masked a deeper malaise. The man who had pulled Wilson back from the brink in the mid-'70s, the psychologist Eugene Landy, had essentially taken over the singer's life as well. And he was doing more than just closely monitoring every movement of his most famous patient. In 1984, Landy had bragged about how his twenty-four-hour therapy had made him incredibly close to Wilson. "I'm practically a member of his band," Landy had confided.[13] It was an omen—and, in the view of many Wilson fans, a bad one.

Landy had helped stage-manage a feat previously thought impossible: he'd gotten Wilson in good enough mental and physical shape to record his first solo album. However, he'd wanted a much larger role on *Brian Wilson* than anyone at Wilson's label, Sire Records, was prepared to allow. Largely thwarted in his efforts to get Wilson to record his own lyrics, Landy was taking no chances now. For Wilson's next album, the good doctor had assumed full control, much to the chagrin of Sire.

When Matt Dike was tapped to work on the project, he was not only the record-spinning king of Los Angeles's nightclub scene, he had become the city's hottest producer as well, thanks to the work he, the Dust Brothers, and Mario Caldato Jr. had done on hip-hop hits by Tone-Loc and Young MC. But when he got a call inviting him to a Brian Wilson recording session, Dike was ecstatic. "They said, 'Brian Wilson wants to do something with you,' and I was like, 'Unbelievable, man!'"

There's more than a little irony in Dike's involvement, brief as it was, with the recording. After the release of the Beastie Boys' *Paul's Boutique* in 1989, Dike would be hailed as a genius, a producer whose psychedelic sampled collages made him the hip-hop heir to

Brian Wilson's creative legacy. Yet, by the early '90s, Dike himself would follow in some of Wilson's less-advisable footsteps.

He became a virtual recluse within his Hollywood apartment, crammed with records and all manner of '70s memorabilia. Battling his own substance-abuse demons, Dike cut all ties to longtime friends, who traded stories about him. They whispered about the food a few remaining intimates would throw over his electric fence, in an effort to make sure he was fed. Or about the time Dike's habit of dropping bags of trash out his window accidentally foiled a robbery; the would-be burglar was allegedly leaving Dike's apartment with his TV when a flying sack of garbage stopped him cold.

But in 2005, Dike emerged briefly from seclusion to reminisce about his career, in which Brian Wilson played a short but memorable role. A student of all types of music, Dike is every bit as enthusiastic about the Beach Boys as the Beasties. "I was really into the Beach Boys' psychedelic era—*Pet Sounds* and 'Good Vibrations' and all that stuff they did around that time," he says excitedly. "That period, I think, is unbelievably cool."

Still, he remembers the 1988 meeting when that enthusiasm suffered at least a temporary hit. When he arrived at the studio, Dike discovered the ubiquitous Dr. Landy behind the recording console, and Wilson lying prone on a couch, "almost comatose. He must've had a stroke or something, because only half of his face and only half of his body was moving. I couldn't believe my eyes. This was a completely surreal situation.

"And Landy is a complete gonzo freak. He's pulling all the strings," Dike adds. "And he says, 'OK, hey, we've got this concept: we're doing a rap song for Brian.' And I went, 'What?!' I mean, for a few minutes I really thought I was on *Candid Camera*."

It was no joke. Several songs have surfaced from the *Sweet Insanity* sessions suggesting that Wilson's muse was still very much intact and functioning. One was a belated duet with Bob Dylan called "The Spirit of Rock 'n' Roll," while three of the better tunes from the disc—"Don't Let Her Know She's an Angel," "Make a Wish," and "Rainbow Smile," which Wilson described as a personal favorite—were filled with the wistful innocence of classic Beach Boys material, and were rerecorded years later for the 2004 album *Gettin' In Over My Head*.

But the track Landy and Wilson were hoping Dike would help produce was a trifle different. In fact, it's fair to say that there is no composition in the Beach Boys' or Brian Wilson's history that has inspired as much enmity as "Smart Girls." Dike recalls,

> They play this song for me. Apparently, what it was, was that Landy was so on his own dick at this point that he had written all the music and the lyrics. And had convinced Brian to rap along with this song.
>
> It was unbelievably embarrassing. It's this swing drum machine beat, and this goofy keyboard going "doot-doot-doot." Like, trying to be Jazzy Jeff, but so not even Jazzy Jeff. And the lyrics—this was Eugene Landy's way of being clever—every line had some kind of a Beach Boys reference. You know like, "Wish they all could be / smart girls."

Dike's description is only the half of it. Even years later, there's simply no way to prepare oneself for the crudely sampled Beach Boys hits, or for Brian's opening declaration, "My name is Brian and I'm the man / I write hit songs with a wave of my hand / Songs of surf and sun and sand / I make great music with my band." And that's before the realization hits that "Smart Girls" was intended to be a proto-feminist disavowal of the Beach Boys' entire back catalog: "All the songs I used to write / Talked about girls who weren't too bright." Now imagine Matt Dike hearing it all for the first time, with its creators waiting expectantly nearby.

"So finally they turn to me and they're like, 'Whaddya think?' And Brian Wilson gets up and kinda lumbers over to me, and he's like, 'We're gonna make *so much* money on this! We're gonna make *millions!*'

"And I'm thinking, 'What are you, fucking *nuts*?!' That's what I feel like saying. But instead I said, 'I'm a really big fan of the Beach Boys. And Brian, you gotta sing, man! People wanna hear you sing. This rap thing is just really not happening,'" recalls Dike. "I tried to explain it as delicately as I could, and they both just looked at me like, 'What the fuck do you know?' They just stared at me, like, 'You don't wanna be part of our million-dollar scheme?!'"

While *Sweet Insanity* would not provide a vehicle for the release of "Smart Girls," the song would eventually see a moment of daylight. In 2006, a writer for *LA Weekly* uncovered an old cassette single of the song,[14] which apparently had been used to help promote Wilson's 1991 autobiography *Wouldn't It Be Nice.*

That book was viewed by many observers as having been at least partially ghostwritten by Landy, and the cassette served as a reminder of a time when his influence over Wilson appeared to be absolute. The insert of the cassette listed songwriting credits for Wilson, Landy, and the doctor's girlfriend, Alexandra Morgan; the tune was described as being presented by "Brains and Genius," the punningly bad name of Landy and Wilson's partnership. According to the text, Wilson evidently gave out 250 of the cassingles as gifts during Christmas of 1990; it's rewarding to imagine the reaction of the lucky recipients.

It was Dike, however, who received the very first copy of this song that will live in infamy. Before taking his disillusioned leave from the studio, he thought to ask for a dub of the track. "Because I'm thinking, 'No one will believe this in a million years!'" Dike laughs. "And I still have it. And I still don't believe it."

Sheryl Crow
This Bird Has Flown

The night Hugh Padgham accepted a demo tape from the girl he'd just met at a mud-wrestling club, he was almost without peer as a producer. He had pulled off one of the most difficult feats in the music business—helping a solo act eclipse a well-known former band—not once, but twice, as Sting and Phil Collins become instantly recognizable brand names on his watch. And Padgham also had credits with both singers' old acts, the Police and Genesis—as well as David Bowie, Peter Gabriel, and Paul McCartney.

But before he was done working with Sheryl Crow, the tables would turn on the polite and talented Englishman. The 1992 debut album he prepared for Crow would be rejected at her request, as the then-unknown session singer found the clout to override the work of one of pop's best-known boardsmen.

"The thing is, I've been in the music business long enough to know that you win some and you lose some. And I can still say with pride that I'm the one who got Sheryl signed in the first place," says Padgham, during a break from sessions in London.[15]

Padgham's discovery of Crow would occur under somewhat bizarre circumstances. "What happened was this: I was working with Sting at A&M studios, and we got asked out one night to see a Billy Idol gig. And we couldn't go because we were working, but we were also asked to go to the afterparty, which was at a mud-wrestling club on Sunset Strip somewhere," Padgham recalls.

> And we went to this party, Sting and myself and Sting's assistant, and this girl starts shouting to me. And I knew her, because she was a friend of Phil Collins's then-wife. And she had in tow with her, Sheryl. So we got them in with us, and started talking, and it turned out that Sheryl was a singer and had these demo tapes. And I said, "Why don't you drop them round to the studio, then?"

Padgham would discover that the Missouri-born Crow was already a session singer of note, who had toured with Michael Jackson and, most recently, as part of Don Henley's *End of the Innocence* revue. But she had been frustrated with the few solo offers she'd received, most of which envisioned her as a dance-pop diva. After he listened to the demo Crow had recorded with St. Louis musician Jay Oliver, Padgham knew immediately that she was capable of far more.

"I thought, 'Wow, there's something good here,'" Padgham recalls. He took the tape to David Anderle, A&M's vice-president of A&R, "and he listened to it and thought it was great, and he took it to Jerry Moss," the cofounder of A&M. "Jerry Moss basically said, 'If Hugh wants to do it, you should sign her.' Because I was Mr. Popular at A&M at the time, with my success with Sting."

Crow would sign a two-album deal that spring, and work began that autumn on her debut at A&M Studios in Hollywood. The budget was a quarter-million dollars, but the game plan for the album was simple, according to Padgham. "All we did, really, once the record company had agreed to sign her, was took the demos and tarted them up," he says, "because that was deemed a quick and cheap way to do this album."

With Crow playing piano and Hammond organ, and with a mixture of her own musicians and Padgham's hand-picked session pros—including drummer Vinnie Colaiuta and guitarist Dominic Miller, two stalwart members of Sting's band, and virtuoso fretless bassist Pino Palladino—work began on the transformation of Crow and Oliver's eight-track demos. The participants soon found the change wouldn't be as easy as it seemed.

"What you have to realise is that the songs had been incepted in a manner where they were integral with the production," Oliver would later say.

> The material had been written using my studio gear, and I had a certain way of playing and working with these interesting sounds that were purely synthetic. They kind of sounded like drums and kind of sounded like guitars, but they couldn't be replaced by humans. They had their own identity and were never intended as substitutes for human tracks. Because of the nature

of the sound, because of the way it was played, and because it was quantised by a computer, it just had a characteristic that couldn't be reproduced in any other way. If you tried to play it, the result wasn't as good; it sounded watered down.

What's more, all of that stuff that I did had a dated production sensibility, and therefore—although I wasn't cognisant of this—Sheryl, Hugh, and David Anderle were all saying, "That's good, but we need to be cutting-edge. We need to do something new," and in retrospect I would have said the same thing. I don't think anyone said it was bad, but where they went wrong was trying to keep the same songs and replace everything with real instruments to make them work. That was a mistake, the wrong move. They tried to take something and turn it into something else, and by the time it became something else it was so watered down that it had not only lost the integrity of the original demos, but it was also just plain confusing. There was no focus in any way.[16]

The effect of all this was, in the minds of many listeners, that Padgham had made Crow sound "too slick"—that he had essentially made a Genesis and Phil Collins record with Crow as the lead singer. It is a criticism that still rankles, especially given that Crow had been awarded a coproduction credit.

"One of the things that sort of pissed me off is that sometimes, I would get the blame for making this 'perfect record.' And she was every bit as involved in making the record as I was," he points out. "It's true, a lot of those Phil Collins records that were hits *were* very kind of produced. But that was the '80s thing. That was what we did then. I mean, I've four Grammies between Sting and Phil Collins, y'know what I mean?

"I'm not saying that I'm not to blame to some extent. I just did what I thought it took to make the best sort of record with those songs at the time."

Another sore spot for Padgham was Crow's constant use of ex-Eagle Don Henley—who would also appear as her duet partner on the ballad "What Does It Matter"—as a sounding board. It was, Padgham thought, a dependence that was starting to have negative effects on the record—especially since Henley had his own ideas about the direction his former backup singer should be taking. "I remember that my relationship with Sheryl was getting a bit strained, because she felt that she was making a record that had to be okayed by Don Henley the whole time," says Padgham. "And that pissed me off as well. So at the end of the day, I was spending days and days mixing songs, when I was overdue to be going home to my family. Because I didn't live in L.A."

As the sessions progressed, Padgham would also have his doubts about some of the material. "I thought there were half a dozen really good songs, for sure," he says. The clear standout, he thought, was "Father Son," a keyboard-dominated number about redemption. Crow evidently agreed, as she continued to play the song well after the accompanying album had been shelved; country star Wynonna Judd also covered "Father Son"—retitled "Father Sun"—the following year.

However, "at the end of the day, we were still two or three songs shy, so she'd written some more songs. And some of those were probably not up to the same standard," says Padgham. "I would be the first person to say that if you listen to that record as a whole, I think a third of it is really good, a third of it is all right, and a third of it isn't all right."

Still, when Padgham had completed what he believed were the final mixes of the album and departed for England, he had no idea that his work would never see release. He was also unaware that nervous A&M executives had decided to turn to Jay Oliver and recut a couple of the tracks, hoping he could reproduce the magic of his demos.

"I went back in there for one or two songs that she wanted to re-sing, and I tried to recreate what I had done," Oliver would say. "Hugh wasn't there for that, and so from his perspective it may have been kind of an unauthorised experiment. Later on I was told that, when he heard the results, he immediately dismissed them as unusable, saying the miking wasn't good enough."[17]

Padgham would later learn about this maneuvering behind his back, which also included A&M allowing Crow's boyfriend Kevin Gilbert to remix the album. "Yeah, that was done without my knowledge," he says with a sigh. "I wasn't really pissed off . . . I was just disappointed.

"The only one I'm angry at was Al Cafaro at A&M. Because I don't think he did the decent thing, as the head of that record company, by not ringing me up and telling me what was going on. He's the only one not on my Christmas card list," jokes Padgham.

With recording costs that now approached half a million dollars, A&M executives undoubtedly felt they were in for a penny, in for a pound. Promotional cassettes of Sheryl Crow were prepared, along with a press release that included an amusingly garbled quote from Henley ("She's one of the best female singers there is right now. Period, bar none.") and the following explanation of the album's contents:

> The songs on *Sheryl Crow* were written when her career had reached a temporary impasse and her personal life was at a low. "I wasn't doing sessions. I was barely making the rent," she explains. "A lot of them were written after a three-year, really rocky relationship. . . . They're dark pop songs."
>
> Sometimes dark, always powerful and stirring, *Sheryl Crow* is the work of a movingly original pop music artist.

That movingly original artist would finally get her way, however. The projected release date of September 22 was abandoned, as was the album. Padgham would receive this news long after the fact, as well. "But by that point, I was busy working on other things," he says. One of them was the breakthrough album of another female singer-songwriter; under Padgham's guidance, Melissa Etheridge's 1993 effort *Yes I Am* became a multiplatinum hit.

That year, Crow would also enjoy a breakthrough, via an album she'd recorded with producer and musician Bill Bottrell at his Toad Hall studio in Pasadena. The disc was an outgrowth of an informal songwriting circle at Bottrell's that Crow recognized in her title, *Tuesday Night Music Club*. There would later be claims she had not given some club members—including Kevin Gilbert—sufficient acknowledgment in the credits, a point Padgham can't resist pointing out. "As you well know, there were a lot of politics that went into the making of that *Tuesday Night Music Club* record as well," he says. "And a lot of people didn't end up very happy from that, either."

Still, Padgham insists he remained a fan of Crow's work. The next time their paths would cross was at the 1995 Grammy Awards, where *Tuesday Night Music Club* racked up a trio of trophies. "And she was kind enough to thank me in her speech, for one of those Grammies she got," he says. "I don't bear any grudges at all."

But he also doesn't believe anyone should expect to see Crow's authentic debut available for official release. Having learned how much clout Crow wielded as a novice artist, he is certain she has more than enough now to ensure that the past stays buried.

"I doubt that it'll get released . . . in her lifetime, anyway," he says, adding with a laugh, "If you know what I'm saying."

Buckethead
Who Needs Mouse Ears?

There are millions of Disney fans around the world, but it's hard to imagine a more singular admirer than Brian Carroll. In his alter ego as the enigmatic guitar prodigy Buckethead, Carroll is never seen without a mask and KFC bucket on his head, and only speaks through a rubber hand puppet named Herbie.

He has played alongside Bootsy Collins, John Zorn, and Axl Rose, earning the ire of the latter by quitting Guns N' Roses shortly before the 2004 Rock in Rio festival. And Ozzy Osbourne, who knows a thing or three about being hard to work with, threw up his hands after auditioning Buckethead for his band. "I met with him and asked him to work with me but only if he got rid of the fucking bucket. So I came back a bit later and he's wearing this green fucking Martian's-hat thing!" Osbourne said. "He told me his name was Brian, so I said that's what I'd call him. He says, 'No one calls me Brian except my mother.' So I said, 'Pretend I'm your mum then!'"[18]

But beneath the fried-chicken bucket, and the china-doll mask inspired by *Halloween*'s Michael Myers, is a shy, lanky kid most comfortable in his own imaginary world. Growing up in the shadow of Disneyland, where he loved to melt into the crowds at the Haunted Mansion or the Pirates of the Caribbean ride, the template Brian Carroll picked for his personal universe was an obvious choice.[19]

"Disneyland was the greatest city he'd ever been to. Everybody was nice, they talked to him and sang songs, and they moved more realistically than his friends in the cemetery," reads one version of Buckethead's official biography. But, allegedly frustrated in his ambition to become one of Disney's animatronic characters, he was forced to create his own theme park—Bucketheadland—instead.

"Well if he couldn't live in Disneyland he had to live some-where. He knew that if he built a park like Mr. Disney did, people all around the world would come visit him," his bio continues. "Or even if they didn't, the park would be full of his audio-animatronic friends. He'd allow chickens inside, and he'd build a huge cemetery in the middle with the statues and tombstones specially lined up to create the best acoustics."[20]

However, the responsibilities of designing and maintaining this one-of-a-kind park aside, Buckethead has never stopped loving its inspiration. In 2005, he even arranged for a tour in support of his solo album *Enter the Chicken* to begin in Orlando, the home of Disney World, and concluded it in Anaheim, not far from Disneyland.

For the better part of a decade, he has also been at work on a more permanent tribute to the genius of Walt Disney. An album full of his versions of Disney songs has been publicly discussed since the late '90s; in 1997, *Buckethead Plays Disney* was announced by saxophonist John Zorn's Avant label, and even got its own catalog number (Avan 053).

The disc never appeared and was later listed by Avant as "canceled," but Buckethead has continued to tinker with it. In an interview with Riffage, he claimed he'd been working on the album when his interviewer had called, and revealed that he'd abandoned one complete version. "Hopefully [it will come out] early in the year, because it's been a long, long time. I just was never happy [with it]. I did it and I didn't like it and I just kept [working on it]," he explained. "But now I'm just gonna do it and let it be, and I'll just make another one if I don't like it."[21]

Despite those encouraging words, the album still didn't materialize, although Buckethead—that is, Herbie—continued to talk about it to interviewers, confessing to MTV's Kurt Loder in 2004 that "When You Wish Upon a Star," from *Pinocchio*, was one of his favorite songs. And he has done live versions of at least a couple of other Disney tunes, faithfully reprising "A Pirate's Life for Me" and "Grim Grinning Ghosts," the twangy theme from his beloved Haunted Mansion.[22]

Recently, Buckethead, with Herbie's help, was ready to talk about his lost Disney album again. But not, however, before bemoaning Disney's recent practice of adding characters from *The Nightmare Before Christmas* to the Haunted Mansion during the holidays. "It bothers me when they alter the mansion. It feels like a phantom limb or something," he complains. "Why can't they just build an attraction solely based on *The Nightmare Before Christmas* and leave the mansion alone? That would be better, cause they could make a great Nightmare ride."[23]

That problem aside, Buckethead says he is once again at work on his Disney masterpiece. "That has been a tough one," he admits.

> I scrapped a couple [versions] already, but finally I think I got it. It will still take some time, but my idea now is to make my own soundtrack for my favorite rides. You could put it on an a cassette or whatever with headphones and go on certain rides.
>
> I have already done it a bunch of times—like on Space Mountain I listened to some wedge[24] off *Cuckoo Clocks*[25] and it was like, "Woooo!" Then there would be a mutated version of some ride songs. Also a storyline too, and (when you) go on the certain ride, there would be a different sound. That is what I am working on now.

It's hard not to speculate that Buckethead will keep working on his Disney music for some time to come. He has admitted it's his most precious personal project, one he has consequently been reluctant to let go. And indeed, his Disney fixation is one of the main components of his bizarrely successful musical persona. "I can work anything into that character and make it totally work: all the things I love in my life, like Disney, Giant Robot, Texas Chainsaw. Even though I'm wearing a mask and have a character, it's more real, more about what I'm really like, because I'm too shy to let a lot of things out," he acknowledged in a rare candid moment some years ago. "Every reason I became Buckethead and am Buckethead has to do with the way I live. It's not because I thought it would be successful. I never use anything that isn't part of what I really loved as a child or love right now."[26]

But if the release of *Buckethead Plays Disney* isn't exactly imminent, the masked guitarist is happy to try compensating with a little advice, drawn from the days he allegedly spent growing up in a chicken coop.

"Thank you for caring, and remember," he advises, "using old wet hay that is moldy may cause aspergillosis."

Julie Christensen
"The female *Sgt. Pepper*"

"The good news," says Julie Christensen with a chuckle, "is there is life after a failed record."[27]

That's a realization it took Christensen some years to accept. But you might feel the same way if you'd recorded an album your producer called "the female *Sgt. Pepper*," but no one else had ever heard it.

"And if you're an artist or an actor or whatever," adds Christensen, "you just wanna be heard."

Todd Rundgren, who oversaw Christensen's rejected 1990 album, understands a little something about making records. Besides producing Meatloaf's *Bat Out of Hell*, which has sold more than forty million copies since its 1977 release, he counts among his credits the 1987 album *Skylarking*, by the British band XTC. Considered a baroque pop masterpiece, its many Beatlesque hallmarks demonstrate that when Rundgren mentions the Fab Four, he knows of what he speaks.

Not that he means Christensen's debut "sounded anything like *Sgt. Pepper*," he now hastens to add. "Just that she was unlike a lot of female singers, who may be creative in their songwriting and write suitably for their own delivery, but don't really try a broad range of styles. It was her ability to sing with conviction in a variety of approaches that made it extraordinary to me."[28]

If Christensen could have been compared to any artist, Rundgren says, it would have been to Icelandic singer Bjork, "but with a stronger voice. Just beyond the performances, there were a lot of interesting things going on sonically in her music. That, I think, is what's unique about Bjork, as opposed to an artist like Sarah McLachlan."

By the time she had been paired with Rundgren, Christensen already owned a rather diverse résumé. An Iowa native who had moved first to Austin, Texas, and then to Los Angeles to pursue a musical career, Christensen would become one of the two lead vocalists in the bluesy punk band the Divine Horsemen. She would wed the group's other singer, Chris Desjardins, but by the close of the '80s, both the Horsemen and the marriage were over.

Christensen's powerful voice, however, suggested life beyond punk, and had attracted admirers. One of them was Roscoe Beck, the musical director for Canadian songwriter Leonard Cohen, for whom she became a backup singer. But she continued to play solo shows in Los Angeles, looking for a record deal. A&R executive Michael Goldstone, who was on his way to PolyGram and had seen some of Christensen's gigs, would help her get it.

Rundgren doesn't recall how he got Christensen's demo, but he found it "remarkable in a lot of respects." He would agree to work with her, allowing her to use several regulars from her own band, and in 1989 in Los Angeles they embarked on a series of recordings Rundgren remembers as "stressless. She had a real good idea of what she wanted. I only had to coach on the basics: that note was a little flat. It was never exhorting her to get into it."

For Rundgren, who had made a career of expertly replicating nearly any musical style, from disco to prog-rock, the breadth of Christensen's musical interests was invigorating.

> There was one song on the demo that hit me right off, because she just attacked it. It was called "Well Enough," and she did a spectacular job when we rerecorded it. But another song that I really loved was called "Traveling Companion," [which was] almost Enya-like, with full orchestration. And then she did an R&B song called "Thunderhead." She sounded almost like Gladys Knight on that one! She was pretty commanding across a wide range of styles.

However, Goldstone had already left PolyGram for Epic, and Christensen was left vulnerable when PolyGram—which was in the midst of an aggressive series of acquisitions, including the Island and A&M labels—began trimming its own roster. She would be dropped and her album shelved, a casualty of which only a select number of music fans were aware.

One of them was Rundgren, who was "terrifically disappointed. I was angry, that the musical merits seemed not to matter." But his anger would not be enough to win the album its deserved release. The female *Sgt. Pepper* would go on the shelf, and Christensen would try to go on with her life.

That was easier said than done. Other producers had expressed interest in working with her; Phil Ramone had once excitedly told Christensen, " 'You're gonna be the next Barbra Streisand, the next Phoebe Snow,' " recalls Christensen. "And I said, y'know, no. I knew he was gonna want to use his homies. Todd was great about letting me use my own band."

Then there was a meeting with the impresario Miles Copeland that Christensen now remembers as "terrifying. He wanted me to work with William Orbit"—the producer who would go on to helm successful albums by Madonna and Blur. "It was just creepy." Instead, Christensen would finally take hold of her own career, rerecording several of her old songs—"Thunderhead" and "Traveling Companion" included—on a pair of solo albums. *Love Is Driving*, released in 1996, and its follow-up, 2000's *Soul Driver*, both appeared on Christensen's Stone Cupid label, and offered a mature blend of her longtime influences: blues, R&B, jazz, and even country. If the results, compared to the colorful recordings Christensen had made with Rundgren, were more sedate, so was she.

Or at least, she was more at peace. Admitting she once harbored secret fantasies of "fire-bombing the record company," she remembers the day in 1996 when she let those dreams go, just as she'd let go of her album years before.

"I put on some Pearl Jam and slam danced with my son, who was three at the time," Christensen says. "It was such a cathartic moment . . . it was really wonderful."

The Bubbleheads
NWA Meets NWO on a UFO

In front of a fist-pumping audience of thousands, Afrika Islam shouldered his guitar and prepared to hit the opening chord of Nine Inch Nails' "Head Like a Hole," when he was struck by a blinding revelation.

He couldn't hit the opening chord. He couldn't hit any chords, in fact—because he had no idea how to play the guitar.

"The worst thing they did was plug me in," Islam says with a laugh, recalling his brief onstage stint alongside guitarist Vernon Reid and Nine Inch Nails at the first-ever Lollapalooza. "I thought I was gonna be Hendrix, a virtuoso. But it was so bad, I basically turned my guitar down until the end, when I could smash it up.

"And then some reporter from *Rolling Stone* came backstage and was like, 'Man, that was the greatest guitar solo *ever!*' "[29]

From those wrong notes, however, came the beginnings of a surprising harmony: a project that featured a who's who of old-school hip-hop and alternative-rock stars, and attempted to obliterate music's color lines once and for all. You may never have heard of the Bubbleheads, but you've lived through many of their ideas.

"I don't know how," Islam muses, from his studio in Berlin, "you can explain being ahead of your time."

It's still worth trying. Islam's Bubbleheads anticipated three of the most important musical trends of the '90s. They were a DJ-led ensemble that mixed rap and rock long before the half-baked Limp Bizkit. Their lyrics were filled with tales of the pre-millennial angst—UFOs and New World Order conspiracies and other strange signs of the end times—that would soon dominate the decade. And Islam's conception of a nearly virtual band with cartoon alter egos predated by some years the work of outfits like Damon Albarn's Gorillaz.

"We were setting a precedent for something else," agrees Islam, who would oversee the recording of more than two albums' worth of Bubbleheads material. But a variety of factors conspired to keep the music unheard—including, most likely, the controversial ideas that undergirded it. It's quite possible the Bubbleheads' support for conspiracy theories also became the reason their work was relegated to the underground—the sort of self-fulfilling prophecy that feeds the persecution complex of the true believer. But Islam had inarguably tapped into a nexus of musical and cultural hot spots.

A native of the Bronx who had brought the ideals of the Zulu Nation—and some much-needed hip-hop credibility—to the West Coast during the early '80s, Charles Glenn became the DJ and producer of Los Angeles rapper Ice-T. As Afrika Islam, he created a spare, drum machine–driven sound that would become legendary. But he was also interested in the plethora of L.A. bands experimenting with fusions of rap and rock: the Red Hot Chili Peppers, What Is This, Fishbone. It was Trulio Disgracias, a spinoff act from the last band, that helped convince Islam and Ice-T to try taking hip-hop into the mosh pit.

The result, Body Count, would forever be remembered for the 1992 song "Cop Killer," which sparked a national firestorm. But a year before that career-defining moment, the band was invited by Jane's Addiction singer Perry Farrell to join the inaugural Lollapalooza festival, a tour that gathered acts from throughout what was still the underground world of alternative music.

Going on two decades later, it is difficult to appreciate how revolutionary the concept seemed at the time. Putting British punk veterans Siouxsie and the Banshees on the same bill as a black heavy metal act like Living Colour was radical enough. But when Farrell and Ice-T performed their frequent duet on Sly Stone's "Don't Call Me Nigger, Whitey"—or when punk icon Henry Rollins and Ice-T would tackle N.W.A.'s gangsta classic "Fuck tha Police," it was easy to imagine hearing musical walls toppling, over the din of screams and feedback.

Afrika Islam was also struck by these juxtapositions backstage, as he watched the tattooed and muscle-bound Rollins psyching himself up for a set by listening to Public Enemy. "That was the white boy on top of the *white boy* to me," he recalls, "so that showed me something." So did the admiration of Nine Inch Nails' Trent Reznor, who invited Islam onstage with his industrial band. "I was around all these guys," he says, "and I just started wondering, 'How come we don't work together?'"

The Bubbleheads would be his attempt to answer that question. Although its lineup was designed for maximum flexibility, at any time it might have comprised three of hip-hop's most revered figures—Zulu nation founder Afrika Bambaataa, Grandmaster Melle Mel, and Ice-T—as well as the rhythm section of Keith LeBlanc and Doug Wimbish, who added drums and bass to multitudes of early hip-hop hits.

Several members of the Los Angeles funk-rock elite, including bassist Flea, Fishbone's drummer Fish, and former Chili Peppers axeman Arik Marshall, were also Bubbleheads. Keyboardist Bernie Worrell added P-Funk lineage, and Vernon Reid lent his guitar pyrotechnics to the ensemble. Most of Ice-T's Body Count was also present, and Melle Mel and Islam manned the turntables. "It was just a tremendous group of players," Islam says. He had even lined up more guests: LL Cool J, Big Daddy Kane, and—perhaps most surprisingly—Will Smith. That connection came via Benny Medina, the record executive who'd helped launch the solo career of the former Fresh Prince. "Benny Medina was the only brother besides me at all the UFO conventions," explains Islam.

A scaled-down version of the band would give the Bubbleheads a London debut in 1993, opening a gig for the industrial funk band Tackhead. There was some talk of the Bubbleheads recording for Tackhead's label, On-U-Sound, but Islam was also getting other interest in the group. The big question, he recalls, was always " 'How are you gonna get all these guys together? Can you tour?' And I'd always say, 'Why would you worry about touring when you can make great videos?' Our thing was all based on animation of all these gray, bubbleheaded aliens."

Those cute, Area 51–style characters, however, were the harmless front for some darker ideas. In the early '90s, Islam had become immersed in the work of Jordan Maxwell, a radio talk show host, author, and researcher touted as an expert in the field of ancient religions. He had a special interest in UFOs and secret societies, and speculated on the possible links between them. Hearing about the shadowy world of blue-blooded groups hit a nerve in Islam, who'd spent time in the Ivy League, home to such mythical brotherhoods as Yale's Skull and Bones. "I'm a Dartmouth graduate," he explains. "When I hear that stuff, I'm gonna look into it."

He would be led to the work of others who ranged even further afield. Milton William Cooper's 1991 book *Behold a Pale Horse* was an apocalyptic mixture of UFO research and survivalist belligerence that predated the militia movement; he would become a martyr a decade later when killed in a shootout with sheriffs' deputies at his Arizona home. Then there was Englishman David Icke. A former football star and TV presenter, Icke became the subject of public ridicule in Britain when he called himself the Son of God on television and forecast the destruction of the isle. His books nonetheless created a substantial audience for his views, which included the belief that several world leaders—among them Queen Elizabeth and both George Bushes—were actually reptilian shape-shifters from another galaxy.

The New World Order theorizing of both men was not exactly new to hip-hop. Public Enemy's Minister of Information, Professor Griff, had been forced to leave the group for a time in 1989, after being quoted as saying that "Jews are responsible for the majority of the wickedness in the world" in the *Washington Times*. Griff would alternately deny or defend the idea, but the fact that many conspiracy theorists based their ideas on the anti-Semitic *Protocols of the Elders of Zion*—an early-twentieth-century hoax—added an uncomfortable edge to their discussions of the Trilateral Commission and Bildabergers.

Islam disavows the anti-Semitic component of such discussions, but acknowledges that the correlation probably didn't help the Bubbleheads in their quest for a record deal. "If I coulda sold the labels popcorn with sugar on it, that would have been a simple thing," he says. "But I didn't shop it that much. I kept it pure."

The controversy, he claims, didn't stop an executive at Fox from offering him $2 million to develop the Bubbleheads as a cartoon series. "He was like, 'This is great! It has it all—it's got rap, it's got rock, and it's got break-dancing aliens!'" Islam remembers, chuckling.

Ultimately, however, he would take the Bubbleheads abroad, signing with Warner Brothers' Teutonic branch and eventually moving to Germany himself. In his new home, far from the funk-rock all-stars of California and surrounded by the thump of techno, Islam's concept would morph into a new band called Machine, which gave the Bubbleheads a Prodigy-style electronic makeover.

However, time has been kind to Islam's original idea of an all-star collective rocking up funk classics like Sly Stone's "Family Affair" and Parliament's "Now I Lay Me Down to Sleep." A cover of the latter song, with Melle Mel taking the lead and featuring funkily vocoderized choruses, shows what could still be, and Islam thinks the death of R&B godfather James Brown could give the Bubbleheads' task some serious purpose. "Now that James is gone," he says, "I see the opening." So the world will just have to wait and see where and when Islam decides to land his own mother ship—the one with all the Bubbleheads on board.

Epilogue

Writing a book about unreleased albums means you feel obligated to ask every musician you encounter if he or she is hiding away some great treasure no one knows about. Most, it can be stated definitively, are not, and a few even find the question odd. Sometimes, however, it provokes a surprising answer.

It is the autumn of 2005, and Paul Weller is reminiscing—briefly—about his days in the late, not-always-lamented Style Council. Even at the height of its popularity, the Bard of Woking's stylish second band always operated in the shadow of his first, British punk legends the Jam. The final straw was an album called *Modernism: A New Decade*, a collection of house music that Polydor refused to release in 1989. That effectively ended the group, and Weller's partnership with keyboardist Mick Talbot.

Weller was one of the lucky ones, however. *Modernism* would eventually reach the public, almost a decade later, as part of the Style Council's 1998 box set. Weller is a proud man, and it is not surprising to hear him say that he viewed the release of *Modernism* as vindication.

"Yeah, there was for me, because it came out on Polydor. I just found it amusing, because we were turned down because of that album, and then however many years later, they put it out on the box set," he says.[1] "I was glad it came out. I still think it's a good album. It's where me head was at the time, and that's the only way you can make records, really.

"It's a shame, though," he continues. "Because there are loads of remixes we did for that album." Among them, he recalls, were reworkings from the New Jersey deep-house duo Blaze, the Chicago producer Joe Smooth—whose "Promised Land" had been covered by the Council—and Detroit techno pioneer Juan Atkins.

"And none of those have ever come out. In fact, I don't even know where the fucking tapes are," Weller says. "But it'd be nice someday to put them all out."

So there's almost a complete album's worth of stuff there, unreleased....

"Well, it would be," admits Weller, who'd previously dismissed the idea of being responsible for any other lost discs. He considers the idea for a moment before responding with his tongue firmly planted in his cheek.

"There's your missing album, mate," Weller says. "There's your Woking *Smile*."

Notes

Introduction
1. Beck, interview by author, October 2006.
2. Juliana Hatfield, interview by author, April 2006.
3. McDonough 2002, p. 469.
4. Sebastian Bach, interview by author, September 2006.
5. Anonymous source, interview by author, November 2005.
6. Bill Laswell, interview by author, September 2006.
7. Green Gartside, interview by author, July 2006.

Chapter 1: Seal
1. Nick Launay, interview by author, March 2004. All quotes from Nick Launay in this chapter are from this interview unless otherwise specified.
2. Gus Isidore, interview by author, March 2004. All quotes from Gus Isidore in this chapter are from this interview unless otherwise specified.
3. Blinston 2004.
4. Seal, interview by *MTV News*, 1998.
5. Seal, interview by Zahlaway, 2001.
6. Cury 1999.
7. Seal, interview by Tannenbaum, 1991.
8. Chris Fogel, interview by author, February 2004. All quotes from Chris Fogel in this chapter are from this interview unless otherwise specified.
9. Doug Wimbish, interview by author, September 2004. All quotes from Doug Wimbish in this chapter are from this interview unless otherwise specified.
10. Seal, interview by Bottomley, 2003.
11. Seal, interview by Thigpen, 1994.
12. Seal, interview by Zahlaway, 2001.
13. Ibid.
14. David Surnow, interview by author, February 2004.
15. Earl Harvin, interview by author, January 2004.
16. Daley 2003.
17. *MTV News* 2003.
18. Seal, interview by Bottomley, 2003.
19. Seal 2007.

Chapter 2: David Bowie
1. Pegg 2002, p. 217.
2. Mike Garson, interview by author, January 2005. All quotes from Mike Garson in this chapter are from this interview unless otherwise specified.

3. Lisa Germano, interview by author, January 2005. All quotes from Lisa Germano in this chapter are from this interview unless otherwise specified.
4. That includes Bowie's critically acclaimed *1.Outside* and *Heathen*—no shabby company indeed.
5. Plati 1999.
6. For the tuba march "Rubber Band," another old-fashioned novelty released that anticipated the Swinging London fascination with things Edwardian.
7. Plati, interview by Gibson.com, 2000.
8. Plati, interview by *Voyeur*, 2001.
9. Ibid.
10. John and Yoko's final album together, which topped the charts after Lennon's 1980 murder.
11. Pete Keppler, interview by author, March 2005. All quotes from Pete Keppler in this chapter are from this interview unless otherwise specified.
12. Plati, interview by *Voyeur*, 2001.
13. With whom she had worked, for a short time, alongside Mike Garson.
14. Plati, interview by *Voyeur*, 2001.
15. Ibid.
16. Which Bowie, of course, co-produced with the late Mick Ronson.
17. Plati, interview by *Voyeur*, 2001.
18. However, he did play bass on the recording.
19. Cocks 1983.
20. David Buckley's excellent Bowie biography *Strange Fascination* also suggests the break had another source: although passed over for the production of *Let's Dance*, Visconti had agreed to mix Bowie's live sound on some European shows of the "Serious Moonlight" tour. He refused to take on the job full-time, however, reportedly angering his old friend and beginning Visconti's 15 years of being, as he put it, "sent to Coventry." (Buckley 2001.)
21. Buckley 2001, pp. 413–14; 578–79.
22. One of which was not, apparently, "In the Heat of the Morning," which removed Visconti's string charts from the original, but otherwise offered a fairly straight—albeit slower—reading of this slightly risqué rocker.
23. Anonymous source, interview by author, June 2005.
24. Ibid.
25. Ibid.
26. Plati, interview by *Voyeur*, 2001.
27. Ibid.
28. Bowie's longtime personal assistant/screener/de facto manager, Coco Schwab.
29. Plati, interview by *Voyeur*, 2001.
30. Pegg 2002, p. 161.
31. Bowie 2000.
32. Bowie July 2001.
33. Bowie Oct. 2001.
34. Bowie Dec. 2001.
35. Bowie Oct. 2001.
36. And is thus similar to the Visconti-produced version that Bowie recorded for the BBC, chronicled on the *Bowie at the Beeb* album.

37. In 2006, according to the *Illustrated David Bowie Discography*, a few fans were able to hear a copy of *Toy* that contained a dozen tracks, plus the probable B-sides "Liza Jane" and "The London Boys." Missing from the running order were "Karma Man" and "Can't Help Thinking About Me"; it's not clear whether the latter song was actually re-recorded.
38. Bowie May 2002.
39. Garson understood this better than most. In 1994, he had participated in the recording for *1.Outside*, joining Brian Eno and guitarist Reeves Gabrels in Montreux, Switzerland, for what Garson thought was "one of the most enjoyable and creative sessions I'd done in my life. I'd rate it up there with *Aladdin Sane* or *Diamond Dogs*. We were basically improvising four to six hours a day, without stopping, and David was painting, and occasionally stepping up to the mic and improvising words. There was no structure. We didn't even tell each other what key we were in. It's like free jazz-slash-fusion-slash-classical."

    These sessions would provide the raw material that Bowie and Eno would sculpt into *1.Outside*, but Bowie had originally envisioned the album as only the first installment in a larger work; at times, a trilogy, at others, an even more ambitious cycle. A follow-up to *1.Outside*, provisionally titled *2. Contamination*, was discussed, and nearly 30 hours of music remained in the vaults, ready to be molded into new songs. "They're not all gems," admits Garson. "But it's not bullshit, either. It could just be instrumentals, ambient or free stuff. It's very creative and very, very good."

    In the event, the tapes would be abandoned in favor of other projects. However, some of the material would leak on a fascinating bootleg that began to circulate in 2004. It offered an aural glimpse of *1.Outside* in its formative stage, with free-flowing jams and improvised lyrics. "I think it's dishonest, whoever did it," says Garson, "but I love that bootleg. It was a very special moment."
40. Tony Visconti, interview by author, January 2005. This interview consisted of an exchange of e-mails between the author and Mr. Visconti, who declined further comment because he was at work on his own autobiography.

Chapter 3: Chicago
1. Bruce Gaitsch, interview by author, November 2005. All quotes from Bruce Gaitsch in this chapter are from this interview unless otherwise specified.
2. Peter Wolf, interview by author, December 2005. All quotes from Peter Wolf in this chapter are from this interview unless otherwise specified.
3. Joseph 2000, p. 134.
4. Dawayne Bailey, interview by author, June 2006. All quotes from Dawayne Bailey in this chapter are from this interview unless otherwise specified.
5. A different musician, obviously, from the singer of the same name who once fronted the J. Geils Band.
6. Joseph 2000, p. 169.
7. Ibid.
8. Although many fans believe Bailey played guitar on *Twenty 1*, he notes that session man Mike Landau instead played all the guitars.
9. Bailey strongly contests this assertion. "I take pride in my rhythm playing," he says. "If that's what Wolf said, then so be it. It's all false though, as far as I'm concerned."

10. Wolf would also try to get another guitarist friend, Sheldon Reynolds, a spot in Chicago, but while Reynolds's audition went well, he decided to join Earth, Wind & Fire instead, and would play on only a couple of songs from *22*.
11. Lamm, interview by Kruger, 1999.
12. Although Scheff was given a writing credit on the song, Bailey says the Wolfs essentially composed "Bigger Than Elvis" themselves. "Peter wrote the music," he asserts, "and Ina Wolf wrote the lyrics based on stories Jason told her."
13. In fact, Loughnane would end up with a co-writing credit on the song.
14. Felicia Parazaider's contributions are, Bailey remembers, "the lines about '[an] empty house full of cages.'"
15. However, the album did receive an official remix. Veteran producer and engineer Tom Lord-Alge first mixed *Sisyphus*, but some of the participants—including Gaitsch— were unhappy with the in-your-face results. Wolf and his longtime engineer, Paul Erikson, then gave the mix a second try. But while Gaitsch and some band members prefer this mix, Wolf insists Lord-Alge's original mix is superior. Both versions have apparently surfaced on bootlegs.
16. In 1999, Pankow admitted to interviewer Debbie Kruger from *Goldmine*, "We're up against this image thing, and no matter how prolific we are, in terms of up-tempo songs, it's like they don't trust it. Our manager comes to us and says, 'Hey man, that'll never get on the radio. We know programmers, our A&R guy in the office couldn't shop that song no matter what he did.'" (Lamm and Pankow, interview by Kruger, 1999.)
17. Sung by Scheff and Lamm, this blistering rocker contains what Bruce Gaitsch says is "the best solo I ever played in my life. So it's perfect that it never came out," he adds, laughing, "so I can keep saying that! Nobody's heard it to tear it apart!"
18. Although the album was shelved, a project the band was working on simultaneously did manage to make its way into stores. Through an arrangement with musical equipment manufacturer Ensoniq, the band had agreed to create a CD-ROM that featured samples of vocal and instrument sounds used on *Sisyphus*. Part of Ensoniq's high-end professional library, the disc also included a Jason Scheff song titled "Evangeline" that was used as sample fodder. Wolf doesn't recall much about the tune, but notes, "We used lots of Ensoniq gear on that record. They were the happening keyboard manufacturer, no doubt about it."
19. Joseph 2000, p. 170.
20. Writer Tim Wood noted on his website, "In 1998, the band went to great lengths to say the album would not be released. Harold Sulman, who ran the now-defunct Chicago Records, emphatically stated at the 1998 fan club convention that the album would not be released, and that he would not take questions on the subject." (Wood 1999–2005.)

Chapter 4: Jungle Brothers

1. Bill Laswell, interview by author, May 2006. All quotes from Bill Laswell in this chapter are from this interview unless otherwise specified.
2. Mike G, interview by author, October 2006. All quotes from Mike G in this chapter are from this interview unless otherwise specified.
3. Tom Silverman, interview by author, May 2006.
4. S. H. Fernando Jr., interview by author, October 2006.

5. Colin Bobb, interview by author, October 2006. All quotes from Colin Bobb in this chapter are from this interview unless otherwise specified.

6. Bizarrely enough, a version of the J. Beez' most avant-garde track somehow managed to see an official release—alongside the Flaming Lips, Daniel Lanois, and a pre-fame Green Day—on the 1993 Warner Brothers compilation *Trademark of Quality, Vol. 2*.

7. Fernando 1996.

8. Matt Stein, interview by author, November 2006. All quotes from Matt Stein in this chapter are from this interview unless otherwise specified.

9. This would presumably have been Collins's 1990 outing *Jungle Bass*, released on the dance-oriented 4th & Broadway label. However, three years earlier, Collins and Laswell had also collaborated on a proposed album for Arista that never saw the light of day, after Clive Davis—who had signed Bootsy—left the label.

   The loss can accurately be described as monumental. The four tracks that survive in Laswell's archives—the final mixes were actually rescued from an old Beta tape that was ready for the landfill—are as potent a funk-rock fusion as the '80s produced, with the powerhouse drumming of Dennis Chambers and the guitar heroics of Eddie Martinez alongside contributions from Bernie Worrell, Fred Wesley, and Senegalese percussionist Aiyb Dieng. Engineered by Power Station stalwart Jason Corsaro, the sound is huge but remains secondary to the almighty groove. Recalls Laswell of the reaction to those Bootsy sessions, "Even George [Clinton] said, 'This is the best thing that's happened to P-Funk in ages.'"

   There is also a splendid, contemporaneous cover of the Sly and the Family Stone chestnut "Family Affair" that Laswell produced for Iggy Pop and later gave to Collins for some overdubs. This recording has occasionally turned up on Iggy bootlegs; Laswell notes that Iggy and his then-collaborator, ex–Sex Pistol Steve Jones, were also considering recording a cover of Jimi Hendrix's "Purple Haze," rough tapes of which may also exist.

10. Both Stein and Laswell also recall James Brown's saxophonist Fred Wesley being present for some of the sessions, although it is not clear on which song or songs he may have played.

11. Off the 1971 funk album *Headless Heroes of the Apocalypse*, a breakbeat favorite.

12. Fernando 1996.

13. Ibid.

14. Meilandt, perhaps best known for his association with Herbie Hancock, would pass away in 2004 at age 46. According to the website of his last roommate, songwriter John Perry Barlow, Meilandt had gone through drug rehab after spending a decade "lost in a blizzard" and "piss[ing] off just about everybody in the industry." (Barlow 2004.) At the time of his death, his music career seemed on the upswing; he was executive-producing an album for the 2004 Olympic Games.

15. Fernando 1996.

16. The song would also be turned into a video, which featured Afrika, Mike G, and a sunglasses-wearing Torture cavorting in a "Hip-Hop Circus" but also included the revealing image of the trio bogging down in quicksand.

17. Christgau 1993.

18. S. H. Fernando Jr., interview by author, September 2006. All quotes from S. H. Fernando Jr. in this chapter are from this interview unless otherwise specified.

19. Fernando 1996.

Chapter 5: Mick Jagger

1. Dave Lee Bartel, interview by author, November 2006. All quotes from Dave Lee Bartel in this chapter are from this interview unless otherwise specified.
2. Johnny Ray Bartel, interview by author, September 2006. All quotes from Johnny Ray Bartel in this chapter are from this interview unless otherwise specified.
3. Bill Bateman, interview by author, September 2006. All quotes from Bill Bateman in this chapter are from this interview unless otherwise specified.
4. May was not a total stranger to the band, however: Los Angeles retro-rockers the Blasters, for whom Bateman had drummed, had opened for Queen during a 1980 tour.
5. Doug Hinman, interview by author, September 2006.
6. The tape was actually running on May 18 at the King King: Jagger's two-song set with the Red Devils has been preserved via an unknown source, and Johnny Ray Bartel adds that "I think it's even better than the stuff we did in the studio."
7. Butler, interview by van der Horst, 1997.
8. Ginny Tura, interview by author, January 2007. All quotes from Ginny Tura in this chapter are from this interview unless otherwise specified.
9. The famed session drummer.
10. Each band member also got an extra $50 for the transport of his equipment. "But we're a neighborhood bar band," notes Dave Lee Bartel, "so we just brought our own stuff."
11. Rob Rio, interview by author, January 2007. All quotes from Rob Rio in this chapter are from this interview unless otherwise specified.
12. This may well have been one of the several infidelities that caused Jagger's wife, former model Jerry Hall, to threaten to file for divorce later that summer. In any event, she and Jagger reconciled, before finally having their 22-year-old marriage annulled in 1999.
13. There were evidently some other tunes Jagger had shortlisted for the session, as well. Dave Lee Bartel's notes from the day list Billy Boy Arnold's "You've Got Me Wrong" and "I Was Fooled" among the songs considered, as well as three additional Muddy Waters compositions: "All Aboard," "Trouble No More," and "Louisiana Blues."
14. The song, sometimes listed as "Two Trains," was recorded at Olympic Studios in May 1968, during the Jimmy Miller–produced sessions for *Beggars Banquet*. It is believed that Brian Jones may have played on the track and that Nicky Hopkins contributed piano. Interestingly, the song finally received its live debut on the Stones' 1995 European tour.
15. This track is also credited to Sonny Boy Williamson II, who also recorded the song.
16. Alternate titles include "I Want Somebody to Love Me" or "You Need Me," which has caused some confusion on bootlegs of this session.
17. In fact, they were quite possibly behind: the album had been scheduled for a November 16, 1992 release, but was instead pushed back until February of the following year. Another reason for the switch might have been to avoid a near-simultaneous release with Stones guitarist Keith Richards, whose second album with the X-Pensive Winos was due for a late-October bow on Virgin Records.
18. While Rubin himself has been quoted as saying that 14 songs were recorded, and while, as previously mentioned, it's obvious that many extra tunes were considered, the actual number completed appears to be 13 different titles. That's according to the

meticulous notekeeping of Dave Lee Bartel—a man whose memory is so good, his brother Johnny Ray reveals, that he was once nicknamed "The Memo Pad."

19. Hochman 1992.
20. *Billboard* 1992.
21. Wild 1992.
22. It still hasn't; things have been downhill ever since his first true solo single, "Just Another Night," peaked at No. 12 in 1985. *Wandering Spirit* did reach No. 11 on the Billboard album chart in 1993, but both its singles—"Don't Tear Me Up" and the discofied "Sweet Thing"—fell well outside the Top 40.
23. Sky 1993.
24. *rpm* 1993.
25. Blake 1993, p. 83.
26. McMahon 1993.
27. Jagger, interview by *Musician*, 1993, p. 44.
28. For the record, Bill Bateman doubts this story. "It hasn't been proven," he says. "Perry Mason wouldn't take the case."
29. Rubin, interview by "Fresh Air," 2004.
30. Ibid.
31. Without crediting Dave Lee Bartel, who played his usual rhythm guitar on the session.
32. Rubin would summon Smokey Hormel back into the studio to overdub a new electric guitar part, which provided the only backing for Cash's vocals. "It sounds really good, but I'd love to hear it with us," says Johnny Ray Bartel. "But I don't think we're gonna be getting that tape out of anyone's drawer."
33. This song, at least, would see official release in 1993—in England, via a licensing deal Def American struck with the British label This Way Up.
34. Dave Lee Bartel, interview by author, January 2007.
35. Ibid.
36. Which also featured guitar from Smokey Hormel.
37. Dave Lee Bartel, interview by author, January 2007.

Chapter 6: Beastie Boys

1 Gettelman 1992.
2. Michael Diamond, interview by author, November 2005. All quotes from Michael Diamond in this chapter are from this interview unless otherwise specified.
3. Sean Carasov, interview by author, March 2005. All quotes from Sean Carasov in this chapter are from this interview unless otherwise specified.
4. During this period in 1987–88, the Beasties also became involved in several side projects, musical and otherwise. The most serious example of the former was Adam Yauch's band Brooklyn, in which he fronted a quartet that also included his friend Tom Cushman on guitar, Murphy's Law drummer Doug E. Beans, and Bad Brains bassist Daryl Jenifer. The group first recorded some home demos of its classic rock–inspired sound, and later laid down some more polished studio performances, with an eye toward scoring a label deal.

   Ultimately, it didn't happen, and Yauch now talks about the possibility with bluntness and barely disguised disgust. "The eight-track demos we did are OK. But then we re-recorded it in a fancy studio," he says. "That stuff is just humiliating. It just sounds *terrible*. My vocals are *awful*." If you're eagerly waiting the official release someday of the *Brooklyn Sessions*, the best advice would seem to be: Don't.

5. Cited on Beastiemania.com (Timeline: 1989).

6. Weizmann 1989.

7. Ibid.

8. If it's accurate, this statement suggests the original idea for *White House* probably dated back as early as the fall of 1987, when the Beasties returned from tour and refused to re-enter the studio to record a follow-up to *Licensed to Ill*. At that point, Simmons might well have decided he could put together his own stopgap release until the Beasties were ready to work again.

9. Chuck D, interview by author, April 2006. All quotes from Chuck D in this chapter are from this interview unless otherwise specified.

10. Bill Adler, interview by author, January 2006. All quotes from Bill Adler in this chapter are from this interview unless otherwise specified.

11. Beastie Boys, interview by *East Coast Rocker*, 1987.

12. The song later appeared, set to a mortifying Christian Slater dance routine, in the film *Pump Up the Volume*.

13. As late as 1999, when the Beasties were assembling their *Sounds of Science* anthology, they were attempting to persuade AC/DC to clear this sample. The effort remained unsuccessful. Mike D would later report, "AC/DC could not get with the sample concept. They were just like, 'Nothing against you guys, but we just don't endorse sampling.'"

14. AKA the New York producer and percussionist Jay Burnett, who was a key figure in the emerging hip-hop scene.

15. Adam Yauch, interview by author, January 2007. All quotes from Adam Yauch in this chapter are from this interview unless otherwise specified.

16. Beastie Boys, interview by *MTV News*, 1995.

17. A film that was apparently never completed.

18. Mario Caldato Jr., interview by author, October 2006. All quotes from Mario Caldato Jr. in this chapter are from this interview unless otherwise specified.

19. Both Yauch and Mike D don't recall this being the case, although Yauch adds that he's "not positive" about whether or not Country Mike material might have been proposed for the album.

20. Williams 1996.

21. One of the songs, Adam Yauch recalls, was completely re-recorded during Baxter's brief visit, although he can't remember which one.

22. When, exactly, the first copies of *Country Mike's Greatest Hits* were distributed is a matter of some conjecture. The most logical date seems to be 1998, although the albums might not have been handed out in December, as would seem logical. According to Beasties scholar Mark Laudenschlager, it has been rumored that the Beasties traditionally observe the holidays during the summer, giving out their gifts at this time. If Country Mike's first appeared at this time, it would square with all other dates involved in this chapter.

On the website Beastiemania.com, an invaluable resource for Beasties fans, it is possible to view a copy of the Christmas card that accompanied the album. The front featured a copy of the old holiday collection *An All-Star Country Christmas*, while the back carried Christmas and Hanukkah greetings from "Country Mike & the Boys."

23. Beastie Boys, interview by MuchMusic, 1998. This Beastie Boys interview and others were provided by Mark Laudenschlager at the incomparable Beastie Boys website Beastiemania.com
24. Unknown interview source. Found at Beastiemania.com (Song Spotlight: "Country Delight").
25. The photos of a cowboy-clad Mike D and Yauch in the *Sounds of Science* book, on the other hand, suggested Glaser's anecdote might have been no tall tale.
26. Beastie Boys, interview by BBC Radio, 1998.
27. Ibid.
28. Ibid.
29. Unknown interview source. Found at Beastiemania.com (Who's Who: Country Mike).
30. Mark Laudenschlager, interview by author, December 2006. All quotes from Mark Laudenschlager in this chapter are from this interview unless otherwise specified.
31. Beastie Boys 1999, pp. 68–69.
32. Beastie Boys, interview by MTV2, 2002.
33. Ibid.

Chapter 7: Ray Davies

1. Des McAnuff, interview by author, April 2006. All quotes from Des McAnuff in this chapter are from this interview unless otherwise specified.
2. E-mail message from Linda McBride, March 2005.
3. Robby Merkin, interview by author, July 2006. All quotes from Mark Robby Merkin in this chapter are from this interview unless otherwise specified.
4. Molenda 1998.
5. Snoo Wilson, interview by author, July 2006. All quotes from Snoo Wilson in this chapter are from this interview unless otherwise specified.
6. Des McAnuff, interview by author, November 2006.
7. Ibid.
8. Savage 1985, p. 158.
9. Ibid., pp. 109–10.
10. Ibid., p. 114.
11. Ibid., pp. 111–14.
12. It was "somewhere on the water, along the Hudson River," McAnuff recalls. According to the exhaustive research of Kinks historian Doug Hinman, it was probably a Kinks concert at Pier 84 on either September 12 or 13, 1985.
13. Bartoldus and Junkerjürgen 2003.
14. Welles's widescreen version of the novel received such poor reviews, in fact, that he felt compelled to take on his critics in person. "Several nights after the critics blasted his efforts," wrote Richard Connema on the Talkin' Broadway website, "Welles came out on stage at the end and told the audience, 'The critics have said I have thrown everything but the kitchen sink into this production.' He went offstage and came back with a kitchen sink and threw it on the stage floor. 'There is the kitchen sink,' he said, and he stormed off stage." (Connema 2006.)
15. Bartoldus and Junkerjürgen 2003.
16. Possibly a place Davies kept on 72nd Street.

17. On the demo, Davies would affect an upper-crust accent to deliver Queen Victoria's contribution to this song, a device he'd used occasionally as a Kink. (See "Yes Sir, No Sir," on *Arthur*, to cite just one example.)
18. Bartoldus and Junkerjürgen 2003.
19. Interestingly, however, this song is the one tune from *80 Days* that has resurfaced. Des McAnuff, who occasionally returns to his garage band days for charity events, sometimes performs songs from Playhouse productions with musicians from the hit musical *Jersey Boys*, based on the songs of Frankie Valli and the Four Seasons. "We've actually played 'When Will It Be Written' [*sic*], and thought about doing another one," says McAnuff. "I think we actually rehearsed it, but didn't perform it.

    "So I love that song. In fact, I can remember Frankie Valli and [Four Seasons member] Bob Gaudio actually saying to me, after an event in New York, 'That's a really great song.' Of course, that's not surprising with Ray."
20. Hinman 2004, p. 296.
21. It's possible all the songs found on the *80 Days* bootleg were recorded during this brief session, although there are differences in sound quality that suggest at least a couple of the tracks might have come from a different source.
22. That didn't happen; Davies had told an interviewer that it would depend "on how (*80 Days*) goes, and how the band feels about it." (Hinman 2004, p. 294.) The opinion of the other Kinks—specifically, Dave Davies—is unknown, but the show's failure might well have foreclosed this possibility.
23. On the demo, it was part of a suite that includes the brief "Mongolia Song" and then "No Surprises," which continued the theme, melodically and lyrically.
24. It also contained the concluding chorus "Cooperation/collaboration/consideration/ around the world," which takes on a slightly ironic cast of its own, considering the show's ultimate fate.
25. That recollection is backed up by an anecdote from Merkin: "There was so much music in the show that Danny Troob volunteered to orchestrate the incidental music, so I could concentrate on the songs. And at one point, I was at rehearsal and listening to some of the transitional music, and I thought, 'God damn, that sounds great. I gotta take my hat off to Danny—I would never have thought of that combination of instruments.' And I went over and told Danny how great it sounded, meaning to be complimentary, and he looked at me funny. And he said, '*You* wrote that,'" Merkin concludes with a laugh. "But I had no memory of it at all."
26. Apart from his demos, Davies would give the creators, cast, and crew of *80 Days* another chance to hear the songs as he'd intended them. Soundman Serge Ossorguine recalled, in a 2004 *Mix* magazine interview, that "With just a guitar, Ray played through all of his songs to the cast, and it sounded great. But we didn't have a DAT machine on hand, and the moment was gone." (Eskow 2004.)
27. According to reviews of the show, which mention the song in passing, it apparently did, although both Wilson and Merkin recall it getting the axe. One of the tunes from the demo that appears to have definitely been cut, however, was "Conspiracy," a vehicle for the Scotland Yard detective Fix. Although presented in the same synth-and-drum-machine format as the rest of the score, the ominous song was notable for its unveiling of Davies's raw-throated rock voice, and it's not inconceivable to imagine it rendered in a more Kinksian, guitar-friendly manner.

28. On the demo, this song is prefaced by "Welcome to India," a short introduction over the music to "On the Map" and "Well-Bred Englishman," that first announces Fogg and Verne's entry to the country.

29. This song does not appear on the *80 Days* bootleg that commonly circulates among collectors.

30. Essentially, a wagon with a sail, used to navigate the flatlands of Middle America.

31. Jones 1988.

32. Ibid.

33. Ibid.

34. Hinman 2004, p. 294.

35. Jones 1988.

36. Doug Hinman, interview by author, September 2006. All quotes from Doug Hinman in this chapter are from this interview unless otherwise specified.

37. Ibid.

38. DeMuir 1993.

39. amorosi 1996.

Chapter 8: Adam Ant

1. Marco Pirroni, interview by author, July 2006. All quotes from Marco Pirroni in this chapter are from this interview unless otherwise specified.

2. Ant, *Stand and Deliver*, 2006, p. 271.

3. Bromberg 1989, pp. 213–17.

4. Ibid., pp. 225–27.

5. Lwin would be joined in Bow Wow Wow, for one memorable gig at London's Rainbow Theatre and a couple of others after it, by guest vocalist Lieutenant Lush—later to become better known as Boy George.

6. Leigh Gorman, interview by author, June 2006. All quotes from Leigh Gorman in this chapter are from this interview unless otherwise specified.

7. As Pirroni remembers it, Gorman had bumped into Adam at a London club, and the chance meeting spurred the invite to produce the sessions.

8. A deal negotiated by Freed, whose primary client, Jody Watley, had also been signed to MCA.

9. It is somewhat unclear when these sessions took place. In his autobiography, Adam Ant remembers spending "two frustrating days" in Miami during the fall of 1990, waiting for Larry Blackmon to call him. The problem, he alleges, was that Blackmon's manager was trying to get his client, who was also signed to MCA, a better deal with the label. According to Adam, he and Blackmon would finally get together later that year and write two songs. It may be these sessions that Pirroni declined to attend. (Ant, *Stand and Deliver*, 2006, p. 265.)

10. Pirroni 2001. "The crowd were oddly enthusiastic," Pirroni also recalled in the same online interview. "I think we nearly got an encore which would have been funny. We would have had to have done it again."

11. In his autobiography, Adam also recalls a writing session with Edwards in New York in September of 1990. Pirroni may have missed this trip as well, thanks to his touring commitments with Sinead O'Connor. (Ant, *Stand and Deliver*, 2006, p. 265.)

12. Ant, *Stand and Deliver*, 2006, p. 266.

13. Marco Pirroni, interview by author, October 2006.

14. Thanks in part, one assumes, to Brian Malouf, who mixed seven of the album's ten tracks.
15. Ant, *Stand and Deliver*, 2006, p. 270.
16. Ibid., p. 272.
17. McOmber 1992.
18. Ant, *Stand and Deliver*, 2006, p. 278.
19. Locey 1993.
20. Boehm 1993.
21. The cinematic equivalent of a demo tape.
22. Ant, interview by Wilde, 2006.

Chapter 9: Juliana Hatfield

1. Juliana Hatfield, interview by author, April 2006. All quotes from Juliana Hatfield in this chapter are from this interview unless otherwise specified.
2. Todd Phillips, interview by author, August 2006. All quotes from Todd Phillips in this chapter are from this interview unless otherwise specified.
3. Gary Smith, interview by author, January 2007. All quotes from Gary Smith in this chapter are from this interview unless otherwise specified.
4. Danny Goldberg, interview by author, February 2007. All quotes from Danny Goldberg in this chapter are from this interview unless otherwise specified.
5. Hatfield, interview by *Alternative Press*, 1993.
6. "The cheaper studio in Woodstock," Hatfield notes. "I never got to record at Bearsville."
7. Although his wife, Rosemary Carroll, was still representing Hatfield, Danny Goldberg says he "didn't follow" the *God's Foot* saga. "Rosemary and I don't talk in much detail about each other's work unless there is something we have in common or can help each other in some way," he says. "I think it's a terrific album musically but I never followed any of the business issues such as marketing, airplay, sales, etc."

    He remains a Hatfield fan, however. "As it happens I have a framed note Juliana faxed me after Kurt Cobain died, which was attached to a fax he had sent her after seeing one of her shows—so I see her name every day," Goldberg says. "I think she was and is a special and brilliant artist, a unique and inner-directed artist that deserves the attention you are giving her."
8. Hatfield, interview by Gary Calamar (KCRW-FM), 1997.
9. Pilvinsky 1997.
10. Milano 1997.
11. Goodman 1998.
12. Hatfield, Launch.com chat, 2001.
13. Milano 2001.

Chapter 10: Should've-Beens, Never-Weres, and Still-Might-Bes

1. Bussy, interview by *Activität*, 1995.
2. Wolfgang Flür, interview by author, February 2005. All quotes from Wolfgang Flür in this chapter are from this interview unless otherwise specified.
3. Hütter, interview by Dalton, 2004.
4. Bussy 1993.

5. "I remember that Ralf and Florian were not too much amused about parts (samples) stolen from our songs to be fitting in another music and genre," says Flür. "The matter led to heavy legal dealings between Ralf and Florian's lawyer and Tommy Boy Records. The result was that Tommy Boy had to pay a pretty big amount of dollars to Kraftwerk."

6. Florian Schneider has stated that Kraftwerk's 1975 song "Autobahn" was inspired, at least in part, by the Beach Boys.

7. One suggestion made by Bartos is that the analog material recorded at Kling Klang was redone in New York. While the album credits state that the disc was recorded at Kling Klang, there is also a credit for "music data transfer" by Fred Maher—better known as a member of Material and Scritti Politti, and the producer of Lou Reed's *New York*. And Wolfgang Flür states that Kling Klang was not upgraded from analog to digital equipment until after *Electric Café* was completed, and he had left the group. "I know from Karl—who was with Kraftwerk some years longer—that this period of retrofitting Kraftwerk on digital equipment happened between 1986 and the release of the unspeakable *The Mix* album (in 1991). Retrofitting was no reason for delaying *Electric Café*."

8. Robbins 1991, p. 371.

9. Beck, interview by author, October 2006. All quotes from Beck in this chapter are from this interview unless otherwise specified.

10. In fact, this abandoned project was apparently a foretaste of the highly acclaimed work Beck would later create with Radiohead producer Nigel Godrich on 1998's *Mutations* and especially the acclaimed 2002 album *Sea Change*. "Sometimes you start working on one thing," Beck acknowledges, "and it doesn't come out, but it points you in the direction of something else."

11. *Mutations*, Beck's first pairing with Godrich, was actually released as the follow-up to *Odelay* in 1998 by Geffen, although this was done against Beck's wishes.

12. Matt Dike, interview by author, September 2005. All quotes from Matt Dike in this chapter are from this interview unless otherwise specified.

13. Carlin 2006, p. 244.

14. Sullivan 2006.

15. Hugh Padgham, interview by author, March 2004. All quotes from Hugh Padgham in this chapter are from this interview unless otherwise specified.

16. Buskin 2003.

17. Ibid.

18. Osbourne, interview by *Revolver*, 2004.

19. It might seem even more obvious upon learning a very obscure bit of Disney trivia: the prince in *Snow White* was nicknamed "Prince Buckethead" by Disney animators. "He got this name from a storyboard, or scene that had been drafted for the animated film but was never used," wrote Chad McCully, who discovered the reference in an article called "Whatever Happened To Prince Buckethead?" written by Henry Mazzeo and published in a 1987 Gladstone periodical about Disney. (McCully's article can be found at http://www.heartlandlibraries.org/news&clues/archive/SU2002/columns.html.)

   Was Brian Carroll aware of this nickname? There's no evidence to support that theory, but he seems just the sort of dedicated Disney fan who might have uncovered it.

20. Witherspoon, date unknown, http://www.bucketheadland.com/story.

21. Kauffman, year unknown, Riffage.com.
22. Ibid. In the same interview, Buckethead revealed that his favorite Disney character is the "Hat Box Ghost," found in the attic of the Mansion. He has also claimed that the Mansion's invisible keyboardist taught him to play Chopin's "Funeral March."
23. Buckethead, interview by author, October 2005. All quotes from Buckethead in this chapter are from this interview unless otherwise specified.
24. Buckethead-ese for "material."
25. Buckethead's 2004 album *Cuckoo Clocks From Hell*, on Disembodied Records.
26. Rotondi 1996.
27. Julie Christensen, interview by author, March 2004. All quotes from Julie Christensen in this chapter are from this interview unless otherwise specified.
28. Todd Rundgren, interview by author, April 2004. All quotes from Todd Rundgren in this chapter are from this interview unless otherwise specified.
29. Afrika Islam, interview by author, February 2007. All quotes from Afrika Islam in this chapter are from this interview unless otherwise specified.

Epilogue

1. Paul Weller, interview by author, September 2005. All quotes from Paul Weller in this chapter are from this interview unless otherwise specified.

Bibliography

amorosi, a. d. 1996. Man Ray. *Philadelphia City Paper* (October 17–24).

Ant, Adam. 2006. Interview by Jon Wilde. *Uncut* (October).

——. 2006. *Stand and Deliver.* London: Pan Macmillan.

Author unknown. 1992. Billboard news brief. *Billboard* (October 10).

Author unknown. 1993. Rumour, Prattle & Murmur. *rpm* (March).

Bailey, Dawayne. Website. http://www.dawaynebailey.com/.

Barlow, John Perry. 2004. The Death of a Room-Mate . . . Tony Meilandt (1957–2004). Barlowfriendz website (March 24): http://barlow. typepad.com/barlowfriendz/2004/03/the_death_of_a_.html.

Bartoldus, Thomas, and Ralf Junkerjürgen. 2003. Une adaptation musicale du Tour du monde en quatre-vingts jours. *Bulletin de la Société Jules Verne* 147 (3): pp. 51–53.

Beastie Boys. 1987. Interview. *East Coast Rocker* (January 21).

——. 1995. Interview. *MTV News.*

——. 1998. Interview. BBC Radio.

——. 1998. Interview. MuchMusic (August).

——. 1999. *The Sounds of Science.* New York: powerHouse Books.

——. 2002. Interview. MTV2.

Blake, Mark. 1993. Review of concert performance by Red Devils at the Borderline, London. *Metal CD* (March 29).

Blinston, Janine. 2004. Seal at the Apollo. Review of concert at the Apollo Theater, New York. BBC Manchester website (March 23): http:// www.bbc.co.uk/manchester/music/2004/03/23/seal_review.shtml.

Boehm, Mike. 1993. Adam Ant Looks Good Enough for Romance. *Los Angeles Times* (February 25).

Bowie, David. 2000–02. Online journal (blog). Bowienet (various dated entries): http://www.davidbowie.com/bowie/journal/.

Bromberg, Craig. 1989. *The Wicked Ways of Malcolm McLaren.* New York: Harper & Row.

Buckley, David. 2001. *Strange Fascination: David Bowie; The Definitive Story.* London: Virgin Books.

Buskin, Richard. 2003. Sheryl Crow and Her Producers. *Sound on Sound* (April).

Bussy, Pascal. 1993. *Kraftwerk: Man, Machine and Music.* London: SAF Publishing.

———. 1996. Interview. *Activität* (August): http://ourworld.compuserve.com/homepages/aktivitaet/8_pascal.htm.

Butler, Lester. 1997. Interview by Herman van der Horst. *OOR* (October).

Carlin, Peter Ames. 2006. *Catch a Wave: The Rise, Fall and Redemption of the Beach Boys' Brian Wilson.* New York: Rodale Press.

Christgau, Robert. 1993. Review of album *J. Beez Wit the Remedy.* *Village Voice* (October 19).

Cocks, Jay. 1983. David Bowie Rockets Onward. *Time* (July 18).

Connema, Richard. 2006. A Wild and Madcap Production of Jules Verne's *Around the World in 80 Days.* Talkin' Broadway website (February 17): http://www.talkinbroadway.com/regional/sanfran/s738.html.

Cury, James Oliver. 1999. If You Post It, They Will Come. Rollingstone.com (November 30): http://www.rollingstone.com/artists/seal/articles/story/5924103/if_you_post_it_they_will_come.

Daley, Niky. 2003. Review of album *Seal IV.* BBC.co.uk (September): http://www.bbc.co.uk/music/release/5925/.

DeMuir, Harold. 1993. Brothers at Arms. *Pulse* (May).

Eskow, Gary. 2004. Serge Audio. *Mix* (April 1) http://bg.mixonline.com/ar/audio_serge_audio_theater/index.htm.

Fernando, S. H. Jr. 1996. Jungle Brothers. (Unpublished feature on *Crazy Wisdom Masters*.)

Flür, Wolfgang. 2003. *Kraftwerk: I Was a Robot*. London: Sanctuary Publishing.

Gettelman, Parry. 1992. Beasties Have Their "Head" Together. *Orlando Sentinel* (May 22).

Goodman, Dean. 1998. Hatfield Bounces Back with "Bed." Reuters (November 16).

Hatfield, Juliana. 1993. Interview. *Alternative Press* (October).

———. 1997. Interview by Gary Calamar on *Open Road*. KCRW-FM (April 5): http://www.kcrw.com/music/programs/or/or970405juliana_hatfield.

———. 2001. Online chat. Launch.com (January 16): http://music.yahoo.com/read/interview/12048566.

Hinman, Doug. 2004. *The Kinks: All Day and All of the Night*. San Francisco: Backbeat.

Hochman, Steve. 1992. Odd Couple Mick and Rick Finish Album. *Los Angeles Times* (October 4).

The Illustrated David Bowie Discography. Ed. Ruud Altenburg. http://www.illustrated-db-discography.nl/Toy

Jagger, Mick. 1993. Interview. *Musician* (March).

Jones, Welton. 1988. "80 Days" A World Away From True Emotion. *San Diego Union* (August 30).

Joseph, Ben. 2000. *Chicago: Feelin' Stronger Every Day*. Toronto: Quarry Press.

Kauffman, Andy. Year unknown. Living with the Chickens: Inside the Head of Buckethead. Riffage.com: http://www.bingebuddies.com/html%20texte/Buckethead%20Interview%20@%20riffage_com.htm.

Kruger, Debbie. 2000. Chicago's Endurance: 34 Years . . . and Counting. *Goldmine* (June 16): http://www.debbiekruger.com/writer/freelance/chicago_goldmine.html.

Lamm, Robert. 1999. Phone interview by Debbie Kruger. Debbie Kruger website (May 5): http://www.debbiekruger.com/writer/freelance/chicago_transcript.html.

Lamm, Robert, and Jimmy Pankow. 1999. Phone interview by Debbie Kruger. Debbie Kruger website (March 4): http://www.debbiekruger.com/writer/freelance/chicago_transcript.html.

Locey, Bill. 1993. Acting Out. *Los Angeles Times* (February 18).

McDonough, Jimmy. 2002. *Shakey: Neil Young's Biography.* New York: Random House.

McMahon, Barbara. 1993. Jagger Goes Back to Basics in Secret Gig. *London Evening Standard* (February 4).

McOmber, J. Martin. 1992. Adam Ant Dusts Off His Moves. *Los Angeles Times* (December 15).

Milano, Brett. 1997. This Year's Model: Catching Up with the New Juliana Hatfield. *Boston Phoenix* (November 13): http://bostonphoenix.com/archive/music/97/11/13/CELLARS.html.

———. 2001. Sweet Returns: The Blake Babies' Blessed Reunion. *Boston Phoenix* (March): http://72.166.46.24/boston/music/cellars/documents/00642836.htm.

Molenda, Michael. 1998. The Kinks: How Ray Davies Penned Some of Rock's Most Literate and Incisive Hits. *Guitar Player* (September).

MTV News. 2003. Segment about album *Seal IV.* MTV.

Osbourne, Ozzy. 2004. Interview. *Revolver*: http://www.roadrunnerrecords.com/blabbermouth.net/news.aspx?mode=Article&newsitemID=31127.

Pegg, Nicholas. 2002. *The Complete David Bowie.* London: Reynolds & Hearn.

Pilvinsky, Marc. 1997. Juliana Hatfield: The Year of Living Dangerously. Flagpole.com (July).

Pirroni, Marco. 2001. Interview. punk77.co.uk: http://www.punk77.co.uk/groups/models_marco_pirroni_interview_2.htm.

Plati, Mark. 1999. The Storytellers Gig. BowieNet: http://www.markplati. net/bits/storytellers.htm.

———. 2000. Interview. Gibson.com (August 24): http://www.gibson. com/Whatsnew/pressrelease/2000/aug24a.html.

———. 2001. Interview. *Voyeur* fanzine.

Ralf Hütter. 2004. Interview by Stephen Dalton. *Scotsman* (March).

Rhoden, Jason. 1999. Website with information about Sheryl Crow's unreleased first album (updated September 17): http://www. jasonrh.com/sc1992.htm.

Robbins, Ira. 1991. *The Trouser Press Record Guide.* 4th ed. New York: Collier Books.

Rotondi, James. 1996. Destroy All Monsters. *Guitar Player* (November).

Rubin, Rick. 2004. Interview. "Fresh Air," NPR (February 16): http:// www.npr.org/templates/story/story.php?storyId=1678537

Savage, Jon. 1985. *The Kinks: The Official Biography.* London: Faber and Faber.

Seal. 1991. Interview by Rob Tannenbaum. *Rolling Stone* (November 28).

———. 1994. Interview by David Thigpen. *Rolling Stone* (August 25).

———. 1994. Interview by Mark Cooper. *Q* (July).

———. 1998. Seal Explains His Turbulent Relationship with Producer Horn. Interview by *MTV News*. MTV (November 30): http://www. mtv.com/news/articles/1433915/19981130/seal.jhtml.

———. 2001. Interview by Jon Zahlaway. liveDaily.com (September 25): http://www.livedaily.com/interviews/liveDaily_Interview_Seal-3692.html.

———. 2003. Seal: Endangered Species. Interview by C. Bottomley. VH1.com (August 13): http://www.vh1.com/artists/ interview/1476844/20030813/seal.jhtml.

———. 2007. Official blog from Seal.com (January 5).

Sky, Rick. 1993. Jumping Jack Dash. *London Daily Mirror* (February 9).

Sullivan, Kate. 2006. Odds/Sods, Bits/Bobs. *LA Weekly* (May 31).

Weizmann, Danny "Shredder." 1989. Boogie and the Beast: Mike D, MCA and King Ad-Rock on U2, Aunt Bea, and the Ozone. *LA Weekly* (September 7).

Wild, David. 1992. Mick: Third Time A Charm? *Rolling Stone* (October 1).

Williams, Paul. 1996. *Watching the River Flow: Observations on Bob Dylan's Art in Progress 1965–1995*. New York: Omnibus.

Wilson, Brian. 1991. *Wouldn't It Be Nice: My Own Story*. New York: Bloomsbury Publishing.

Witherspoon, Ronald L. 2003. The Buckethead Story. Bucketheadland website: http://www.bucketheadland.com/story.

Wood, Tim. 1999 (updated 2005). Chicago's Lost Album: The Stone of Sisyphus. Tim Wood website (July): http://www.timmwood.com/sos.html.

Index